Neolithic Britain and Ireland

Caroline Malone

For Charlotte and Lucy, who have already seen too many megaliths!

TEMPUS

First published 2001

PUBLISHED IN THE UNITED KINGDOM BY:

Tempus Publishing Ltd
The Mill, Brimscombe Port
Stroud, Gloucestershire GL5 2QG
www.tempus-publishing.com

PUBLISHED IN THE UNITED STATES OF AMERICA BY:

Tempus Publishing Inc.
2 Cumberland Street
Charleston, SC 29401
1-888-313-2665
www.arcadiapublishing.com

Tempus books are available in France and Germany
from the following addresses:

Tempus Publishing Group   Tempus Publishing Group
21 Avenue de la République   Gustav-Adolf-Straße 3
37300 Joué-lès-Tours   99084 Erfurt
FRANCE   GERMANY

British Library Cataloguing in Publication Data.
A catalogue record for this book is available from the British Library.

ISBN 0 7524 1442 9

Typesetting and origination by Tempus Publishing.
PRINTED AND BOUND IN GREAT BRITAIN

Contents

List of illustrations

Acknowledgements

I am indebted to help from the following people and wish to thank: the Tempus team (Peter Kemmis Betty, Tim Clarke and Claire Brittain) who managed to put the multiplicity of text and figures together and create a book, to Roger Mercer, Jill Cook, the British Museum, Cambridge University Committee for Aerial Photography, the Cambridge University Museum of Archaeology and Anthropology and Mick Sharp for providing additional photographs and much enhancing my own limited images, to Frances Healey for useful advice on lithics, and especially to my family for tolerating the writing of this book which took far longer than anyone predicted.

Preface

My aim is to introduce the reader to the archaeology of Neolithic Britain and Ireland, and to the sites, data and many approaches that have come to characterise a very particular episode of cultural development. The Neolithic is a vast subject, so vast and complex that for too long scholars have skimmed over the bigger picture in favour of applying contemporary theory to often well-known sites (usually Stonehenge and its relatives) rather than re-assessing the whole for the student. Having taught Neolithic archaeology for many years, and seen the confusion and frustration that frequently result from students' efforts with the available literature, and the difficult task they have in disentangling fact from interpretation, I hope to simplify their first encounter with the subject. There are many published studies of individual types of monuments, regions, artefacts and arguments for the specialist, but a lack of synthesis to pull the many strands together. Chapters here tackle the different topics of landscape, economy, settlement, monuments, burials, artefacts and technologies, so that a fair range of types and characteristics are explained and illustrated — if simply. This is not a book intended for the expert who already knows about the Neolithic and delights in monographs and journal papers, and who will doubtless see many flaws in what is or is not included. Instead it is for the newcomer to the subject, in the hope that they too will delight in the archaeology of Neolithic Britain and Ireland.

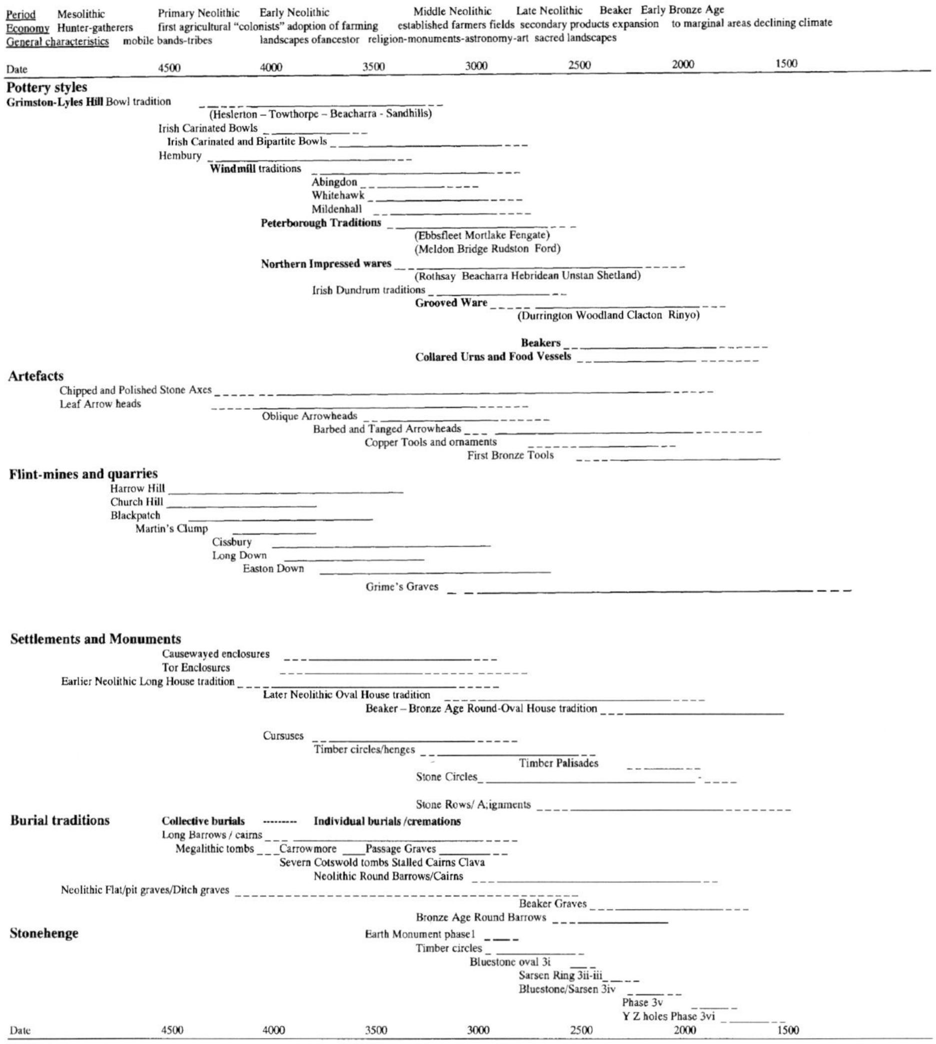

Period / Economy / General characteristics

Period	Mesolithic	Primary Neolithic	Early Neolithic	Middle Neolithic	Late Neolithic	Beaker	Early Bronze Age
Economy	Hunter-gatherers	first agricultural "colonists"	adoption of farming	established farmers fields	secondary products expansion		to marginal areas declining climate
General characteristics	mobile bands-tribes		landscapes of ancestor religion-monuments-astronomy-art		sacred landscapes		

| Date | 4500 | 4000 | 3500 | 3000 | 2500 | 2000 | 1500 |

Pottery styles

Grimston-Lyles Hill Bowl tradition
(Heslerton – Towthorpe – Beacharra - Sandhills)
Irish Carinated Bowls
Irish Carinated and Bipartite Bowls
Hembury
Windmill traditions
Abingdon
Whitehawk
Mildenhall
Peterborough Traditions
(Ebbsfleet Mortlake Fengate)
(Meldon Bridge Rudston Ford)
Northern Impressed wares
(Rothsay Beacharra Hebridean Unstan Shetland)
Irish Dundrum traditions
Grooved Ware
(Durrington Woodland Clacton Rinyo)
Beakers
Collared Urns and Food Vessels

Artefacts

Chipped and Polished Stone Axes
Leaf Arrow heads
Oblique Arrowheads
Barbed and Tanged Arrowheads
Copper Tools and ornaments
First Bronze Tools

Flint-mines and quarries

Harrow Hill
Church Hill
Blackpatch
Martin's Clump
Cissbury
Long Down
Easton Down
Grime's Graves

Settlements and Monuments

Causewayed enclosures
Tor Enclosures
Earlier Neolithic Long House tradition
Later Neolithic Oval House tradition
Beaker – Bronze Age Round-Oval House tradition
Cursuses
Timber circles/henges
Timber Palisades
Stone Circles
Stone Rows/ Alignments

Burial traditions

Collective burials -------- **Individual burials /cremations**
Long Barrows / cairns
Megalithic tombs ___ Carrowmore ___ Passage Graves
Severn Cotswold tombs Stalled Cairns Clava
Neolithic Round Barrows/Cairns
Neolithic Flat/pit graves/Ditch graves
Beaker Graves
Bronze Age Round Barrows

Stonehenge

Earth Monument phase 1
Timber circles
Bluestone oval 3i
Sarsen Ring 3ii-iii
Bluestone/Sarsen 3iv
Phase 3v
Y Z holes Phase 3vi

| Date | 4500 | 4000 | 3500 | 3000 | 2500 | 2000 | 1500 |

1 Introduction

This book is about the beginnings of settled societies in the British Isles, from the moment that agriculture and food production began to offer alternatives to the annual round of hunting and gathering. The Neolithic period is one of remarkable changes in landscapes, societies and technologies, which changed a wild, forested world, to one of orderly agricultural production and settled communities on the brink of socially complex 'civilisation'. It was a period that saw the arrival of new ideas and domesticated plants and animals, perhaps new communities, and the transformation of the native peoples of Britain. The Neolithic opened an entirely new episode in human history. It took place in Britain over a relatively short space of time, lasting in total only about 2000 years — in human terms little more than 80-100 generations.

Neolithic remnants abound in the British Isles, especially in the northern and western areas where stone monuments have survived the ravages of time and more recent destructive occupation. Evidence in the form of stone tombs, houses, monuments, economic remains, pottery, flints and stone tools, combined with evidence for landscape changes, forest clearance and human remains, provides a tangible link to the first farming societies of Britain and Ireland. Chapters are focused on different topics and aim to explain the evidence and the problems involved in its interpretation. Sites and museums for the reader to explore are listed, and an extensive bibliography should encourage a follow-up to the discussions introduced.

The islands of Britain, including Ireland (**1**), lie on the north-west of Europe — an area in prehistory on the edge of the civilized world, far from the action of the Mediterranean and the Near East. Unlike the western Europe of modern times which has generated new technologies and been influential across the world, 6000 years ago the area remained a technological backwater of sparsely populated hunter-gatherer communities. Only the northern regions of Scandinavia and Eurasia were slower in adopting new forms of subsistence, settlement and technology than the British Isles. Until the arrival of agricultural practices and the Neolithic social world that accompanied them, the landscapes of Britain were the product of nature with little human intervention evident. Within a thousand years of the arrival of farming — a short time in terms of human history — a transformation so complete had taken place that never has the landscape of the islands reverted to its natural state. Between about 4000 and 3000 BC, communities increasingly focused on agriculture, and native hunter-gatherers became farmers alongside the established food producers. They cleared great areas of forested land, and constructed a distinctive landscape that epitomised their enduring civilization. As time passed, they built monuments to celebrate their dead ancestors, created ceremonial places out of earth, timber and standing stones, manufactured an impressive array of tools, pots, ornamental

1 *The regions of Britain and Ireland*

objects and built houses. By the end of the Neolithic period around 2000 BC, a diversity of regional cultures and economic adaptations to the wet, cool islands of north-west Europe had developed and left their indelible mark.

Neolithic Britain has long been a perplexing and difficult period to write about and present, and there are many reasons for this, not least the relative rarity of sites and their preservation. However, many developments over recent decades have brought the Neolithic period to prominence. Scientific dating methods and material analysis, as well as the environmental reconstruction of past landscapes, have enabled scholars to be much more precise about

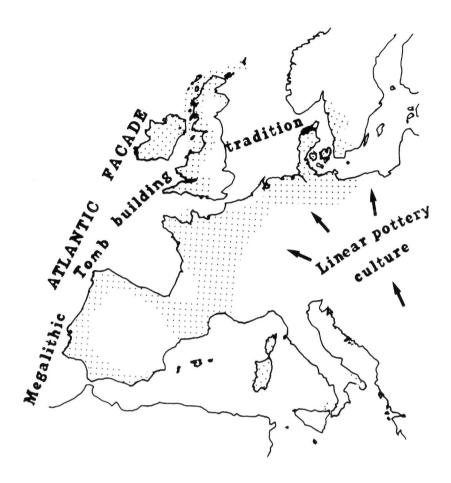

2 The Atlantic façade stretches from Iberia to Scandinavia and has long been associated with prehistoric Megalithic traditions. Neolithic central Europe was characterised by the Linear pottery or LBK tradition of farming communities, who represented a very different culture to the possibly indigenous Megalith builders of the west.

technology and change. Technological developments since the Neolithic (Bronze-Iron Ages and later) are distinguished by artefacts in particular styles made at very precise times, such as bronze swords, pottery, coins or even historical documents. In comparison, the Neolithic world moved slowly and communities left often vague and insubstantial clues behind, making detailed historical reconstruction difficult. But, in spite of the relative lack of archaeological clues to this 2000-year long period of history, an astonishing mass of information is yet available, along with many impressive and well-preserved monuments. The sites and materials of the Neolithic are real and tangible, as anyone who has held a polished axe or visited a megalithic chambered tomb will agree. There is much to explore and learn from this period, which enhances our understanding of how the societies and landscapes of Britain and Ireland developed. Such understanding is important for appreciating the emergence of the Bronze Age

3   *Kalahari hunter-gatherer.*
From the collection of the Museum of
Archaeology and Anthropology,
Cambridge University

that follows and the demise of the Mesolithic period that precedes the Neolithic, as well as the
origins of many components of our present world.

The background

The major changes of lifestyle and technology that punctuate human development are the
very stuff of archaeology. Change can be identified and measured, for example by the
methods of production of stone tools, or the ratio of wild to domesticated food in the diet.
Archaeologists spend a good proportion of their research effort trying to define how much
one period or site differs from another, and thus how much 'change' has taken place and
why. Nineteenth-century scholars were concerned with simply recognising the different
episodes of human technological development. They divided the past into material stages
of Stone, Bronze and Iron (the Three-Age Classification), and this ordering has long
dominated archaeological studies, as a means to create an order from the chaos of random
fragments. Much of the twentieth century (see below) was taken up with refining the
classification of types of site and of artefact and in trying to recognise patterns in economic
behaviour and assess the length of time of episodes of prehistory. As absolute dating
methods, especially C14 dating, have become routine procedure, the quest for sequence
and date has become less of a preoccupation and an ever more refined understanding of
time has been achieved. Since these developments liberated scholars from working
through sequence and typology as an end in itself, recent trends have instead been towards
the reconstruction of societies, of what behaviour and material culture might have
symbolised in the past and towards more elaborate theory building. Contemporary
thought has been especially interested in social structures, in the 'Phenomenology' of

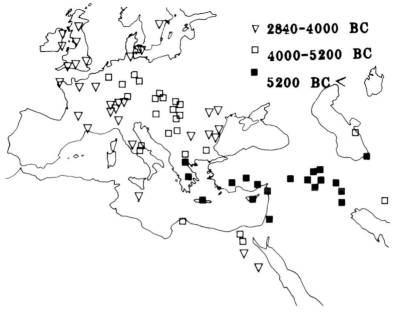

4   *Chronological maps showing the spread of agriculture to Europe. That above is based on Clark 1965. The breakthrough in C14 dating allowed early dates of domestic plants and animals to be plotted, and these showed that farming spread to Europe from the near east. Recalibration and many new dates still confirm the pattern identified by Clark nearly 40 years ago. More recent simulation models and revised dates suggest a 'Wave of advance' of farmers westwards and northwards across Europe, colonising indigenous Mesolithic territories. The diagram from Ammerman and Cavalli-Sforza (below) was constructed in the 1980s before the recent re-calibration of C14 dates, which instead are expressed as bc (approximate calendar dates are expressed in brackets BC). The broken lines show where farming penetrated into Mesolithic areas, before the full 'Wave of advance' arrived.*

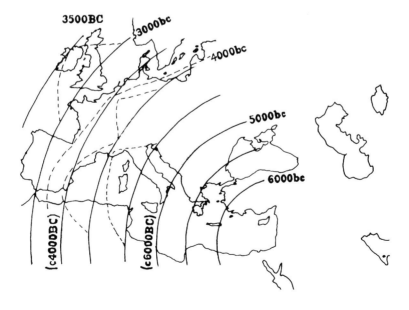

5 *Stukeley's engraving of the West Kennet Long Barrow, Wiltshire*

landscape, comparing the experience of the past with the present, in the impact of sensory perceptions on landscapes and sites, and how they might have operated in the past.

The synthesis of data, and the development of testable hypotheses and models which attempt to explain how changes occurred in the past, is important for opening a debate into how and why things happened. The most important model was proposed by Gordon Childe, and posited the notion of a *Neolithic* and an *Urban Revolution* (Childe 1934). He suggested that farming came about in the Near East through a combination of factors — climatic desiccation, the development of oases and population increase — that encouraged human proximity to plants and animals, which were forced to live together at water sources, and triggered domestication and the Neolithic economic and technological 'revolution'. Childe listed a number of characteristics that typified the Neolithic Revolution. These included sedentary villages, pottery making, arts and crafts such as textiles and carpentry, ground and polished stone tools, an economy based on domesticated plants and animals, and finally a coherent system of beliefs. At a time when scientific evidence was not available and Childe's theories were simply untested ideas, they had a great impact on the way scholars began to think about Neolithic societies, and their enormous differences to hunting and gathering societies. Many scholars have examined and challenged Childe's ideas over the succeeding decades. New data have of course provided the material for refinement and revision of his original theory, but in many ways much is still valid today. Childe was correct in assuming that the Neolithic represented a major 'revolution' in human and social development, in part triggered by environmental change, but there are now controlled and scientific ways of extracting information and examining it and measuring change from one economic strategy to another.

The Neolithic concept

Hunting and collecting economies have dominated the human and hominid past, and only in the last 10,000 years has there been a change from this form of subsistence, to one where food production has become the norm. Now we take it for granted that our food is largely produced through husbandry and agriculture. Only fishing still persists as a form of hunting for food on a large scale; otherwise, hunted and collected foods such as rabbit, mushrooms or blackberries are considered as free bonus foods. Our mental picture of the

The Stone Age

Ancient Swedish civilisation

The Iron Age

STONE ⟶ BRONZE ⟶ IRON

6   Three-age system of Thomsen and Worsaae as represented by Oscar Montelius and de Mortillet at the end of the nineteenth century

status of food differs vastly from that of the hunting and gathering people in the distant or recent past. Today, if we want more, we grow more, we tend it more intensively or breed more productive types of plant or animal, and food is seen as a sedentary item, planted in the landscape or confined within in a field or garden. It is not a mobile, unpredictable and elusive thing, as it is for hunter-gatherers. Important observations were made by anthropologists who studied mobile hunting and gathering groups in various parts of the tropical world (Lee and Devore 1968; Sahlins 1972). These studies showed that hunter-gatherers rarely stored food, or planned what to eat the next day. Being mobile, they followed their food, often in seasonal rounds, in small bands of perhaps 10-25 people, and only came together for larger social gatherings when food was especially plentiful. They carried very little with them, and children were spaced over several years, with infants carried by their mother until fully weaned. Amongst the !Kung bushmen of the Kalahari desert (**3**) in southern Africa, women are the main food collectors, often walking great distances each day to gather nuts or tubers, and these nutritious foods sustain quite large groups. The men — who regard themselves as hunters — spend some time in pursing small game, usually unsuccessfully, but most of their time sitting around their camps, gambling, storytelling and generally not engaged in food procurement or food processing.

Similar patterns of food procurement have been observed in tropical and sub-tropical hunter-gatherer groups in Australia and the Philippines, who similarly spend little time procuring food. Cold climate hunter-gatherers, such as the Inuit of Canada had, however, to plan their hunting expeditions with care and precision in very marginal environments and never enjoyed similar leisure. Parallel trends may also have happened in prehistory. Such findings confound the conventional assumption that hunter-gatherers had to spend all their time on the food quest, with no time for the arts and crafts in which more leisured, sedentary societies indulged. However, it is clear that such lifestyles of successful hunter-gatherer subsistence can only succeed where the population levels are very low, probably below one person per km², and where there are seasonally rich and predictable foods. In the richest environments, such as the swamps and forests of California, up to five people per km² might have been supported, but in general, much lower hunter-gatherer population densities existed, perhaps averaging one person per 10 or even 20km². If this was the density for Britain over its 244100 km² then Mesolithic hunter-gatherer populations might have numbered only 24,400 people (Malone 1999).

Studies by anthropologists of simple farming societies have shown that farming with primitive tools and crops is much more labour intensive than hunting and gathering. For relatively small returns, prehistoric farmers (like their modern tropical counterparts) had to invest massively in several activities which enabled them to produce food. Firstly, they had to clear land of forest cover, remove the timber (a practice sometimes called *slash and burn*), and then break the forest soil through digging and tilling. This long and arduous process would have promoted ideas of ownership and property, very different from the relaxed territorial concepts held by mobile hunters. In order to safeguard their land and its new crops, farmers would usually have to live close by in settlements, which may have been permanent. Seed corn of domestic crops, such as wheat, barley, beans and peas, had to be collected and stored safely from vermin and damp until planting. Once sprouted, crops had to be tended, weeded, protected from destructive animals and birds, and finally harvested. Grain then had to be threshed to remove the seed heads and winnowed to remove the chaff, before being stored or processed into food. All the main cereal crops (wheat, barley, oats, rye, rice, millet and maize) are annual grasses, requiring a yearly cycle of planting and harvesting. Their processing into food requires a surprising level of preparation, including grinding and milling, and not least cooking, to break down the starch into a digestible form. Compared with the almost instantaneous return of wild collected fruits, nuts, fungi or tubers and hunted meat, cereal plants are immensely labour-intensive foods. It is hardly surprising to find that some modern hunter-gatherer groups have told anthropologists that they prefer to stick to their ways of obtaining food and enjoy their leisured sociable lives.

Broad spectrum economies and farming origins in the Near East

The transition to agriculture occurred in the Early Holocene, about 10,000-8000 years ago, in several parts of the world, including the Near East, China and, a little later, in Mesoamerica, south east Asia, Africa and India. Climatic changes at the end of the last glacial period some 12,000-10,000 years ago resulted in much wetter and warmer conditions (see B. Smith, 1995). From landscapes of cold desert steppe and coniferous tree cover, new landscapes of species-rich deciduous forest and grassland developed rapidly, colonising formerly inhospitable regions and forming humus-rich soils. Europe, the Mediterranean region and the Near East especially saw flourishing new ecosystems developing which supported not only great varieties of plants, but also animals and human communities who subsisted on them. Even areas like the Sahara desert were moist and covered with vegetation, and supported herds of animals and mobile hunters. From the north of Scotland to the Sahara, new communities of

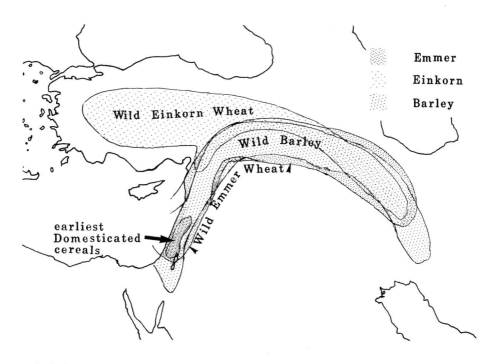

7a   *The fertile crescent: natural distribution of cereals in the Near East and early areas of domestication*

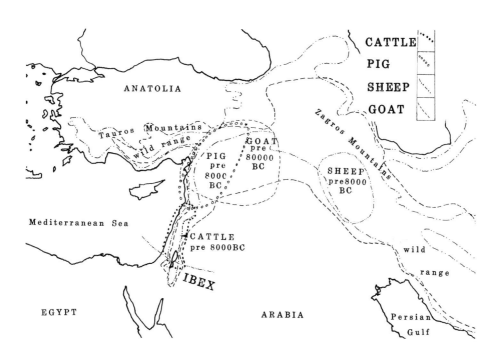

7b   *The fertile crescent — natural distributions of animals and early centres of domestication*

hunter-gatherers developed from their Ice Age predecessors, and instead of subsisting mainly on mammal meat (such as reindeer, mammoth or horse) these new communities experimented with a vast array of foods. The Mesolithic (middle Stone Age) bridges the period between the last Ice Age and the Neolithic, and was typified by new toolkits of small geometrically shaped stone and flint flakes called microliths. These offered the means to make new and flexible multi-component tools including graters, knives, scrapers and harpoons. Bone and wood were shaped into a variety of tools, including pins, spatulae and handles, sometimes carved and ornamented with animal heads or geometric patterns.

The most important developments in early farming in western Eurasia took place in the Levant and the mountains surrounding Syria, Israel, Jordan, Turkey, Iraq and Iran. From the beginning of the Holocene 12,000-10,000 years ago, the massive climatic and vegetation changes in this region offered the already successful late Palaeolithic hunters a very rich landscape with many different ecological niches to explore. With the Mediterranean Sea to the west, and grassland steppe and desert to the east and north, from coastal plains and valleys to hills and high mountains, the area offered different seasonal environments and resources in a compact area. Hunter-gatherers had the perfect environment for easy subsistence. The 'fertile crescent', as the hilly-mountainous area is known, was uniquely provided with natural distributions of the wild grasses ancestral to domesticated cereals (wheat, barley, oats), pulses (lentils, vetches, flax, peas and beans) and pistachios and almonds. It offered a rich juxtaposition of agricultural potential that enabled the Mesolithic intensive food collectors to experiment with a broad spectrum of resources from the diverse landscape of woods, grasslands and scrub, and develop technology and husbandry to become ever more dependent on domestic plants and animals (**3a**).

Excavations of sites in the Levant area of west Asia, especially of the Natufian culture (Henry 1989; Bar Yosef and Valla 1991; Moore *et al.* 2000; Redman 1976) have shown how hunter-gatherers in the area became steadily more sedentary, lived in larger communities of several dozen people, and began to store the wild foods collected from the landscape around them. They constructed oval-round huts or tent-bases in small settlement concentrations in strategic positions overlooking streams and the grazing areas of gazelle and goats, such as the sites of Abu Hureyra and Jericho. The houses included storage facilities such as grain bins and pits, hearths, grind stones, ground and decorated stone bowls and elaborate burials beneath the floors. These Natufian communities systematically hunted and perhaps also herded and controlled the wild goats, gazelle, cattle, sheep and pig naturally distributed within the area. Fish supplemented the other foods on the coast, rivers and lakes.

The Natufian culture was a wholly Mesolithic hunter-gatherer culture, and no element of the economy they practiced was based on domestic species. However, the selection of plants, and their harvesting, manipulation, replanting and use, precipitated a process that resulted eventually in the domestication of food plants. Animals were also being managed and manipulated and probably over-hunted. This resulted in the near-extinction of wild gazelle and goats and thus the main food of many Natufian communities. Many large new sites emerged during the 2000 years or so of Natufian culture, and seem to represent a massive population increase, responding to the bountiful food supplies and the easy environment. One explanation for the increase of human populations proposes that cereals cooked into a porridge would have enabled the early weaning of children, allowing mothers to have their offspring more closely together, and thus triggering a rapid rise in population levels.

The optimal conditions of the early post-glacial period did not last however, and there was a period of sustained return to glacial conditions in the ninth millennium BC, which in the Near East resulted in colder and drier environments. The climatic episode (known as the 'Younger Dryas') formed minor glaciers and across Europe tough cold conditions prevailed for perhaps two or three centuries — a short time, but highly significant for dense hunter-gatherer populations in crowded and suddenly unproductive environments. The restricted area of the Near East Levant offered little escape for hunter-gatherers; with the Mediterranean Sea, mountains and new and expanding deserts enclosing it on all sides there was nowhere to migrate. So a logical and obvious step appears to have been taken during the period between 8000 and 7000 BC — a transformation from hunting and gathering food, to one of growing plants and breeding and herding animals.

Domestication

However, the very process of intervention by humans on some plants and animals had a decisive effect. In cereal plants, the harvesting and manipulation involved the inadvertent selection of particular characteristics, especially those that ensured the seed remained within the seedhead rather than dispersed naturally. The selection for seedheads that were tough and held large seeds led in turn to genetic mutations that irreversibly changed wild emmer and einkorn wheat types, for example, into domestic species. Their structure, the shape of the seeds and their mechanisms of seed dispersal became 'man-made' or domestic.

The same process of mutation can be detected in some animals, principally the ungulates or typical farm animals. By managing the wild flocks of sheep and goats for example, humans began to control their food supply, their breeding patterns and even their behaviour. Cramped artificial conditions, poor food, infestations, and doubtless intentional selection of smaller, more docile animals, led to physical changes in the animals' skeletons. Their teeth became crowded, jaws shorter, brain size decreased, horn shapes changed, and their size generally became smaller. At a later stage of animal breeding, other characteristics such as wool rather than hair, and colour and appearance, were also selected, gradually creating domestic 'breeds' from what had simply been 'species' in their wild state.

The centuries of experience gained from the optimal environments were turned to benefit, as the dense populations of sophisticated hunter-gatherers began to direct their efforts to food production. By the early Pre-pottery Neolithic (PPN-A) levels at tell sites such as Jericho (between *c.*7600-6000 BC), wild animal bones still dominated the assemblages of faunal material, but plant remains were mainly domesticated wheat and barley. Soon after, in the Pre-pottery Neolithic (PPN-BC – *c.*6000-5600 BC) levels almost all the wild animals had also disappeared from the economy, presumably hunted so destructively, that only managed herds and flocks of increasingly domestic animals were reliable food. Thus began the major transition from taking food to making food, and from wandering across a landscape to living in a closely demarcated one. A change took place from small mobile social groups, of no fixed abode other than a territory, to larger sedentary communities who for generations honoured their ancestors and changed the land.

The economic and social changes seen in the Near East were gradually adopted by adjacent hunter-gatherers in Turkey, Greece, the Balkans, across Europe and the Mediterranean (see Clark 1965; Ammerman and Cavalli-Sforza 1973, 1984). They may have copied or been encouraged to adopt some of the elements of farming and Neolithic technology by actual migrants, who had perhaps moved from crowded areas to new and more open land. Certainly, farming and pottery spread rapidly across Europe, and over the space of less than 2000 years, most parts of central and southern Europe had taken on many aspects of the new way of life. Only Britain, Ireland and the northern lands remained unchanged. Separated by the English Channel, the North Sea and the Baltic, Mesolithic communities seem to have remained unaware of the massive economic changes taking place in France and the north European plain for several centuries, but eventually, change came. In Britain, there is much debate and discussion about the origins of agricultural communities, and some current ideas (such as proposed by Alasdair Whittle 1996) prefer to explain the coming of agriculture through adoption rather than social migration. Nevertheless, fully domestic plants and animals, and the technology and know-how to deal with them did arrive in Britain as a complete subsistence package. Future research using ancient DNA may be one means to assess whether populations moved or whether only the technologies and products of the Neolithic crossed the English Channel (**2**).

Carbon 14 dating

Developments over half a century in absolute dating techniques (principally C14) have had an extraordinary impact on Neolithic studies.

Before the 1950s, estimation of the date or length of the Neolithic period was simply speculation based on stratographics and typological sequences. In summary (for detail see Bowman 1995): Carbon 14 dating essentially measures the variations in the three atomic isotopes (12, 13, 14) that occur in carbon. Carbon 14 is unstable and radioactive. It occurs in all living things, and generally decays at a constant rate from the time the plant or animal dies. It has a half-life of 5730 years, that is the time taken for its original concentration of C14 atoms to halve.

However, estimating a calendar date from a C14 sample is complex. The rate of decay of atomic matter is not constant and thus a radiocarbon date is estimated in three ways: a date before present or BP (1950 being taken as BP), an uncalibrated radio-carbon date, or bc, and, through the application of statistics combined with dendrochronology (measuring tree rings, which also have 'radio-carbon' ages), the calendrical date BC. However, recent re-calibration programmes have changed archaeological expression of dating, from a precise date ±100, for example, to several levels of increasing accuracy. These are now expressed as sigma 1, 2, etc, and introduce cal BC, to show the whole date range; for example 3800-3300 cal BC. The Neolithic period is especially dependent on C14 dating because the half-life effectively covers the British/European Neolithic.

Where samples are very small, such as individual cereal grains, or where conventional C14 methods are unsuitable, AMS or Acceleration Mass Spectrometer dating can be used. This method measures the number of atoms present by mass spectrometry.

Research history of the Neolithic

Neolithic research in the British Isles has a long and impressive history. From the seventeenth century onwards antiquarians and historians speculated extensively about megalithic tombs and stone circles and recorded their encounters, even though the very concept of 'prehistory' had not been born. John Aubrey, famous as the antiquarian writer of the never-published *Monumenta Britannica* and founder member of the Royal Society, 'discovered' the great henge at Avebury and made a survey of it in 1663 and Robert Plot recorded the Rollright stones in Oxfordshire in 1677. The latter half of the seventeenth century was a period of great scientific inquiry, marked by debate and numerous observations and studies. By the eighteenth century, landscape studies had matured, and the greatest researcher of his time was William Stukeley (**5**). He devoted much of his life to recording sites which ranged from Medieval and Roman remains and buildings to Stonehenge and Avebury. He started sensibly in the 1720s, and sketched and recorded sites, observing construction methods and site settings, and also the recent destruction of many sites. However, carried away with the romanticism of the mid-late eighteenth century, he became obsessed with Druids and his acute observations were hidden by a veil of absurd speculation and classical mythology. His volumes on *Stonehenge* (1740) and *Avebury* (1743) epitomise the extremes of Druidic megalithomania.

The beginnings of more serious archaeology, and especially excavation, were led by a number of antiquarians and scholars. Foremost amongst these were William Cunnington and Richard Colt Hoare who set up a remarkable partnership at the beginning of the nineteenth century, and over a few years excavated a great number of barrows and sites in Wiltshire. Most were Bronze Age barrows, but several instances included Neolithic and Beaker discoveries. They demonstrated the importance of prehistoric sites and their material contents at a time when the Classical world was particularly dominant. By 1812 two great volumes had been published — *Ancient Wiltshire* (north and south), which recorded in careful detail the individual tombs and the material found. Much of this is now displayed by the Wiltshire Archaeological Society in its museum at Devizes. The very idea of human antiquity was still new and considered *avant garde* in the middle of the nineteenth century, when the established theory for human origins was changing from biblical to evolutionary. The publication of Charles Lyell's *Principles of Geology* in the 1830s and then Charles Darwin's *Origin of Species* in 1859 transformed the scholarly view of human antiquity and evolution, and archaeological evidence that had long been known was quite rapidly reinterpreted within the hugely extended timescale into which humanity was now seen to be included. The importance of the scientific acceptance of human origins was that prehistoric sites (which were clearly older than biblical and historical records) were recognised as human constructions, and thus part of the continuous history of humanity. In 1865, with the recognition of human antiquity and a systematic means of exploring the early human past, Sir John Lubbock (later Lord Avebury 1834-1913) wrote *Prehistoric Times*, the first use of the word 'prehistoric' in a popular context. This book was a best seller in its day and went through many editions. It presented material from Britain and elsewhere and included examples from ethnography which showed how ancient tools were made and used, and provided a context for the ancient sites of Britain. The division of the timescale into logical, technological segments was pioneered first by the

Danes, in the persons of Christian Thomsen (1788-1865) and his student Worsaae (1821-85). Thomsen organised the antiquities of the National Museum in Copenhagen in terms of their materials — stone, bronze and iron. He wrote an influential guide to the museum which was widely translated and had a profound impact on scholars across Europe and especially in Britain. It provided a logical means to organise and put into sequence undatable pre-history, and thus a route to explore the non-historical past (**6**).

By the end of the nineteenth century field methods were also becoming more systematic, and particularly so under the direction of General Pitt Rivers. This extraordinary individual retired from a military career and took up field archaeology with energy. Throughout a life of travel, he had collected artefacts as examples of technology and raw material, and accumulated a vast collection of exotic and mundane objects. He housed these in his own private museum in Dorset, and then set about excavating prehistoric sites on his estates at Cranborne Chase. His findings were published and set new scientific standards for excavation and publication. By the end of the nineteenth century the study of prehistory — including Neolithic Britain — had become a respected and recognised branch of archaeology [Bowden 1991].

Major developments for prehistory in Britain in the twentieth century began with the synthesis of large bodies of data. Abercrombie defined the Bronze Age pottery of Britain (1912) and his student, Gordon Childe — the great synthesiser — extended his research across Europe, providing a setting for the development of prehistoric societies. Alongside his 1925 survey of Europe, *The Dawn of European Civilisation*, his major contribution was to focus on the so-called 'Neolithic Revolution' in the later 1920s and 1930s, and investigate how this social and economic transformation came about. He was restricted in his research because many methodological and scientific developments in economic and environmental archaeology had not been made. For instance, carbonised seeds were almost impossible to extract from the soil, precise dates were still 20 years away and studies of climatic and environmental change immature. Instead Childe focused on social explanations, cultures and cultural sequences and provided a series of models that are still being tested today. During the early decades of the twentieth century several important projects were initiated that enabled rapid progress in the study of British Neolithic sites. These included the excavations of the causewayed enclosure sites of southern England. Alexander Keiller at Windmill Hill (Smith 1965), Cecil Curwen on the South Downs (1929, 1930, 1934, 1936), and Dorothy Liddell at Hembury in Devon (1930, 1931, 1932, 1935) which demonstrated that Neolithic sites of great size and complexity and related to tombs and henge sites survived in Britain. However, the larger picture was only put together by Stuart Piggott's great work, *Neolithic Cultures of the British Isles* (1954). Although over 40 years later we have absolute dates, many more sites and splendid economic and environmental evidence, the book was and probably still is the major synthetic contribution to Neolithic research in Britain. It did not stand alone, however, and research by Graham Clark on the Mesolithic (1935) over the same period provided economic antecedents and an environment against which the Neolithic of Britain could be viewed. Alongside these histories of early Britain, studies were made of particular monument types, especially megalithic sites and here I pick just a handful of names to paint a picture of a rapidly moving and growing discipline. From the late 1930s to the 1960s, Glyn Daniel classified Neolithic megalithic tombs in Britain, drew broad links with the European megaliths, speculated on their spread and development (Daniel 1950), and excavated the site of Barclodiad y Gawres with Terence Powell (Powell and Daniel 1956). Over the same period, several scholars pioneered Neolithic research on settlements and tombs in Ireland (e.g. Powell 1938, Sean O'Riordain1954, Hugh Henken 1939, R. de Valera and S.O'Nuallain 1961). Since the 1960s, when a great increase in knowledge resulted from archaeological rescue work and local government Sites and Monument Records, there have been studies of every imaginable area of the Neolithic: Henges (Wainwright 1989), stone circles and rows (Burl 1993, 2000), long barrows (Ashbee 1984), Irish passage graves (Eogan 1986), cursus monuments (Barclay and Harding 1999), houses (Darvill and Thomas 1996) and Neolithic landscapes (Bradley 1998, the Royal Commission on Historical Monuments, and many others). Objects such as pottery, lithics, and artefacts have also been subjected to scrutiny: for example Clarke et al.. (1985) *Symbols of Power in the Age of Stonehenge*. Incredibly perhaps, in the light of the mass of new and factual information on the Neolithic, the so-called 'lunatic fringe' remains in that earlier tradition of William Stukeley. It has flourished and grown ever more fantastic in speculative New Age theory about Neolithic sites, earth mothers, ley-lines and such like. In the politically aware environment in which archaeologists now work, few would dare dismiss the claims of the competing groups for their share of the interpretation of the ancient and megalithic past of Britain!

Theoretical and practical issues and current debates

This book is not the place to expand on the many debates challenging the approaches to the study of prehistoric cultures, other than to point the reader towards the many volumes and papers that tackle the theoretical issues of prehistory (see Renfrew and Bahn 2000 for an introduction). Academic traditions primarily aim to build clear structures, to order information, and archaeological attempts aim to clarify the prehistory that reflects these scholarly preoccupations. Invariably a tripartite division has been favoured, with culture sequences organised as early, middle and late, or developing, flourishing and declining. With the British Neolithic, the tripartite approach has given way to a two-part process — earlier and later, which has been increasingly confirmed by C14 and dendrochronological dating, and a growing understanding of cultural material and sites. The earliest or primary Neolithic is poorly known in Britain, because the data are still scanty, and very early sites are generally identified in environmental work rather than in substantial monuments or settlements.

One scholarly tradition that has left an indelible mark on the Neolithic in Britain and across Europe has been the link identified between pottery types or styles and groups of people. A typical example is the 'Linear Pottery People' (LBK), based on the Linearbandkeramik of early Neolithic central Europe, a distinctive early incised pottery associated with the first agricultural peoples and their longhouses. Similarly, theories of the Beaker culture and folk of the Copper Age are based on the presence of Beaker pottery. Gordon Childe, in trying to define prehistoric cultures, noted that similar pottery, tools, houses and burials would recur together over a defined geographical and temporal space and thus a 'culture' could be identified. However, the last half-century has seen much debate over the question of whether artefacts really constitute the ethnic identities of the past, or whether people simply developed and adopted objects suitable for particular uses. At one end of the scale, functional explanations of artefact style see this as simply part of adaptation, and on the other, a host of social and ideological explanations are used to describe the ethnic identity, meaning and symbolism of the material culture of early communities. A balance is needed between the social, functional and scientific approaches to prehistoric cultures which goes beyond simple pottery names for entire cultures, environmental episodes or technological stages, but recognises the real limitations we have in reconstructing the remote and nameless societies of the Neolithic. There are many valid approaches to the study of Neolithic Britain, each one contributing to increasing understanding and appreciation of the period, yet rarely are they combined into an integrated study of the past.

At one extreme, a popular approach aims to explain social life in the past, through empathy and trying to explore aspects of memory, perception, senses and meaning, and to offer a narrative of the past (see for example Edmonds 1999, Tilley 1994 and Edmonds and Seaborne 2001. At the other, the approach is dominated by the more mundane matters of environmental reconstruction and economic understanding of the Neolithic of Britain. Yet another is focused on landscape studies (Topping 1997), prospecting and recording traces of sites and undertaking reconnaissance as part of multi-period, interdisciplinary research. More traditional artefact researchers create and organise catalogues of material, such as arrowheads or pottery, in an attempt to see broader patterns in distributions and style. Each approach makes its own contributions to the increase of knowledge about the Neolithic period, and when combined together and with other complementary disciplines, they offer much scope for new discovery and understanding.

At a broader academic level, the Neolithic period falls between very different scholarly approaches, and rather than being studied as a continuum from the Mesolithic, or as part of the sequence towards the Bronze Age, it has developed its own rigour and priorities. Mesolithic research tends towards pragmatic studies of environments, subsistence, artefact procurement and manufacture, and ecological work on territories and economic seasonality. Very little is written about Mesolithic societies, or their beliefs and perceptions, and indeed, they are treated as part of their natural world, much as one might study ecology. In sharp contrast, research on the British Neolithic tends to assume no continuity with the Mesolithic. Instead, a fascination with a perception that Neolithic people thought differently about their world and themselves to their predecessors has dominated recent research. Scholars like Ian Hodder (Hodder 1990) and Julian Thomas (Thomas 1999) continue, rather as Childe did decades before, to assume different intellectual frameworks for the Neolithic and the preceding Mesolithic. Richard Bradley, however, has explored aspects of continuity with the Mesolithic with some success (1998). Current research is stimulating and fun, but there are practical problems in demonstrating how archaeological evidence may relate to the Neolithic ideas and meanings which intrigue modern researchers. Conversely, the second-first millennia BC Bronze Age are rich in tangible material — tools, pots, weapons, personal items, settlements, fields, and tombs. The rich material culture provides ample evidence for technological innovation and variation, exchange, the status of individuals and gender, and can be subjected to typological analysis. As a result, rather less scholarly emphasis is placed on the ideological, ritual and monumental in later prehistory and the approaches to the period and its archaeology are also surprisingly different to those of Neolithic research.

2 Living off the land

Introduction

The land in which the first farming communities of Britain began to settle in the late fifth and early fourth millennia BC was one little changed from its natural state. This had developed over the preceding millennia of glacial, inter-glacial and post-glacial climatic episodes, each with distinctive plant communities adapted to the particular conditions (**8 &1**).

By 6500 BC the British landscape was predominantly one of trees and their surrounding vegetation, with reedy wetlands of willows, open coastal grasslands on

Climatic Zone	Pollen Zone (Godwin and West + *Irish*)	Archaeological Period	Climate and Vegetation	Approximate date (cal BC and unclaibrated bc.
FLANDRIAN				
Sub-Atlantic	VIII	Roman, Late Iron Age, Late Bronze Age	DETERIORATION Cold and wet, general deterioration, high rainfall, decline of lime, increase of ash, birch and beech.	
	FL III			1100BC / 950bc
Sub-Boreal	VIIb *ILWCdl*	Middle Bronze Age, Early Bronze Age, Late Neolithic	STABLE Warm and dry, low rainfall, wind-bown deposits. Woodland regeneration in southern England.	2500 BC /2000 bc
	ILWC	Late Neolithic, Middle Neolithic, Early Neolithic	Declining warmth. Landnam and first agriculture. Elm decline – 3350 BC / 2300 bc.	4000 BC /3200 bc
Atlantic	**FL.II** VIIa *ILWB*	Later Mesolithic	OPTIMUM Climatic Optimum, warm and wet. Increase of 2 C, Poly-climax forest. Increase of Alder, some clearances.	6000 BC/ 5500 bc
Boreal	VI V	Mesolithic	AMELIORATING Continental climate, warm and dry. Assynchronous expansion of mixed oak forest with hazel and successional from pine	7500 bc
Pre-Boreal	**FL1** IV *ILWA*	Early Mesolithic	RAPID AMELIORATION Sharp increase in warmth at 7800 bc. Birch, juniper and pine woodland.	8300 bc
LATE GLACIAL Loch Lomond/ Younger Dryas Stadial	III	Later Upper Palaeolithic	Sub-arctic climate: Loch Lomond readvance, Tundra	9000 bc
Windermere (Allerod) Interstadial	II	Later Upper Palaeolithic	Interstadial rapid amelioration. Birch, pine, and tundra.	
Late Devensian	I	Later Upper Palaeolithic	Sub Arctic climate.	11,000bc
Main Devensian		Upper Palaeolithic	Sub-arctic climate, full glacial advance. Humans absent from the British Isles.	14,000 bc
MID GLACIAL Sub-arctic – Upton Warren – Interstadial Sub-Arctic.		Earlier Upper Palaeolithic ?Mousterian	Sub arctic climate – interstadial

Sub-arctic climate | 22,000 bc

60-70,000 bc |

8   Vegetation and climatic phases — Holocene — Atlantic. After Allen in Green

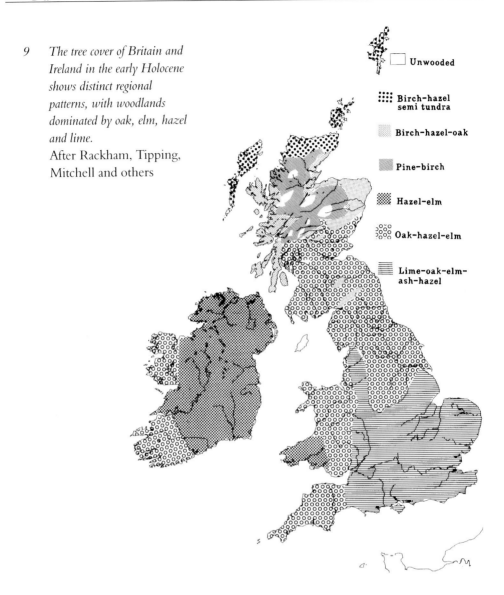

9   *The tree cover of Britain and Ireland in the early Holocene shows distinct regional patterns, with woodlands dominated by oak, elm, hazel and lime.*
After Rackham, Tipping, Mitchell and others

Unwooded

Birch-hazel semi tundra

Birch-hazel-oak

Pine-birch

Hazel-elm

Oak-hazel-elm

Lime-oak-elm-ash-hazel

terraces, dunes and floodplains, and their various forests depending on latitude, altitude and rainfall. Mesolithic communities had exploited parts of the landscape, especially the coastal inlets, lakes and rivers and the more open scrubland. However, apart from areas where the intentional burning of undergrowth may have improved deer hunting and woodland living space, little physical change can be detected. Mesolithic people do not seem to have broken the soil, built earthworks or manipulated the landscape to any degree. In comparison, Neolithic communities had a profound and rapid impact on the natural wooded landscape, and cleared immense areas for cultivation. Over the space of 2000 years the landscape became one of open fields and discrete woodlands. As trees were felled, grass, weeds and cereals took their place. Landscape change from the Mesolithic to the Neolithic has been steadily reconstructed through the work of environmental archaeologists, botanists, soil scientists and geographers over the last half century (see for example Evans 1971). In combination with C14 dating, they have established a clear sequence of vegetational change, and have been able to detect local and general changes resulting from human activity and from natural events (for an introduction to methods see Evans and O'Connor 1999 and Harding (ed) 1982.

Vegetation

The landscape of Britain at the beginning of the Neolithic was essentially the product of local climate and soil, and minimal intervention from the indigenous communities. Different plant communities flourished according to moisture levels, aspect and the underlying soil and rock. Pine and birch forests grew in the cool and damp of the Scottish uplands, the Wicklow hills and the west of Ireland. Hazel flourished as the understory shrub almost everywhere, especially in western areas and Ireland. Elm and mixed elm-oak and lime forests covered much of Ireland, SW England and Wales, with pockets in the north and Scotland and were dense on all but the heaviest wet soils of the islands, where only alder woods flourished. The original natural woodland is sometimes called 'wildwood' and it no longer exists anywhere in Britain, where woodlands have been manipulated for more than 6000 years (**9**).

Scholars have built up an elaborate scheme of vegetation and change over time, based on pollen samples taken as vertical cores sliced through peat bogs and wet deposits. The preservation of tree pollen is very variable, and depends on the robustness of the species of pollen grains, on where and when it falls, and the conditions that allow its long-term preservation in bogs or buried soils.

Pollen studies show that Mesolithic forests changed considerably in composition towards the end of the Boreal climatic phase in Europe. There was a huge increase in trees like alder that prefer warmer wetter conditions, just when trees of cooler conditions like birch, pine and hazel declined. The Neolithic period falls into the Atlantic to the Sub-Boreal phases (British phases VIIa-VIIIa, and Irish phases VII and VIIIa). The Atlantic phase (*c*.5800-3800 BC) was characterised by dense deciduous forests consisting of alder, oak, and elm, with lime in East Anglia, and pine and birch on the uplands. The warmer Sub-Boreal period (*c*.3800-2500 BC) saw the rise of hazel, together with elm and oak, the decline of pine, and there is considerable evidence for clearance of tree cover and the growth of blanket bog in the west, reflecting climate change and human intervention. Finally, the Sub-Atlantic phase extends to historic times, and represented climatic deterioration shown by an increase in ash, and a massive decline in elm.

The elm decline

Much has been written about the elm decline in Neolithic Britain. Elm forests were especially dense in southern and eastern England, just the areas where the first relatively intensive farming was adopted, and the decline may simply have been the result of catastrophic clearance for arable plots. However, the elm decline may have also been triggered by disease (similar to the Dutch Elm Disease outbreak in Britain in the 1970s which destroyed most elm trees) from the beetles that accompanied the first crops and farming regimes imported from other areas of Europe (Robinson 2000).

Sea levels

Following the massive climatic changes of the Ice Age, sea levels were rarely stable, even though present sea levels are within 2m of the levels of 5000 BC. During the Neolithic some lowland areas of Britain were affected by at least three marine transgressions, when glacial melt-water caused sea levels to rise and drown lowlands. North-west England, the Cambridgeshire Fenland and the Somerset Levels are areas where research has been able demonstrate these changes, through studies of marine clay deposits and sedimentation. Many of the islands and inlets that supported Mesolithic fishing communities, as in western Scotland, were drowned, leaving rare shell-midden sites on raised beaches and camps on higher land, as in Cumbria and parts of Argyll. Alongside sea-level change, some areas were affected by isostatic recovery, where land depressed from the weight of earlier glaciers rose up to earlier levels, often changing local drainage patterns and causing raised areas, tilting and sinking. The coasts of eastern England (such as Yorkshire and East Anglia) were particularly affected, and substantial areas of land were inundated by the sea or by lakes, a process which is still underway (for example at Dunwich, Suffolk). Across Europe, and presumably Britain, the earliest sites that demonstrate the transition to farming and Neolithic economy are located on the very edge of wetland environments. These were the ideal locations for mixed, broad-spectrum economies, spreading the risk of food failures across a wide range of possible sources, fished, farmed, hunted and gathered.

Charting the changes — some regional examples

The Fenland

The flat damp lands of Cambridgeshire and Lincolnshire surrounding the Wash of eastern England were inviting places for Neolithic settlement. Far from being monotonously flat, the landscape is marked by small gravel islands and ridges of higher land surrounding what was once a huge river basin, draining to a plain under what is now the North Sea. Rising sea levels some 7000-6000 years ago drowned the landscape, including oak forests, and the area became a vast wetland. Perhaps surprisingly, it was the great variety of local environments in such a landscape that provided a rich and hospitable place for Mesolithic and Neolithic communities, where food resources could easily be found. These included fish and fowl and various mammals as well as abundant plants, from trees to tubers, that could be eaten or exploited in various ways. The islands and terrace lands around the basin and rivers provided dry land for living and cultivation, and the low wet areas, a seasonally changing land to exploit for hunting and grazing. Early camps and settlements were usually situated in areas beyond the seasonal floods, but still easily in reach of the great variety of rich landscapes in the wet mire. Over time, the region became increasingly wet, and areas settled in the Neolithic and Bronze Age were gradually abandoned in the Iron Age and Roman period.

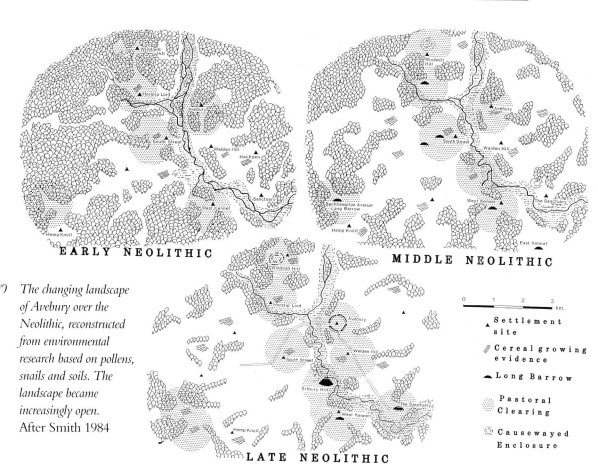

EARLY NEOLITHIC

MIDDLE NEOLITHIC

LATE NEOLITHIC

The changing landscape of Avebury over the Neolithic, reconstructed from environmental research based on pollens, snails and soils. The landscape became increasingly open.
After Smith 1984

▲ Settlement site

/ Cereal growing evidence

◤ Long Barrow

Pastoral Clearing

◉ Causewayed Enclosure

Drainage projects over the last two to three centuries have changed the traditional regime of summer grazing and winter wetland, so that now the area is the most productive agricultural land in Britain. Since the 1930s, realisation of the potential for finding organic remains and especially pollen evidence, stratified in the wet soils, has meant that the Fenland has been particularly well studied. It became (from the 1930s onwards) one of the most important areas for the environmental reconstructions of Professor Harry Godwin from Cambridge University, who pioneered techniques of pollen extraction and study. Since then, intensive agriculture and gravel quarry activity has promoted rich archaeological discoveries, especially so for the Mesolithic-Neolithic periods. Flint scatters remain the most common form of evidence for Mesolithic communities who lived in the area. The Neolithic evidence, from random finds of axes and flints to large lowland monuments, barrows and settlements is potentially very rich. Graham Clark, also based at Cambridge University, examined sites including early Neolithic sites Hurst Fen (Clark and Longworth 1960) and Shippea Hill (3000-2920 bc). More recently, the work of Francis Pryor at Fengate, Flag Fen, Maxey and Etton (Pryor 1974, 1984, 1988, 1999) has vastly expanded knowledge about the use of landscapes and the interrelationship of sites and activities, and work on the Ouse Valley has similarly added to out knowledge of the wider area (Dawson 2000).

31

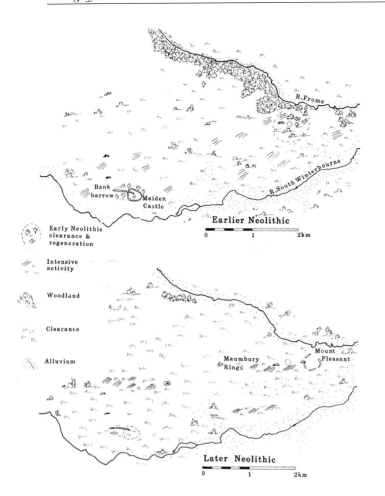

11 *The Maiden Castle landscapes changed from wooded to an open and intensely used agricultural landscape between the earlier and later Neolithic. Lack of secure and intact ancient deposits prevent a more detailed reconstruction .* After Allen

The Wessex chalklands

Intensive surveys in the Wessex chalk downlands around Avebury, Stonehenge, Maiden Castle and Cranborne Chase have located sites and information about their local environments enabling landscape reconstruction over the period of the Neolithic. Surface survey has picked up scatters of material (some of which can be dated), located actual sites, established datable soil sequences of snail shells, buried pollens, erosion and alluviation. These, together with plough marks etched into the subsoil from agriculture, field systems and evidence for clearance such as felling, have promoted general models of landscape development. The evidence has been usefully mapped, and shown over a sequence from early to late Neolithic. Smith's work at Avebury (Wiltshire) (1984) (**10**) showed an early Neolithic wooded landscape with very limited clearings around sparsely scattered settlements and areas of cultivation. By the later Neolithic, the bulk of the landscape was open, and 'wildwood' remained only as isolated patches, interspersed by cultivated land, settlement and large monuments.

A rather different scenario existed at Maiden Castle in Dorset (Allen 2000) (**11**) where the Frome river valley and areas around it were heavily wooded, but areas surrounding Maiden Castle appeared to be recently cleared. The open rolling downland of the area has been so

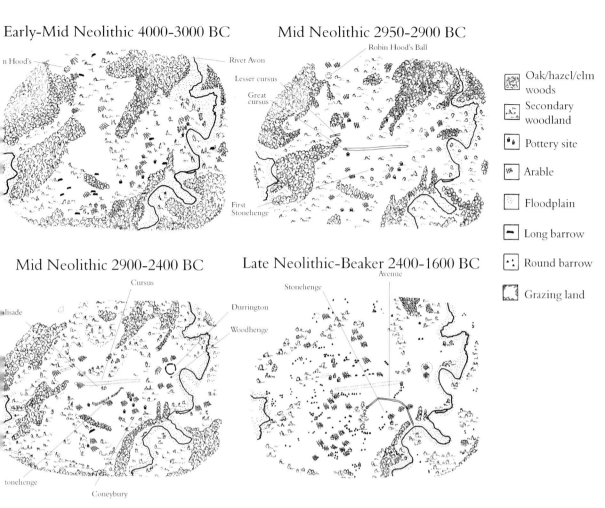

Early-Mid Neolithic 4000-3000 BC

Mid Neolithic 2950-2900 BC

n Hood's — River Avon
Lesser cursus
Great cursus
First Stonehenge

Robin Hood's Ball

Mid Neolithic 2900-2400 BC

Late Neolithic-Beaker 2400-1600 BC

Cursus
lisade
Durrington
Woodhenge
tonehenge
Coneybury

Stonehenge
Avenue

Legend:
- Oak/hazel/elm woods
- Secondary woodland
- Pottery site
- Arable
- Floodplain
- Long barrow
- Round barrow
- Grazing land

12   *The Stonehenge landscapes and its many monuments have been subject to intense archaeological study, allowing the reconstruction of a detailed four-stage development over the Neolithic. In the Early Neolithic Robin Hood's Ball enclosure, long barrows and scattered settlements occupied clearings in the woodland; by the Middle Neolithic the two cursus monuments and the ditch of what became Stonehenge were added, followed by Durrington Walls and Woodehenge and a palisade across the centre of an increasingly open landscape of cultivation and settlement. By the end of the Neolithic, the landscape was open, and only Stonehenge remained as a monument.* After Allen

heavily farmed that no environmental data has been forthcoming, but it might be inferred that much was still wooded in the early Neolithic. By the later Neolithic there is evidence for widespread clearance across the landscape, with areas of intense agricultural activity, and all the river valley areas were cleared but for a small patch of woodland around Poundbury.

A different picture emerges for the earlier Neolithic Stonehenge landscape (Allen 1997) (**12**). The floodplains of the rivers Avon and Till were the only substantially open areas apart from a limited amount of grazed land that surrounded the earlier monuments such as Robin

Hood's Ball, and the small arable plots on King Barrow Ridge in the Earlier Neolithic. The landscape was dominated by oak, hazel and elm woods with secondary open woodland.

In the middle Neolithic around 2900 BC the surrounding wildwood remained much as before, but around Stonehenge and the cursus monuments there were more arable plots and open areas, and an increase in secondary woodland. This regeneration continued in the later Neolithic between 2900-2400 and broke up the swathes of semi-cleared grassland and arable landscape into scrubby patches of woodland, with the denser elm-oak-hazel woods still enclosing much of the landscape. In the final Neolithic to early Bronze Age period (2400-1600 BC), which corresponds to the culmination of Stonehenge, the landscape was much more open, with grazed downland, arable areas, small isolated patches of secondary wood; only at the fringes on steep or heavy land did the elm, oak and hazel woods remain intact.

Cranborne Chase (Dorset) is another chalkland area that has been subjected to intensive research (Barrett et al 1991) which expands the understanding of the pattern of forest clearance and agricultural expansion seen elsewhere in Wessex. Data have been collected from the Down Farm shaft (Green 2000), a natural solution-hole some 4-5m in diameter, and over 25m deep. It was carefully excavated and sampled for a range of environmental indicators, including pollens, snail shells and dating materials. The shaft was filled in through natural weathering, and its contents bridge the important Mesolithic-Neolithic transition with some rich environmental data. It shows a wooded Mesolithic landscape of hazel and forest trees, gradually becoming more open, even in the late Mesolithic period *c*.4350-4000 BC, when areas were cleared and then reverted to woodland. The samples taken from the later levels of the shaft support evidence from nearby sites such as Hambledon Hill causewayed enclosure ditches (3660-3380 BC) where massive tree felling had cleared the upper part of the hill. Buried soils beneath local long barrows and enclosures such as Handley Down contained snails of various woodland species, including old forest species, and these continued throughout the life of the sites showing local woodland persisted over a long time. The construction of the nearby Dorset cursus had cut through the woodlands, and the local pollen and snail shell sequence shows that periodic clearance around the monument took place, followed by local regeneration. For 40 years, the experimental earthwork on Overton Down (Bell et al 1996) has focused on the processes of erosion, and plant, animal and human effects on earthworks, and has become an important means of measuring changes to landscapes since the Neolithic.

Scotland

Forest clearance and intensive use of the landscape took place some time later in much of north, west and highland Scotland. Not only was much of the landscape generally harsher and less suitable for agricultural activities than the south, but it was also more thinly populated and endowed with adequate wild foods to support the local hunter-gatherer communities. The pollen sequence is particularly important in Scotland, where local peat formations provide suitable samples. The Elm decline is identified in Scotland, and it seems associated with increased quantities of grass pollens, but at an earlier date than the main Neolithic clearance phases (Braeroddach Loch, Aberdeenshire, 4340-3960 cal. BC). Pollen studies from Loch Rae near the Cleaven Dyke (Barclay and Maxwell 1998) show local clearance episodes and a decline in tree pollens.

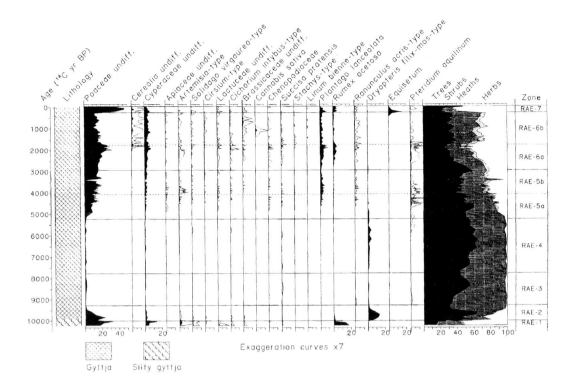

13   *Loch Rae (Scotland) pollen diagram shows the marked decline of tree and shrub pollens and the rise of herbs (grass and cereals) from c.3000 BC (right hand column) that is typical of Neolithic forest clearance.* After Edwards and Whittington

By the middle Neolithic, woodland regeneration has been identified at several sites such as the settlement at Scord of Brouster on Shetland (**38**)and at Machrie Moor on Arran. Some scholars suggest that rather than simply major phases of tree clearance followed by regeneration, there may have been various forms of forest exploitation, such as coppicing, stock foraging and management. A good sequence of C14 dates demonstrates that at many Neolithic sites clearance came only in the third millennium BC. Callanish (or Calanais) on Lewis was cleared only *c.*2780 BC, and Kinloch on Rhum (where late Mesolithic communities are recorded) in *c.*2460 BC. Many others suggest major clearance only in the second millennium BC, as at Machrie Moor on Arran *c.*1340 BC. And as time went on, the pace quickened and rarely did forests fully regenerate. Climatic variation is marked in Scotland and Ireland by the growth of peat deposits as rainfall increased during the third millennium BC. On Shetland, blanket peat covered the site of Saxa Vord from *c.*2290-2030 BC, but elsewhere peat formations began over a wide timespan, from after the last glaciation until recent times.

Cleaven dyke

A good case study has been made of the area around the Cleaven Dyke in Perthshire, showing the locally changing environment from *c.*8000 BC to recent times, based on pollens

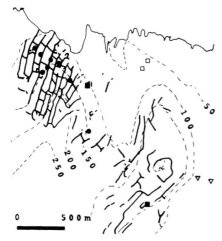

14a The Neolithic co-axial Ceide field systems of Behy Glenura date from as early as 4000 BC, and were probably used as cattle pastures. The earlier Neolithic house of Ballyglass is located just off the right of the map, and was probably in use at the same time as the field systems

14b The buried Neolithic walls in the peat of Behy Glenura which grew over them after c.3200 BC, with Seamus Caulfield the excvator. Photo C. Malone

from Rae Loch (Edwards and Whittington 1998) (**13**). In the late glacial around 8000 BC the area was dominated by willows, docks, sedges and grasses, indicating a cold climate and very little woodland cover. By the early Holocene *c.*7000 BC, woodlands of birch trees and juniper were already being replaced by hazel woods, and very little grassland seems to have been present in the area. Hazel then decreased as warmer conditions spread into eastern Scotland, allowing oak and elm to become established, followed by alder, forming a dense forested landscape *c.*6000 BC. There was no suggestion in the sequence for human intervention in the woodlands through coppicing or burning, and it was only around 4000 BC that change came with the rapid decrease in elm, together with the other main tree species. Alongside the tree pollen decline, there was an increase in grass, weeds and bracken,

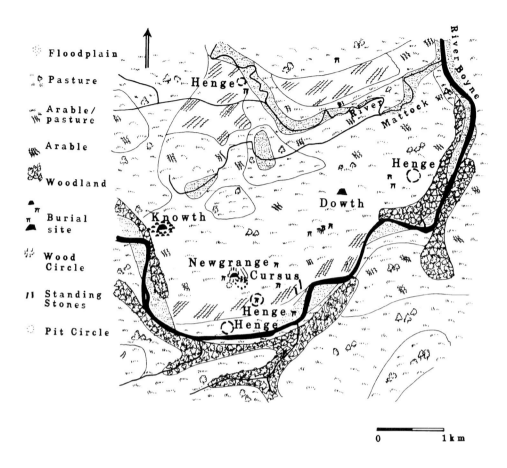

Legend:
- Floodplain
- Pasture
- Arable/pasture
- Arable
- Woodland
- Burial site
- Wood Circle
- Standing Stones
- Pit Circle

15 Probable landuse around the passage graves and associated monuments of the Boyne valley, Co. Meath. After Cooney 1997

all indicative of clearance and agricultural activities. By 3000 BC cereal pollen was present together with weeds specific to arable farming. However, by the Bronze Age over a millennium later, cereals declined suggesting a reduction in the intensity of farming in the area, which could relate to more extensive forms of farming and pastoralism as landscape reverted to grass and scrub. Throughout the long sequence, woodlands persisted around the edge of the cultivated areas, and only really declined in later prehistory.

Western Ireland

Similar trends can be seen in Ireland, where agricultural economies were gradually replaced by peat formations and more extensive grazing regimes. The field systems of Behy Glenura (or Ceide Fields) in north Mayo (**14a & b**) were entirely buried in peat that began to grow from *c*.2700 BC, burying a landscape of pines and grassland that had been growing from before 4000 BC. The fields that had been laid out to contain cattle and small arable plots were abandoned by 2500 BC, and the landscape became a blanket bog.

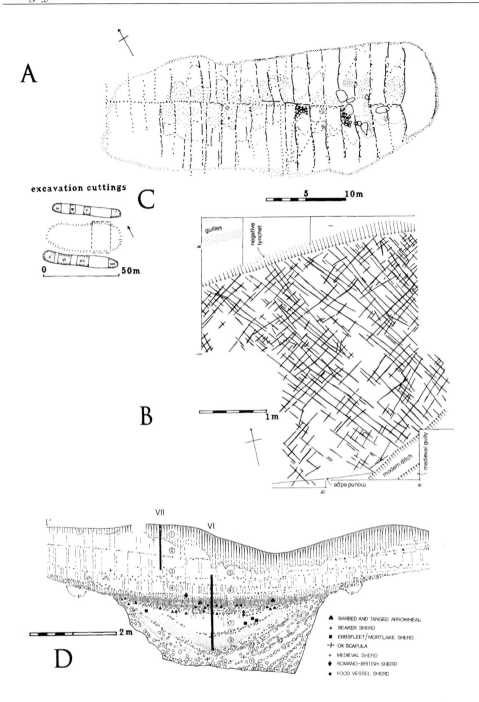

16 *Excavations at South Street Long Barrow (Wiltshire) revealed evidence for Neolithic cultivation using an ard (C), important information on the changing landscape, and (A) how the barrow had been sub-divided by internal hurdles into discrete bays. B is the location of the excavation trenches and area of ard marks; D is a section through cutting VII, showing the mollusc and pollen sample columns VI and VII. After Ashbee et al.*

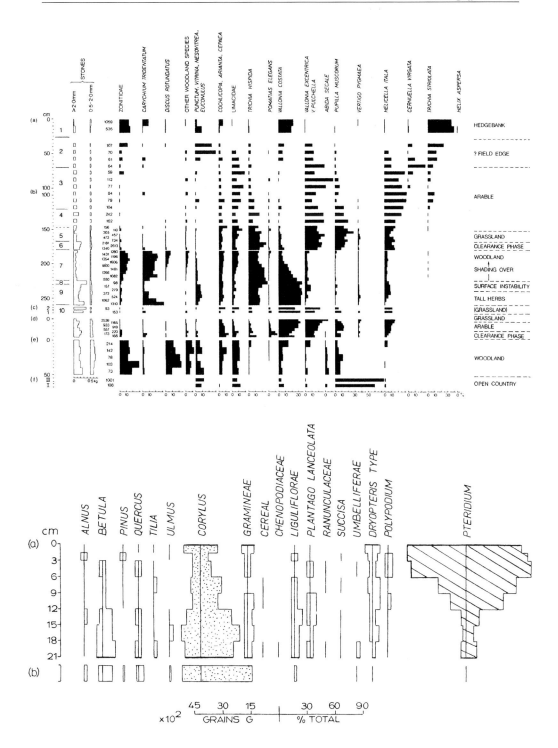

17   *Excavations at South Street Long Barrow. A: Landsnail diagram from column VII. B: Pollen diagram; 'a' represents the buried soil beneath the barrow; 'b' is a roothole cast at the base of the buried soil.* After Evans

Modern soils are often good indicators of the potential of agriculture in the Neolithic, and soil maps, combined with the environmental record of archaeological sites, can sometimes estimate where arable activities may have been in the landscape. Such work has been attempted in the Boyne valley around the great passage graves (**15**). It shows how the monuments were generally located away from the prime farming land, and on poorer quality soils. It also suggested that by the later Neolithic, the landscape was fairly open, with tracts of woodland interspersed with grazing and arable land providing a suitable background to the conspicuous and dramatic monuments.

Farming

Cultivation and management of the landscape brought marked changes to the formerly forested natural environment of Britain and Ireland. There are a number of characteristics of all farming regimes that may leave archaeological traces, and provide a means to explore the economic world of the Neolithic. As discussed above, the clearance of trees was a major activity and had the greatest single impact on the landscape in which people lived. Initially, the cutting of small clearings for settlement and arable plots must have been sufficient for low levels of population, and forest blanketed the bulk of the landscape. However, as the Wessex data implies, over the space of half a millennium from *c*.3800-3200 BC tree cover was progressively removed and the landscape became much more open and covered by individual plots and settlements. Evidence for this is demonstrated by the existence of ard marks from early cultivation, beneath later mounds, as in the example of South Street Long Barrow at Avebury (Ashbee et al 1979) (**16 & 17**). Ards were the first forms of plough and

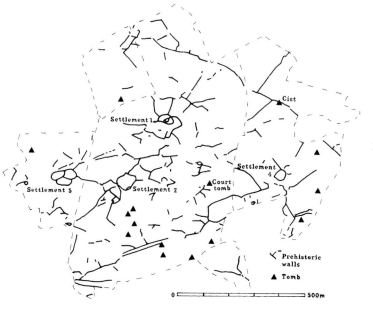

18 *Rougham Hill, Co. Clare in Ireland has revealed an extensive landscape of fields, tombs and settlements from the later Neolithic, comparable to the landscapes recorded on Shetland. After Jones and Gilmer*

were designed to score the ground and break the soil. The pollen and snail shell sequence associated with the earlier Neolithic cultivation showed trees had been cleared from the area and replaced by more open grassland, arable and later scrub regrowth (**17**).

By the later Neolithic, declining soil fertility, more extensive pastoral farming practices, expansion into more marginal landscapes, and, on prime areas, perhaps better crop management and higher productivity, meant that woodlands regenerated. They did not consist of the large forest trees of the primary 'wildwood' but instead of scrub and heathland species such as the bracken, gorse, and thorn that predominated with the grasslands. Farmers would have marked their plots with fences, hedges and ditches, in an attempt to contain their stock and keep scavengers off their growing crops. The evidence from Behy Glenura and Shetland shows categorically that fields existed. New research at Rougham Hill in Co. Clare (**18**)has recorded an extensive later Neolithic landscape of fieldwalls and associated prehistoric settlement (Jones and Gilmer 1999). It is likely that some of the remnant walls of west Cornwall had their origin in the Neolithic. Controls for herded animals, such as cross dykes (for a third millennium example on Hambledon Hill see **44 & 46**) or droveways (Fengate) demarcated routes for animals to access grazing land. These usually fragile structures are rarely located on Neolithic sites other than as gullies and post-holes. Much more research and extensive excavation is needed to demonstrate the regional and the chronological nature of Neolithic farming sites, of which at present too little is known.

Plants and animals

The earliest farming communities used imported animals (domesticated cattle, sheep, goat (ungulates) and pig). There has long been speculation over whether any indigenous animals could have been locally domesticated, and wild boar are particularly strong candidates along with Exmoor ponies. The domestication of the primary farm animals is well documented in the east Mediterranean and Near East, and evidence across early Neolithic Europe shows how these animals were transported, adopted and bred in local situations. The domestic species that reached Britain were of very similar stock, and almost certainly were introduced fully domesticated and adapted already to a cool north European climate. The first sheep to be introduced were probably similar in size and appearance to the Soay sheep of Scotland. They were small, rugged and had hair rather than wool. The cattle were small, and in comparison to the wild, indigenous and huge *Bos Primigenus* very docile. Pigs were probably brought in from Europe, although there may have been local domestication of the native *Sus Scrofa* wild boar, which is relatively easily tamed. As woodlands diminished, it is quite likely that both introduced and local species made up pig populations.

The identification of animals from archaeological sites is relatively straightforward, provided that the animal bones are properly sampled and recorded. Age and sex can be determined from the bones so that a population can be reconstructed. Much of course depends on the sample size, and many thousands of bones, ideally with many scores of individual skeletons, are needed to give an accurate account of the prehistoric economy of a site. A predominance of young male sheep bones and a high number of mature female

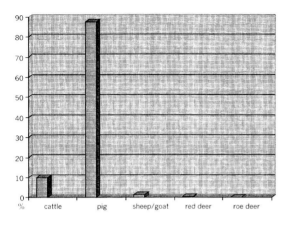
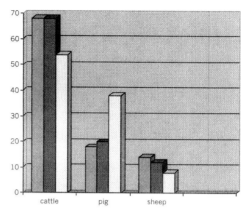

19a *Relative ungulate proportions at the West Kennet enclosures.*
Edwards and Horne in Whittle (ed.) 1997

19b *Relative ungulate proportions from Windmill Hill. Percentage of numbers of bones from the
1988 excavations, showing changing proportions of animals during the Neolithic.*
After Grigson in Whittle 1999

sheep would imply that the flock was kept for wool and breeding. Similarly, a large percentage of older female cows might imply the same, together with an emphasis on milk production. The culling of young animals at a particular part of the annual cycle, for example at the end of the summer, could suggest that fodder was directed to only part of the breeding herd over the autumn and winter. There are many subtleties and complex statistical tests that need to be applied to animal bone data in order to extract a reasonably accurate scenario of food supply and economic strategy. Equally, the archaeological contexts from which the bones come need to be clearly phased and accurately sampled. In many instances, bone does not survive well in acid or sandy soils, and these conditions thus remove the possibility of reconstructing a large part of the economy.

In the wetlands of Somerset and the Fens, other strategies were employed, such as coppicing the willow and hazel to provide animal fodder from the leafy branches and grazing around the shrubs. Early experiments with making silage and hay were probably underway as well.

Animal bones have been found and studied from Neolithic sites across Britain, and in many instances the basic economic composition is not the main interest. Instead, the association of particular animals and body parts with special contexts, such as causewayed enclosure ditches or burials, offers an important insight into the symbolic and conceptual world of the period. The site of Windmill Hill has been subjected to three different excavations, the most recent in 1988 (Whittle et al.. 1999). These have provided a very complete picture of the fauna of the causewayed enclosure, and its economic and symbolic practices. Domestic ungulates were the most frequent species in each of the discrete contexts excavated, with cattle representing between 50 and 80 per cent of the total, pigs between 10 and 50 per cent and sheep/goat between 5 and 50 per cent. In some instances, crania, horncores and groups of bones were placed in the ditches, which together with the meat-bearing bones placed there implies perhaps conspicuous consumption or symbolic offerings. (**19**)

The research on Cranborne Chase showed that the Neolithic domestic fauna was well adapted to a woodland environment, predominantly consisting of pigs and cattle, alongside wild deer and cattle. Sheep were relatively rare in the earlier Neolithic, and only became more common in the Bronze Age.

At the causewayed site of Hambledon Hill in Dorset (Mercer 1981 and forthcoming) cattle were also the most numerous animal, well suited to the downland and the Blackmore Vale grazing. The same emphasis is thought to be the case in the Boyne valley of eastern Ireland, where traditionally cattle have been grazed on the river terraces. Whereas sheep/goat were the primary stock animal of much of Europe, cattle appear to have been well adapted to the rich grass and woodland of Britain and Ireland. Pigs too, flourished in the mixed woodlands and browse of the Neolithic landscape. The recently excavated enclosure of Etton on the Fenland edge was rich in animal remains, and plots were made of the excavated ditch sections containing bones (Pryor 1999). And at Staines, deposits in ditches implied symbolic and carefully structured arrangements of animal and human bones and objects. By the Middle-Later Neolithic, feasting activities may have focused on pigs. For example, the excavations at the enclosures at West Kennet (Wiltshire) (Whittle 1997) revealed that pig were the most frequently butchered animals, and occurred in great quantities in the ditches (**19**). Although the excavated sample was small, it can be inferred from the total number of pigs that they were used for feasting on a large scale. Cattle too seem to have been valued for feasting although in smaller numbers. What makes the deposits interesting is the placement of the bones around the large timber uprights which marked the enclosures and the emphasis on particular sides of the animal — perhaps implying symbolic significance.

Agriculture and economic expansion — interpretation

The farming of Neolithic Britain has been extensively studied over the decades, and many papers, books and reports have resulted. We know much that was simply assumed three decades ago about landscape changes, soils, dating, crops and animals. But there is still considerable detail missing, and the lack of settlement sites or large and comprehensive samples of seeds and bones means that our understanding of changes from early to late Neolithic economic strategy is still often based on broad assumptions. Many scholars have adopted this viewpoint, and made studies of 'prehistoric' (rather than Neolithic) agriculture, incorporating data that are strictly from later episodes and more intensive farming regimes.

In general, the earlier Neolithic is assumed to have been one of household levels of food production, supplemented by gathered and hunted foods. However, from the beginning of the Neolithic it is certain that fields were laid out (Ceide Fields, Fengate) and that ards or simple ploughs were employed to break the soil for crops (the ard marks under the South Street long barrow, Wiltshire, and the Donnerupland ard from Denmark are good evidence) for what were probably little more than garden-sized plots. Much of the impetus for woodland clearance and control came from the need to make space for the newly introduced crops of einkorn, emmer and bread wheat, six-rowed and naked varieties of barley, and rye.

Although pulses such as pea and bean are assumed to have come to Britain, only flax is unequivocally recorded in the Neolithic. Wild plants that were routinely exploited alongside these domestic cereals included grasses, hazelnuts, acorns, wild fruits (sloe, berries, elder, hawthorn), fungi and tubers. The evidence for early farming remains, however, unclear and incomplete. Relatively few sites have been sampled extensively, and of those that have, enclosures seem to have the highest concentrations of seed remains, since burial and ritual sites such as cursuses were hardly used for food processing or eating. Fairbairn (2000) argues that the take up of new plant foods was not necessarily an economic choice, but one that had social implications. Feasting and exchange at causewayed enclosures may have been one way that local indigenous groups acquired seed for planting, and indeed seeds may well have been an important and prestigious gift between different groups. The rather limited range of plants that have been identified in Neolithic Britain implies that not all the possible varieties, including pulses and rye, actually crossed the English Channel to Britain. However, exotic plants sometimes did, such as a grape pip found at Hambledon Hill from fourth millennium BC deposits. Changes in crops over the Neolithic are poorly charted, since almost no sites span occupations long enough to show different economic episodes, unlike for example occupation in a deeply stratified cave. Late Neolithic enclosures such as the West Kennet site produce relatively few seeds, and of those found even the different types of wheat and barley are difficult to distinguish.

Animal remains provide a better idea of changing economic practices over the Neolithic, and from a cattle-dominated earlier-middle Neolithic, pigs became increasingly important as feasting food in the later Neolithic. There is no obvious explanation for this, other than the fact that pigs are extremely efficient meat producers with rapid breeding cycles and growth rates. Pigs also forage on woodland undergrowth and scrub and would have flourished in the increasingly degraded landscapes that surrounded areas of dense Neolithic occupation when more intensive farming had failed. The pollen and mollusc record indicate that some landscapes reverted to scrub during the middle-later Neolithic perhaps from soil exhaustion, erosion, and changing farming practices, and this seems to tally with the rise in pig keeping. However, it did not mean the wholesale reduction of cattle rearing, and instead we can identify the employment of different practices in cattle and sheep farming. The secondary products of these animals included wool, leather, horn, milk and (from cattle) traction to pull ards, logs and, later on, wheeled carts. Animals probably began to have different values and were regarded not simply as food, but as the producers of many different resources. In continental Europe the third millennium BC is distinguished by pottery developed to make cheese and yoghurt, by combs and weaving equipment, and special kit designed to harness animal energy (see Sherratt 1997). The technology must have spread to Britain, but left little secure artefactual evidence until well into the second millennium BC when loom weights, needles, and spindle whorls become common. One obvious reason for the lack of evidence is the almost complete lack of settlement excavation in lowland or southern Britain where such practices would have been commonplace. Instead, settlement evidence is from the marginal areas where intensive and sophisticated economic use of animals was lacking. Much remains to be done on the reserch of Neolithic Britain, and fieldwork that might supply evidence needs to be developed if knowledge is to be advanced.

3 Hearth and home:
domestic settlements in the Neolithic

This chapter discusses the evidence for domestic settlement, while chapter 4 examines the larger enclosure — the causewayed camps which may also have had a settlement function. In some examples discussed below, the distinction between domestic site and enclosure is not really clear, and archaeological evidence often presents a confusingly mixed picture of categories of data.

The concept 'settlement' underpins our ideas about Neolithic societies. It was the fundamental change from mobile hunter-gatherer groups to farming communities. At a broad level, it represents the change from temporary camps to a more permanent occupation of places, with communities remaining for generations rather than seasons. One of the most distinctive characteristics of farming communities in the Near East and Europe was the development of villages, houses and architecture. Many sites in Europe have revealed the archaeological remains of houses, implied from post-holes, trenches and slots which once held planks and posts of wood, together with their associated ditches, hearths and storage pits. Such remains are virtually unknown from Mesolithic hunter-gatherer sites in NW Europe, so archaeological evidence for settlement and houses is a key to recognising Neolithic societies. However, the evidence from Britain is problematic because very few settlements survive. Much recent discussion (see especially Whittle 1996) has focused on this lack of evidence, and some current ideas favour a Neolithic world which was far more mobile and less settled than its central-southern European counterparts. The survival of evidence may be the main problem, and the history of intensive agriculture of Britain, coupled with forest clearance, soil movement and the alluviation of the valleys of the south and east where many early farmers lived, may have removed or covered much settlement evidence. In many areas, burial mounds seem to cover earlier settlement debris and features, and there may well be a link between the former living places of people and their burial sites. Indeed, there is a strong similarity between the architecture of tombs and houses. Some north European and Orkney evidence is particularly impressive, and provides a parallel to the longhouses in the TRB and Lengyel cultures on the north European plain which seem, for example, to be mirrored in long burial mounds and burial enclosures, even down to details of their orientation (Bradley 1998, ch. 3; Hodder 1990, 142-56; Whittle 1996, 192-5).

The remoter parts of north and west Britain and Ireland have some remarkable examples of surviving earlier Neolithic settlements and individual houses. These show that the Neolithic people lived in small social units, mostly farmsteads, scattered thinly across the landscape. Mixed grain and stock agriculture was not, it seems, the only form

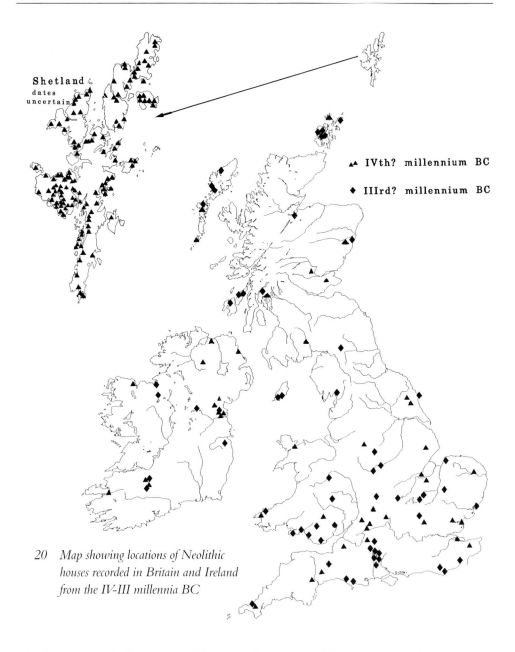

IVth? millennium BC

IIIrd? millennium BC

20   *Map showing locations of Neolithic*
     houses recorded in Britain and Ireland
     from the IV-III millennia BC

of subsistence at the beginning of the Neolithic. Many of the surviving settlements were located in places where hunted, gathered and marine resources were especially rich, such as in the Orkney islands, western Ireland and west Wales, and these foods clearly supplemented an otherwise farmed diet. Most of the evidence for early farming is not based on grain but on stock rearing, and especially on cattle. Pastoral economies favoured farmsteads spread across the landscape, where each unit would have had grazing land and water, as well as areas for cereals and garden production. The rather temporary buildings and structures associated with cattle keeping would not have been of a scale that would survive as archaeological evidence over 5000-6000 years of successive cultivation and disturbance. Hedges, small byres, haystacks, fences and suchlike are the types of structure expected, and indeed found, at rare sites like Fengate. The houses seem to have been just as temporary.

Finding and recognising settlement evidence

The simplest method for locating settlement evidence and economic activities from most prehistoric periods is a combination of fieldwalking, aerial reconnaissance, geophysical and soil survey, and excavation. Fieldwalking the surface of ploughed fields often reveals flint scatters, stone material, pottery, bone and burnt daub. Ploughing often clips the top of buried features and brings these diagnostic materials to the surface. But most do not survive for long in the frosty winters of Britain, and pottery, bone and daub will rapidly disappear leaving just stone material. In upland stony areas, remnants of Neolithic field systems, wall foundations, terraces and clearance cairns are sometimes preserved, as in the Shetland Isles (**38**) and Cornwall. Buried sites may be apparent from the air and, if photographs are taken at the right season or light level, the form of a site is recorded. Once a concentration of artefactual material is found, geophysical survey and other investigations may provide detailed information on buried features, such as ditches and banks (Clark 1996). Soil studies sometimes pick up areas of ancient settlement, through the concentration in the soil of high phosphates from animal pens and middens, from burnt soils and hearths though magnetometry, or from particular environmental remains such as snail shells that were specific to a recognisable type of landscape use or ecology. Microscopic remains in the soil structure may indicate local activities such as stone-working, bone-working and other domestic, industrial or natural processes resulting in erosion and burial (Soil Micromorphology). As discussed in chapter 2, plant pollens preserved in buried soils and peat show episodes of cultivation and clearance over time, and may link with settlement development. Many of these analytical techniques are routinely applied to archaeological sites, but the circumstances of site discovery are rarely designed to make the most of Neolithic settlement. More often, sites are found through routine excavations designed to sample areas of landscape prior to destructive development. Specially designed research programmes for Neolithic settlement are not part of the usual research agenda. However, one or two recent projects have brought exceptional material to light. One is the survey of intertidal areas around the River Blackwater (Hullbridge) in Essex (Wilkinson and Murphy 1995, forthcoming). In the wet tidal zone, Neolithic settlement evidence has been discovered and plotted, together with extensive samples of environmental data. Another is Whittle's work on Shetland at Scord of Brouster (Whittle et al 1986). This was able to link together a long sequence of settlement, houses and field systems. Similarly, the work in Mayo has shown how the boulder walls of the Ceide fields were linked to Ballyglass and its domestic structure and court cairns and other tombs in the are (see below).

Evidence

The lack of obvious or intact Neolithic settlement evidence in many areas of Britain may result from the biases of research strategy, and a failure to recognise (or perhaps even look for) buried or eroded remnants. For centuries interest has centred on the prominent Neolithic remains of Megalithic monuments. Chambered tombs, standing stones, henges and circles naturally attract attention because they are visible and often remarkably intact. They provide a tangible link with the 'mysterious' and monumental Neolithic, rather than the more mundane domestic world of settlement. In contrast, later prehistory is dominated by substantial settlements and hillforts, which tend to distort our expectations for earlier and less obvious settlement. Most Neolithic settlement evidence has come to light accidentally in small-scale excavations that have not aimed to examine a whole settlement. Although too little is known about typical Neolithic communities and their settlement, work over recent decades has shown distinctions between early and late settlement types with house forms changing from rectangular to circular as time passed.

The evidence for settlement falls into a number of different categories:

1. House structures, pits, post-holes, and associated evidence.
2. Surface scatters of material (pot, flint, bone, stone) from fieldwalking and excavations.
3. Settlement/burial/ceremonial foci around causewayed enclosures or camps (Smith 1971; Oswald *et al.* 2001).
4. Soil evidence, phosphates, molluscs, pollens etc.
5. Crop marks of buried structures (such as Balbridie).

Much of the literature on Neolithic settlement, not surprisingly, is very negative, and suggests that little is known (or indeed can be known) about how people lived or the sorts of structures which they constructed. A recent book on Neolithic houses (Darvill et al.. 1996) successfully reverses this negative impression by showing that across Britain and Ireland, there are hundreds of sites, a few of which provide a tangible view of the domestic world of the Neolithic. Settlement sizes and thus their populations are not easily estimated, since most sites consist of individual or, rarely, groups of buildings, although quite a number are associated with enclosures. Skara Brae, the most complete settlement known in Britain, had a total of 10 rooms or houses surviving, and seven to fifteen structures have been recorded elsewhere. In 1996 England and Wales had an estimated 65 sites, containing over 109 buildings. Scotland has some particularly well-preserved settlements, such as the dozen or so Neolithic settlements on Orkney, the very dense settlement of the Shetland Islands (which has some 140 structures recorded), and the Western Isles. Fieldwork in Ireland has recorded over 50 settlements with houses (Grogan 1996). It is often the least fertile, inhospitable areas that preserve the best Neolithic settlement evidence. Agriculturally richer areas like east Scotland, East Anglia and the chalklands of southern Britain are remarkably poor in coherent survivals, as cultivation has destroyed the fragile remains of post-holes, beam slots, floors and middens. The most common location for settlement survival is under later barrows and cairns, and some 21 per cent of the English/Welsh examples have been located beneath such structures.

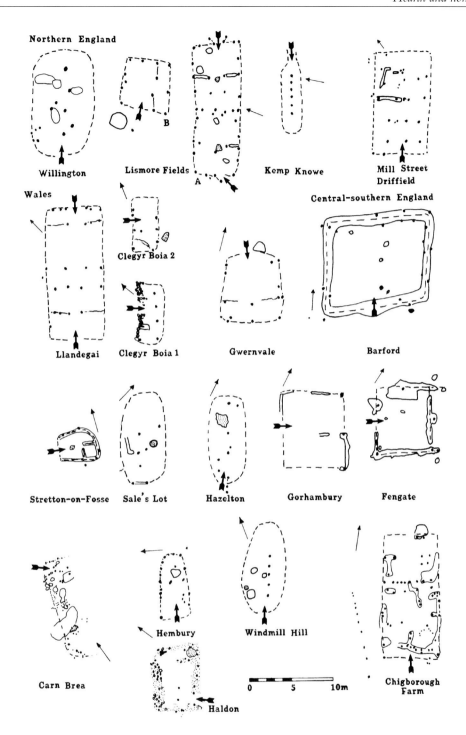

21   *Earlier Neolithic rectangular house plans from England and Wales built of posts, planks and stone. The heavy arrow shows the likely entrance and the small arrow points north. Stippled areas are hearths.* After Darvill and others

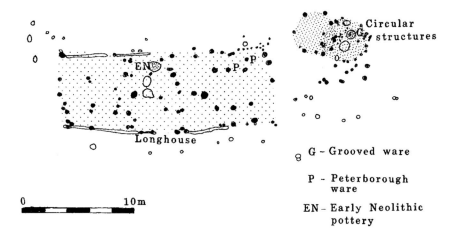

22   The long house from White Horse Stone, Kent is similar in plan to contemporary European examples. After Glass

Examples of early settlements — houses

The earlier Neolithic sites seem to reflect European prototypes — typically the rectangular timber-built halls or longhouses of the north European plain, which were common in the fifth millennium BC Linearbandkeramik (LBK) Culture. Sites as far apart as Kent and Aberdeenshire have revealed very substantial timber-built structures similar to these prototypes (Barclay 1996, Fairweather and Ralston 1993). Balbridie on Deeside was some 24.5m long, 13m wide and probably had a roof height of 8.5m. It was located through aerial photography. The recently discovered example at White Horse Stone near Maidstone, Kent, is smaller — 18m long by 8m wide (**22**). The building was buried under 4m of hillwash, which had protected the slight post-hole and slot traces. The structure has linear slots at one end, and a number of post-holes which supported a roof and porch. Within were hearths and pits, and close by the south-east end is another circular structure 3.75m in diameter, but perhaps of a later Neolithic date than the longhouse. The pottery (early bowls) suggests that it is earlier Neolithic, but absolute dates are awaited (Glass 2000).

Most houses of the earlier Neolithic in England and Wales are rectangular to squarish in plan, and smaller than the examples described above. They range from 2x1m to 15x5m, although average sizes are 4-10m long and 3-7m wide. Wood was the major building material of most houses, either set as upright posts in sockets, or resting on stone footings. The larger buildings consumed enormous numbers of felled trees and much labour. Preparation involved straightening posts and splitting planks and working lengths of wood for roof purlins and beams, stakes, wattle and internal divisions. In addition, great quantities of reed, straw or turf were required for roof thatch, and clay, mud and animal dung for daubing the walls. Experimental reconstructions of Neolithic longhouses imply that an entire community might have been involved for months in building the larger houses (Startin 1978). Examples of wood survive from wet sites like the Somerset Levels

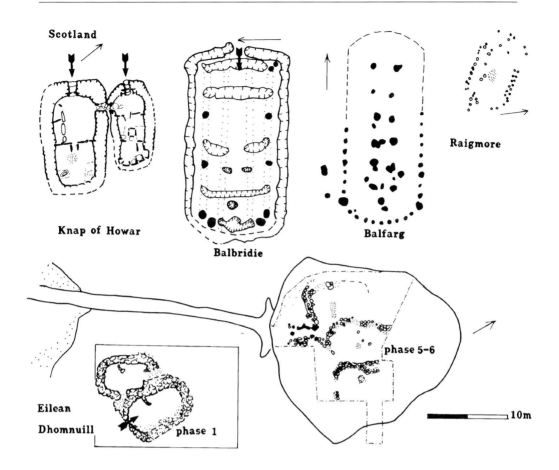

23 (above and following page) Earlier Neolithic rectangular house plans from Scotland and
    Ireland built of posts, planks and stone. The heavy arrow shows likely entrance, the small
    arrow points north. Stippled areas are hearths. After Barclay, Grogan and Armit

Sweet Track and the Cambridgeshire Fens at Etton, which show how skilled Neolithic
woodworkers were. It is likely that houses were elaborately finished, and doubtless
decorated with carvings, although the ground evidence for timber houses does not
preserve any part of the superstructures to prove this.

Enclosed early Neolithic settlement

Many earlier Neolithic houses were associated with enclosures which functioned as
settlements as well as ceremonial and defensive sites. The embanked promontory fort of
Hembury in Devon (Liddell 1931) was one of the first sites to demonstrate the potential of
Neolithic settlement. Just inside the entrance was a rectangular post-built house 7.1x3.6m
(**21**), together with evidence of distinctive pottery and flintwork. Also in Devon, a trapezoidal

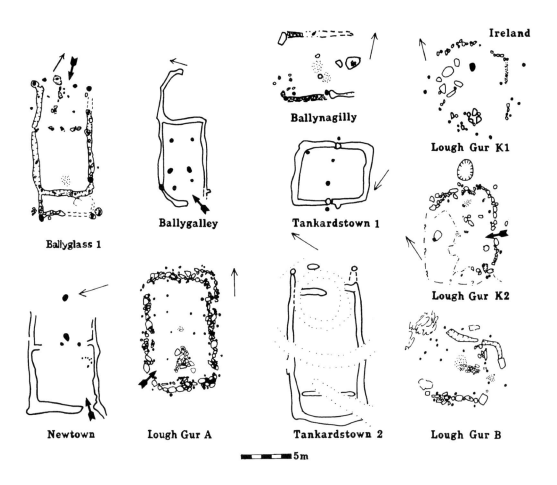

Ballynagilly

Ireland

Lough Gur K1

Ballygalley

Tankardstown 1

Lough Gur K2

Ballyglass 1

Newtown

Lough Gur A

Tankardstown 2

Lough Gur B

5m

house was found at Haldon similarly associated with an enclosure (**21**). Measuring 6m long and from 4.4-5.3m wide, it incorporated a stone wall that probably supported the wall and roof timbers. Inside there may have been a partition and a hearth was located in one corner (Willock 1936; 1937). The site of Carn Brea in Cornwall is particularly important for the information it provides on an unusually extensive fortified site. This consisted of massive, granite boulder-built defensive walls linking natural rock outcrops, which enclose an area less than a hectare, within a larger defended area of some 3-4ha. Several post- and stake-built structures were built as lean-tos against lengths of stone wall (**27 & 21**). Hearths, pits, Hembury pottery with distinctive trumpet lugs, axes, flints, a midden and industrial waste were found, and a radiocarbon date indicated occupation between *c.*3940-3704 BC. Around the enclosure, areas of cleared stones may represent cultivation activities (Mercer 1981).

Another prominent site is the causewayed enclosure/fort of Crickley Hill in Gloucestershire (**53 & 54**) where numerous Neolithic buildings have been identified, some predating the enclosure. These appear to be oval domestic post-built houses (2 x 1m and 2 x 3m) on top of the hill. Later buildings relating to the enclosure were more substantial rectangular post-built structures, and one isolated example built of timber and stone may have been a shrine (Dixon 1981; 1988 a & b). At Windmill Hill, several lines of

24   Reconstructed Neolithic house based on Irish examples at the Wexford Heritage Park.
      Photo C. Malone

post-holes, stake holes and slots suggest pre-enclosure and post-enclosure buildings (Smith 1965) (**21**). One example has a line of five post-holes over 4.5m with a hearth at one end, which might have supported a building of some 4.5 x 3m. The recently excavated enclosure at Etton exposed several structures within and close to the ditched enclosure (Pryor 1999). One post-built rectangular house 7 x 4m lay immediately inside the enclosure entrance at Etton Woodgate, and another squarish house was hard against causeway B. Other causewayed enclosure sites doubtless had similar buildings, but few excavations have been rigorous enough to locate them.

Unenclosed early Neolithic settlement

Many early Neolithic houses were not related to enclosures. Traces of field-systems and boundary walls have occasionally been identified and it seems more likely that farmsteads would normally have been associated with defined areas of fields, yards, pens, middens and other necessary farming structures.

However, some late Mesolithic structures may predate full farming, and in particular four houses of ring-slot and beam construction came to light at Bowman's Farm in Hampshire. Three were roughly rectangular measuring 4 x 4m, 5 x 4.5m and 5 x 4.5m, the latter being sub-circular, about 4.5m in diameter. The finds were Mesolithic in

25-6 The Neolithic houses of Knap of Howar, (Papa Westray, Orkney). The two structures are oval in form and are amongst the earliest domestic structures surviving in north-west Europe
Photos C. Malone

character and an accelerator date for the sub-circular building was 4934-4721 BC (Green 1996). Another site with Mesolithic elements (post-holes) and Neolithic structures is Lismore Fields in the Derbyshire Peak District. Occupation at this upland site shows that the houses were occupied from *c.*3800-3650 BC (structure A, of 15 x 5m) and 3650-3350 BC (structure B of 5 x 5m) (**21**).

Also in Derbyshire, the river valley settlement at Willington consisted of seven houses spanning the earlier to later Neolithic. The earliest building of 8x4m had post-holes and flanking slots and gullies and was associated with typical earlier Neolithic Grimston-Lyles Hill pottery. Excavations at Fengate in the 1970s on the fen edge at Peterborough in Cambridgeshire (Pryor 1974; 1984) uncovered an extensive buried prehistoric landscape on the gravel terrace above the wet fen, occupied from Neolithic to Iron Age times. The site had early Neolithic Grimston-Lyles Hill pottery types spread across the area, but the most significant structure was the Padholme Road rectangular house (7 x 8.5m) constructed of planks and posts set in slots, which probably supported a wattle frame, clay walls and a thatched roof. Within the structure, pottery, flint, a Great Langdale axe fragment and a jet bead were found. Carbon 14 dates ranged from 3900-2900 BC (**21**). Later structures were sub-circular in form and associated with Grooved Ware and Beaker pottery styles. Middle Neolithic lowland sites have been identified in the drowned inlets of intertidal river estuaries of the Essex coastal, where settlement was originally situated close to inlets. Square stake and wattle houses were noted at Stone Point at Walton on Naze, and excavations at The Stumble, Goldhanger identified a post-built rectangular house (7 x 5m) associated with plain Neolithic pottery and flint (Wilkinson and Murphy 1995; forthcoming). In Wales, a number of more marginal locations have shown that earlier Neolithic houses were being occupied. At Clegyr Boia (St David's, Pembrokeshire) two rectangular post and gully structures overlay each other. The earlier measured 6.7 x 3.6m and was linked to a low wall. There was an external hearth, and the site contained domestic rubbish (Williams 1953). A much more extensive site of at least seven buildings (predating standing stones of Late (?) Neolithic date) has been identified at Rhos-y-clegyrn (St Nicholas, Pembokeshire). An impressive timber 'long house' was excavated at Llandegai, Bangor associated with Grimiston-Lyles Hill earlier Neolithic pottery. It measured 13m long, and bears similarities to White Horse Hill, Lismore fields and Balbridie, reflecting house forms known from Europe.

Early Neolithic settlements in Scotland

Settlements located along rivers and coasts enabled Neolithic communities to exploit important marine resources, especially in northern and western zones, where conventional cereal agriculture was only slowly adopted. Coastal settlement was naturally significant in the Orkney and Shetland islands with their deeply indented coasts and lakes. Traces of Neolithic settlement occur in situations where marine resources could be exploited, and sites were often located close to the sea. Sand dunes have buried a number of settlements providing remarkable preservation. From the earlier Neolithic, the only likely houses are at the Knap of Howar on Papa Westray (Ritchie 1983) (**23, 25, 26**). Now exposed on the sea edge, but once situated in grassland behind dunes, two structures were built side-by-side within a 50cm-deep midden which probably predated the houses. Carbon 14 from the site suggests a date of 3600-3100BC. The houses were buried by 2.5m of blown sand, which preserved door lintels and walls to almost full height. The houses give a vivid sense of a small community. The buildings faced the sea and both had front doors. House 1 was entered through a low paved passage with a door once attached to stone jambs. Within, the house was divided into two parts, overall measuring 9.5 x 4.5m.

The first section had a stone bench at one side and a central post pit. The inner room had a central hearth surrounded by a clay floor and a shelf built into the depth of the wall. The second house was slightly smaller, 7.5m long, but divided into three sections by large sandstone slabs set on end. It is less substantial and seems to have been built against the larger one, with a passage linking the two cut through the central wall. The outer room was an entrance area and led into a central room which had evidence for two successive hearths and much occupation material. The inner room was a storage area containing stone shelves and cupboards and a stone-lined pit in the floor. The passage between the houses had apparently been blocked at some late stage. The two structures would have been roofed in timber and perhaps even whale-bone, and thatched in turf, straw and reed.

Another settlement is the artificial island of Eilean Domhnuill, in Loch Olabhat on North Uist (Western Isles) located in a shallow loch and connected to the surrounding land by a causeway of stones and a wooden walkway. Within the palisaded perimeter, the settlement had a long occupation, with at least 11 distinct levels, each containing two or three houses and various other structures and middens. The houses had stone and turf walls which supported wooden superstructures, and they measured 5-6.8m long and 3.4-4m wide. The early phases represent earlier Neolithic occupation (**23**) and whilst the artefacts provide a good indication of this C14 dates are awaited. The fragile nature of the structures as well as the dense succession of buildings makes reconstruction difficult, but a fine indication has nevertheless been achieved.

Ireland — early Neolithic

Fieldwork in Ireland has unearthed a great number of domestic houses of the earlier and later Neolithic, preserved in the less intensively exploited landscapes of heath, peat and pasture (**23**) (Grogan 1996, Cooney 1999). Circular or oval structures are most numerous, although quite a number of early oval/rectangular ones have been recorded. These latter seem to date from 3900-3600 BC and are found at several locations across Ireland numbering at least 32 recorded buildings. The structures have from one to three compartments, and some are associated with other buildings or have open fronted areas facing the south. At Ballyglass in Mayo, a 12m-long house was constructed from plank walls and post-holes with a large entrance section and a two-part main structure. It was later demolished and buried by a court cairn and thus partly preserved, perhaps closely linked with the field systems found at Behy Glenura (Ceide). Similar buildings were found in Northern Ireland and the Ballynagilly house survives as a single roomed house 6.5 x 5.5m, but it now lacks ends, so it might have been larger and more complex. It produced some extremely early dates which are now questioned. Two larger houses at Ballygalley were more complex; the first was tripartite, 13 x 4.2m in size, and had a curved entrance area forming a semi-open porch (**23**). The second smaller house was 5m wide, but of unknown length. Other rectangular houses have been recorded from Tankardstown and Lough Gur in Limerick in the south, and at Newtown, Slieve Breagh and Knowth in Meath. The average length of plank and post houses ranges from 12-15m, and their width is usually of a 2:1 or 3:1 ratio. Floor areas, which provide some means to assess the possible number of inhabitants of these structures, range from 42m^2

down to 9m². Less substantial post and wattle houses have been found in some number at Lough Gur. These are structurally similar to the Shetland houses (see below), with thick walls holding a double line of posts and stone footings, which may have had a fill of turf, rushes or straw. Houses at Lough Gur were rectangular, oval and circular, and probably extended over a long time range conforming broadly to the sequence of earlier rectangular houses and later Neolithic circular houses found across the British Isles. They had Neolithic and Beaker pottery associated with them dating from *c*.3500 BC to after 2500 BC (**29 & 23**).

Examples of later Neolithic settlements — houses

England and Wales

Later Neolithic houses on mainland Britain differ from the earlier examples described above, and most typically they become circular/sub-circular in plan, as former rectangular forms were gradually abandoned in many areas (Darvill 1996). Some house structures appear to have been intentionally buried under later barrows, sealing in a 'house for the dead', and their ground-plans have been preserved; in other cases, sand-dunes, alluvial deposits and middens have buried settlements. The house found at Gwithian in Cornwall typifies the trend towards circular buildings, with its two post-built oval structures. The earlier one was 4.5m in diameter, and had a substantial porch and a slightly off-centre hearth. The later and larger house measured 8.1m diameter and was built directly over the earlier one, using less substantial stake holes to support wattle and daub walls. The house was set within a palisaded enclosure. A very similar stake-built house associated with later Neolithic and Beaker material was located under a later Bronze Age barrow at Chippenham in Cambridgeshire, and measured 12m diameter. A comparable site sequence was found at Playden in East Sussex with its curious rectangular post-in-slot building (dated to the last centuries of the third millennium BC). In the uplands, rectangular structures were still in use in the later Neolithic, as shown by the five structures associated with Grooved Ware pottery at Aleck Low in Derbyshire. Similarly, the site of Swarkeston in Derbyshire preserved two set of post and stake holes beneath a barrow. These were squarish buildings, *c*.3.6m across, associated with pits, Beaker pottery and a hearth. A round barrow covered a house at Mount Pleasant (Glamorgan) and consisted of a rectangular 6 x 3m stone wall (up to eight courses high) and post structure. There was a central line of three post-holes supporting the main roof ridge and a substantial doorway marked by doorposts. It was dated with Peterborough style pottery to the later Neolithic (Savory 1952). In Powys, the site of Trelystan was similarly covered by Bronze Age barrows, and two squarish post and stake houses were located. One measured 4.5 x 4m and the other 4.2 x 3.9m; they both had central hearths plus internal pits and debris, including Grooved ware pottery and flint. Carbon 14 dates place both structures in the middle of the third millennium BC. Of similar date was the rectangular house at Ronaldsway on the Isle of Man, measuring 7.3 x 4.1m, and built in a rock hollow, with stone and post footings for walls around a central hearth, midden remains, and local Ronaldsway pottery. Nearby the recent excavations at Billowan have revealed further evidence of this culture and its structures from the fourth-third millennia BC. Meldon Bridge in Peeblesshire, Scotland (discussed in chapter 6) is unique amongst later Neolithic settlements with its defended promontory of massive posts and wall enclosing some 8ha. Pits and a large timber structure some 9m diameter, plus later Neolithic pottery within this area, signal that it may be similar to the southern henge buildings (**28 & 30**).

The Northern Isles — Orkney and Shetland

Skara Brea on Mainland, Orkney, is one of the most impressive settlement sites of the later Neolithic (**31, 33-5**). A 'village' of at least 10 houses was originally located on grassland behind dunes close to the coast and was constructed within midden deposits. Gordon Childe, one of the excavators of the site in the 1930s, speculated that the inhabitants must have been living in a steaming compost heap, protected from the winds and warmed by the middens (Childe 1931, Clarke 1976a & b and Clarke and Sharples 1990). Today, the houses survive to the 3m high roof line and provide the most tangible and evocative picture of domestic life in the British Isles for the period 3100-2500 BC. The form of the houses was sub-

27   *Excavations at Carn Brea, Cornwall, showing the post-hole structures built against the surrounding stone wall.* Photo R. Mercer

rectangular, and each covered about 36m², with walls built of the local sandstone slabs. These facilitated the construction of characteristic 'built-in' furniture. Each house had a central stone kerbed hearth, and on the wall opposite the entrance was a two-shelved dresser supported by three stone piers. There were often additional shelves and cupboards set into the walls, and flanking the hearth on each side was a stone box bed. The right-hand bed was usually the larger and the left hand one the smaller. The discovery of paint pots in the latter has led to speculation that the smaller beds were for women. Stone seats and benches were sometimes placed next to the dresser, and set into the floor were stone-lined tanks (for bait, limpets or water) and grindstones. Each house had a doorway that could be sealed with either a stone or wood door, and this led into a covered passage that linked other houses together. One house had a peephole through the wall into the passage, and others had cells connected with drains, which may have functioned as internal toilets. The houses are similar in design at Skara Brae, and similar elsewhere in the Orkneys (Rinyo, Barnhouse and others). The houses functioned as a unit, within a tightly enclosed area, protected from the worst wind by the linking passages (**34**) and the semi-subterranean design. Under roofs of wood, whale bone, skins and turf, they would have been warm, and the internal design provided space and storage for various activities, as well as the more symbolic aspects of life. Decorated stones are found in several areas, especially houses 7 and

28 *Later oval Houses in England, Wales and Ireland. H = hearth.* After Darvill and Grogan

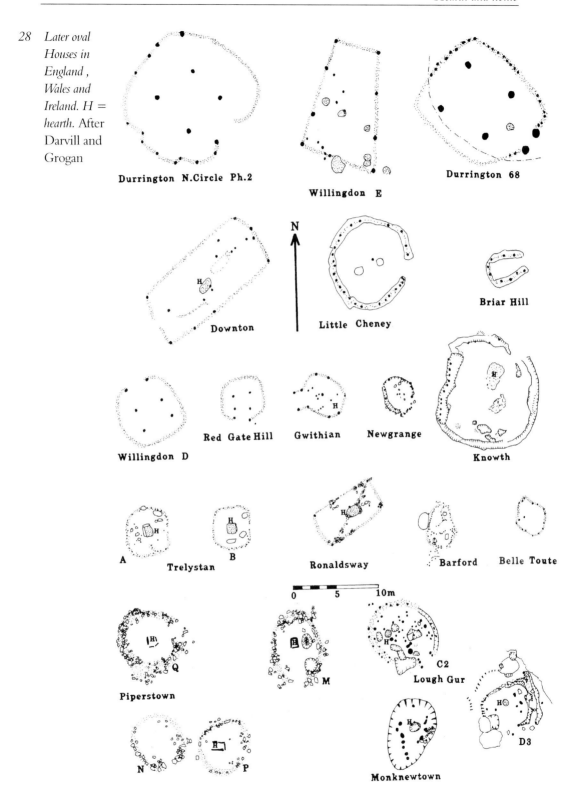

Durrington N.Circle Ph.2

Willingdon E

Durrington 68

Downton

N

Little Cheney

Briar Hill

Willingdon D

Red Gate Hill

Gwithian

Newgrange

Knowth

A Trelystan B

Ronaldsway

Barford

Belle Toute

0 5 10m

Piperstown

M

C2 Lough Gur

D3

N P

Monknewtown

8, which may have had special status. House 7 especially may have been symbolic, with two females buried under the box bed before the house was constructed (**31**).

Industrial activities were undertaken in house 8 which was set apart from the rest, and had no dresser, beds or limpet boxes, but instead had a large hearth. The floor had been littered with chert debris which may have been heated before knapping to improve its flaking quality. Subsistence evidence at the site shows that, like the Knap of Howar, Skara Brae was dependent on mixed agriculture, barley, and some wheat, supplemented by deer, whale, crustacea, fish and birds (see Chapter 2).

Other sites in the Orkney Isles provide further details of remarkable settlement from the later Neolithic (**31**). The site of Rinyo on Rousay was discovered in the 1930s and excavated until 1946. Several houses were found, although much damaged from ploughing. Gordon Childe assisted with the work, and noted several phases of building and ancient demolition over an extensive terrace, larger in total than Skara Brae, and similarly, Rinyo employed midden material in its construction, plus a cutting in the hillside to provide depth (Childe *et al.* 1939, 1947). Houses had the same components as Skara Brae, including drains, hearths, beds and dressers. The wet hillside location required particularly good drainage solutions, and some drains may have been wood lined. Next to one hearth, a clay oven (internally 37cm^2) set over a stone slab was located, and others were traced, showing that cooking may have been quite sophisticated. Similar material equipment to Skara Brae's was found, including the eponymous Rinyo pottery (see Chapter 7). In recent years other later Neolithic settlements have been traced in several locations in the Orkneys, at Pool on Sanday, and Barnhouse on Mainland. The latter is close to some of the main ceremonial monuments of the Loch Harray area. It was found, along with several other possible settlement sites around the internal lochs, through fieldwalking by Colin Richards (Richards 1990). Barnhouse consists of some 15 excavated houses (and others still unexplored) spanning a long sequence of occupation (**31 & 36**).

Unlike Skara Brae, the Barnhouse buildings are freestanding and do not appear to have covered passages between them or middens within the walls, perhaps because the site was more sheltered. The houses had similar internal layouts to Skara Brae but appeared more circular outside, and were carefully faced in stone. Roofs were probably wood and turf. Two distinctive buildings were much larger than the rest and may have had special functions or status. House 2 was well built and had six rectangular recesses, and unlike the other houses appears to have remained unchanged, but for two additional hearths, over a long period. The very large house 8 was later, set on a yellow clay platform and enclosed by a wall 3m thick. This surrounded an inner square room 7m across which had a large central hearth and traces of a huge stone dresser on the wall opposite the doorway. The doorway was monumental, with stone monoliths close to the hearth; it led outside through a 3m-long passage to an area of hearths, pits and stone boxes, enclosed within the building. Food and waste materials from preparation were found on the south side of this area, out of sight of what was probably the performance and public area of this strange building. The excavator speculates that the house combines elements from both the domestic and mortuary spheres, and appears to bridge these different cosmological themes. It may also symbolise social authority and changes in the social order and functioned as a communal meeting house or religious building.

The late Neolithic settlement at Links of Noltland (Westray) has yet to be fully explored but covers an area possibly four times larger than Skara Brae. A very large midden was heaped over 1100m², perhaps in anticipation of additional building. Those located so far are different to the rectangular style found elsewhere, and over a very large site, houses seem to be lobate in shape and closely similar in floor plan to some of the chambered tombs. The Orcadian settlements contain the characteristic Rinyo Grooved ware pottery, which places them in the mid-third millennium BC.

The Shetland Isles are especially rich in later Neolithic occupation sites. These include house remains and their surrounding field systems, which once supported the scattered farms of the islands. There are some similarities to the Orcadian forms in the structures, and houses are mostly oval, heel-shaped stone buildings entered at one end. Similar construction techniques and ground plans were used in the building of tombs and houses, where large upright stones at intervals had niches, portals and dividing walls between them. From evidence excavated at Scord of Brouster in the 1980s, this form of house was in use for over a millennium, from *c*.3300 to after 2000 BC. (Whittle *et al.* 1986). The houses are solidly built and simple, and the walls, which survive to about a metre, probably supported timber roof beams. One of the most impressive houses is the so-called Stanydale Temple. This large structure measures 13 x 6m, in a 'horseshoe' shape, and has a concave façade at the entrance. The roof beams appear to have been of spruce wood (probably carried from Canada as driftwood) were supported on two large posts and the regularly-spaced stone piers which jut from the internal walls, dividing the space into sections. The house — if indeed it is one — is the largest (94m²) known from Shetland; other structures are much smaller and average 33m². Although called a temple, the building might have functioned as a communal or even a ceremonial place. Far more typical perhaps are the smaller structures such as the nearby and recently excavated Scord of Brouster houses which ranged from 14-28m square. Here is a succession of three houses, all linked into a complex of field walls and boundary dykes (Map). Like the Stanydale temple, they had a central hearth, set lower than the surrounding floor, connected to drains. Niches for beds at the sides are typical of some oval houses; others were simpler. The land enclosed in the field walls was between 100 and 200ha, and probably served a small community. Settlement patterns across the Shetland Isles suggest that clusters of houses were located at a low level in particular locations. (**32, 38**).

Ireland

Irish later Neolithic houses were mostly circular-oval in shape, and well over 50 examples now provide a rich source of information on later Neolithic settlements, which are less aggregated than earlier sites. The extensive excavations at Lough Gur (Limerick) have located six house structures over the Knockadoon peninsula (**29**), and new work in Meath has located more than nine houses at Knowth and in excess of 18 at Newgrange from the final Neolithic, suggesting that settlements were becoming larger foci than in the fourth millennium BC. Irish houses were constructed in two ways, either with a ring of posts supporting the walls or as less substantial structures with some supporting posts for a roof (?tent), and an often well-constructed central hearth, as at Townleyhall 2 (Co Lough). The circular houses are mostly smaller than the rectangular examples and covered an area

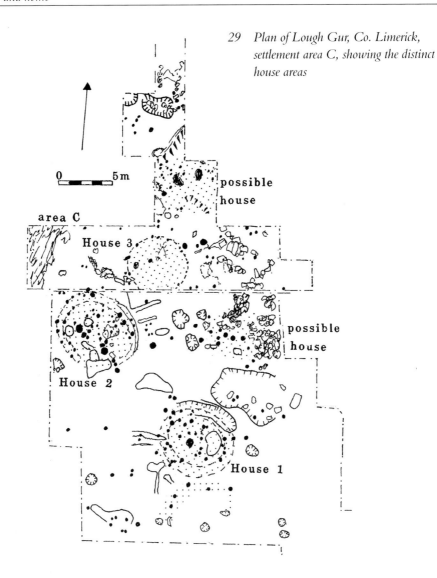

29 *Plan of Lough Gur, Co. Limerick, settlement area C, showing the distinct house areas*

between 13-28m², with diameters of between 4 and 8m. Some of the largest houses are the Knowth examples with floor areas up to 39m². These are concentrated close to the main mound of Knowth, over an area of 2100m², and were partly sealed by satellite tombs. Elsewhere, associated with other structures and isolated, smaller, less tangible structures have been recorded from various sites, such as Knocknarea (Sligo) and Piperstown (Dublin). As in Britain there seems to be a strong association with settlements and later cemeteries overlying the structures, and evidence from Carrowkeel (Sligo), Ballyglass (Co Mayo), the Antrim sites of Ballybriest, Ballintoy, Ballymarkagh and Dun Ruadh, and Knowth, Newgrange and Townleyhall indicate earlier houses, demolished to make way for tombs or perhaps transformed from houses for the living into houses for the dead. Other examples, such as Ballygalley 2 (Antrim) and Lough Gur site B, show a succession of houses on one site (**28**). Some prominent sites, such as Lyles Hill and Doneygore Hill in

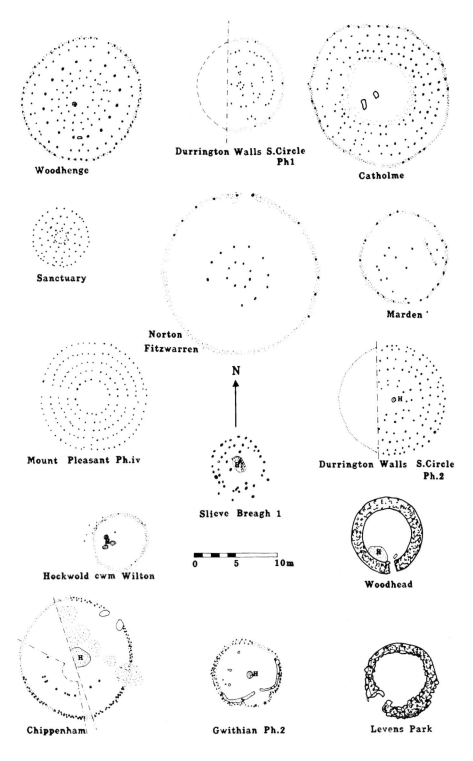

30   Circular houses/structures of the Later Neolithic. H = hearth. After Darvill and Grogan

Antrim, and Feltrim Hill, Co Dublin, were clearly used as strongholds and settlements, but have produced no evidence for houses or permanent settlement. Such constructions may be closely related to the English causewayed enclosures sites (discussed in chapter 4).

The Somerset Levels

Not all settlement evidence has to be in the form of house plans, and other structures, such as trackways, related to settlement can be equally revealing on how communities lived, moved around and subsisted. In particular, wetland locations were exploited for settlement and subsistence around Britain, but most have been lost to deep alluvial cover or the sea. Remarkable survivals have been located in the Somerset Levels in south-west England, and others are know from Corlea Bog and elswhere in Ireland (O'Sullivan 1996). Sites like the Somerset Sweet Track show how communication routes between earlier Neolithic communities were constructed and maintained (Coles and Coles 1986). The trackway linked a low hillock — Westhay Island — to the foot of the Polden Hills on the south side of the Levels by means of a raised wooden walk-way above the wet reed swamp. During winter the area was prone to flooding and even in summer was wet and boggy, and the trackway provided a dry path between settlements. The wood used in the trackway was carefully selected from trees in the Levels — oak, elm, dogwood, hazel, ash, willow and holly were employed for specific parts of the structure. Oak planks, for example, were used for the main walkway. Much of the wood survived with tool marks, notches and evidence of quite sophisticated carpentry. The structure has been accurately dated to *c*.4000 BC through dendrochronology and C14. Lost or discarded Neolithic tools were distributed all along the trackway, including axes, flints, pottery and wooden objects. Fieldwork in the areas has located flint scatters on the 'islands' in the Levels, which may relate to settlements. The exploitation of the Levels may have been seasonal, with communities from around the area hunting, harvesting and grazing the damp lowlands in summer, before retreating to higher land in the flooded wintertime.

Several later Neolithic trackways have been located, though not in such lengths as the Sweet Track which extended over almost 2km. The Honeygore and Abbot's Way both linked Westhay Meare Island with Edington Burtle, and other shorter lengths were clustered around the south side of Edington Burtle and at the foot of the Poldens. The Walton trackway was made from hazel hurdles, and the Garvin track from brushwood. Beside one track on Meare Heath an entire decorated yew-wood long bow was found dating from a few centuries later than the Sweet Track (**40, 175**). Third millennium BC hazel bow fragments have also been found in the area. Pollen studies show that the construction of the tracks coincided with woodland regeneration and changes in agricultural activity, where clearance, coppicing of the hazel and willow, cereal crops and grazing were practised by the Neolithic communities.

In conclusion, the survival and recognition of settlements and their dwellings for much of the Neolithic in the British isles is still poorly known in comparison to later prehistory, but knowledge has nevertheless grown very rapidly over recent years with new field projects focused on the problem. The general picture of settlement and its changes over the Neolithic is now much clearer than three decades ago, and begins at last to divide into two clear phases of settlement development. The less intensively cultivated fringes of the country in uplands,

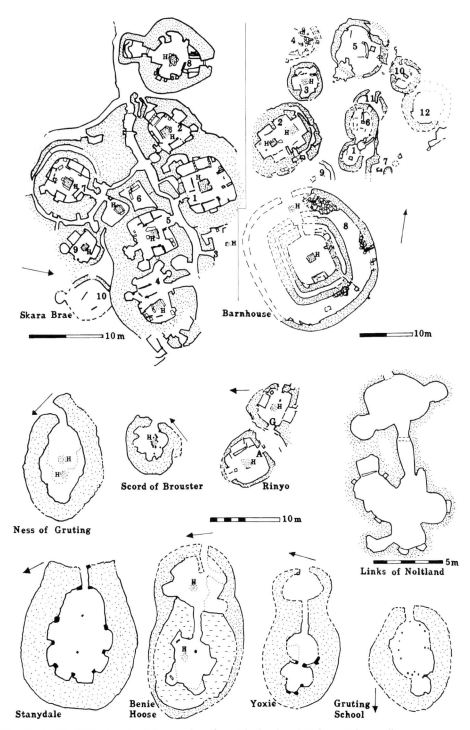

31   *Later Neolithic stone built house plans from Shetland and Orkney. The small arrow points*
      north and H represents hearths. Skara Brea, Barnhouse and Rinyo houses are known by their
      individual numbers as shown. After Clarke, Richards, Barclays and Sharples

32   *Culsetta Neolithic settlement, Mavis Grind (on Shetland), showing house structures still visible as earthworks and walls.* Photo Mick Sharp

33-5   *(above and right) Skara Brae showing the settlement, the houses and the details of dressers, beds, drains, cupboards and internal fitments.* Photos C. Malone

34

35

36   *The restored central building and domestic structures at Barnhouse Neolithic settlement on Orkney.* Photo Mick Sharp

37   *Staneydale 'Temple' on Shetland, the Neolithic settlement, showing the massive stone walls with uprights for roof supports.* Photo Mick Sharp

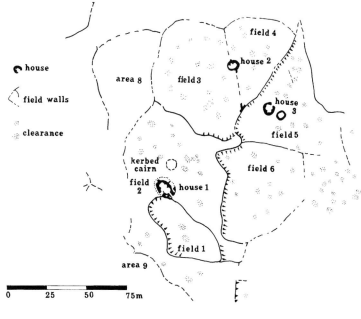

38a Scord of
    Brouster; detail

house

field walls

clearance

area 8

field 3

field 4

house 2

house 3

field 5

field 6

kerbed cairn

field 2

house 1

field 1

area 9

0   25   50   75m

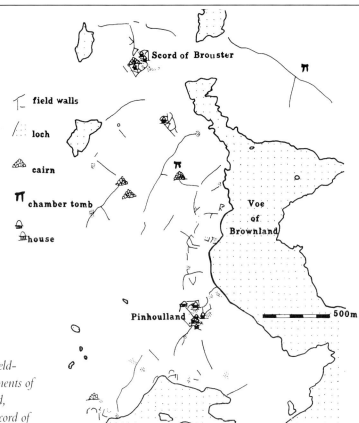

Scord of Brouster

field walls

loch

cairn

chamber tomb

house

Voe of Brownland

Pinhoulland

500m

38b The remarkable field-
    systems and settlements of
    Neolithic Shetland,
    mapped around Scord of
    Brouster. After Whittle

39   *Staneydale (Shetland) — excavated house remains showing walls and entrance porch on the far side.* Photo Mick Sharp

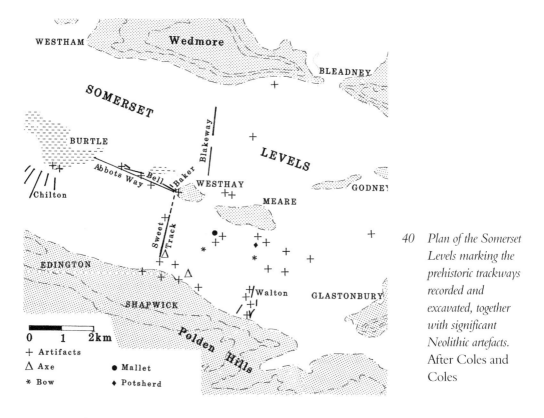

40   *Plan of the Somerset Levels marking the prehistoric trackways recorded and excavated, together with significant Neolithic artefacts.* After Coles and Coles

pasture and coastal dune still offer the best opportunity to explore this key element of the Neolithic world. Fieldwork on tracing settlement in the agriculturally richer zones of the south of Britain remains a priority for future research, if a broader context for the ceremonial landscapes are to be more fully understood and appreciated.

4 Causewayed enclosures:
communal monuments of the earlier Neolithic

The first sites constructed during the Neolithic that represent a major input of communal effort and organisation were the causewayed enclosures. Ancestral tombs (chapter 5) were the earliest constructions (from around 3800 cal. BC onwards) that we are able to recognise today, but it is the enclosures that marked the landscapes with central places for social activities and focus. They are defined through their enclosing ditches, which were usually dug in short sections and backed by a bank to form a large open area covering from about one to 10 hectares in size. Over the decades there has been much speculation about the role and function of causewayed enclosures, and as each new site is excavated and interpreted, the range of possibilities increases. In truth, there is no single explanation for what the sites were, or why they were built. What seems to be emerging, though, is that the landscape in which the first enclosures stood was generally densely wooded, and that the enclosures must have represented rare open spaces used for a host of different social and economic activities.

> The Windmill Hill enclosure was built in a world of low population, tethered mobility or short term sedentism, woodland, cattle-keeping and limited cultivation and episodic contact between social groups. The enclosure itself represents the largest accumulation of residues and materials for many miles around. (Whittle et al. 1999:348).

This quotation represents a typical current scholarly view of causewayed sites — and is the result of cumulative fieldwork in recent years. Another view emphasises the significance of these monuments:

> . . . they are of extraordinary importance, for they represent the earliest form of non-funerary monument and the first instance of artificial enclosure of open space in the British Isles. [But] Despite their importance, the activities that went on within the enclosed areas remain only dimly understood.(Oswald et al. 2001:1).

Causewayed enclosures were first recognised as Neolithic monuments in the 1920s with the advent of aerial photography, and the excavation of Windmill Hill (1925-9) in Wiltshire. Before this the existence of large ditched communal monuments was an unknown dimension of the earlier Neolithic. Since then about 70 sites have been systematically mapped, excavated and dated. More are recognised each year, and increasingly in areas outside the main distribution of southern-eastern England. Much recent interest has resulted in some fine new studies which bring a rather muddled and disparate body of data together (e.g. Topping and Varndell 2002, Darvill et al 2001, Oswald et al.. 2001, Whittle et al.. 1999). Recent systematic work began with Isobel Smith's assessment of enclosures (Smith 1971) which was followed by Roger Palmer's study (Palmer 1976) of aerial photographic evidence. This showed that sites are either small, often upland sites below 4ha. or larger lowland sites. He tentatively suggested regional groups — South-western, Sussex, Thames and Midlands (**42**).

The early excavations of Windmill Hill (**43**), the Trundle (**50**), Abingdon, Hembury (**26**), Whitesheet Hill (Piggott 1952) and Whitehawk Hill in the 1920-40s gave the impression that causewayed sites were always in prominent locations in the landscape. More recent research has revealed sites in lowland situations at the confluence of streams or on river terraces, such as Etton and Haddenham in Cambridgeshire (**49**) or Staines in Surrey. Typically the enclosures have one to four concentric rings of ditches around a central area. The name 'causeway' is given because the ditches were excavated in pit-like segments, interrupted by unexcavated sections forming bridges or causeways between them. The main function of the ditches was presumably as a source for soil and rock to make up the banks. They formed not only useful repositories for offerings and dumps of tools, flint knapping waste, rubbish, human and animal burials, but also created a symbolic division between inside and outside the enclosure. The banks constructed from the ditch material were not always continuous and seem to have had several entrances and gaps. They were sometimes reinforced with palisades of timbers set into the earthwork (as at Hambledon Hill), plus additional stacks of turf and this doubtless created an impressive sight to onlookers. Some sites, like Windmill Hill, were already occupied before enclosure, and plank and post buildings and pits lay within the interior. The act of enclosing the site probably created an identity for the interior space that became increasingly formalised by a succession of additional ditches and palisaded banks, yet possessed a sense of openness in a closed and wooded landscape.

Interpretations of causewayed enclosures — with rich evidence from their physical structure and the materials deposited within them — have prompted a wide range of possible explanations including economic, topographic, political, social, ritual and defensive functions (see Oswald et al 2001, 120-32, Darvill and Thomas 2001 1-23. and Mercer 1998 for comprehensive discussion). Some classic interpretations include the following:
Prominent locations enable enclosures to be:—
Defensive sites (Dixon 1988, Liddell 1930-5, Mercer 1980, 1981a, 1988).
Political statements of power, territory and possession.
Central places for social activities, festivals, ceremonies, seasonal gatherings (Smith 1965).
Elite centres symbolising the power of tribal identity, kin groups, religious specialists.

Interrupted ditches-causeways may have represented:
Communal acts of creation for a fragmented/dispersed society, where the causeways = access and individual group enterprises (Megaw and Simpson 1979, Startin and Bradley 1981, Mercer 1980).
Multi-directional access to scattered communities through the causeways (Evans 1988, Hodder 1990, Edmonds 1993).
Folk-memory from Europe (Bradley 1993).

Economic functions may have been as:

Kraals for cattle and sheep and Centres for animal culls and butchery (Piggott 1954).

Market places for exchange, fairs, barter, bride-giving (Smith 1965, Edmonds 1995, Pryor 1998).

Industrial workshops for flint knapping, mining, bone work, potting, antler and bone working (Piggott 1954, Smith (Keiller) (1965, 1971), Case 1982).

Settlement sites may have a settlement function, as suggested by structure and food-industrial rubbish.

(Curwen 1930, Mercer 1980a; Evans 1988b; Liddell 1931; Pryor 1999)

Social and religious functions are suggested, including:

Funerary centres Places to expose human remains on platforms or place body parts in ditches (Mercer 1980 and Drewett 1977).

Liminal zone Ritual place between life and death (Pryor 1999).

Cult and religious centre (Drewett 1977, Pryor 1999).

Feasting centre (Smith 1965, Legge 1981, Robertson MacKay 1987)

Evidence

Excavation has revealed many aspects of the use of causewayed sites from durable evidence in the form of bones, artefacts, structures and deposits. Interpretations hinge on the relative importance scholars put on the many possible factors listed above.

From an economic perspective, studies of animal bones show that cattle were the most common animals, and enclosures with palisades, banks and ditches would have formed effective kraals for them. Some sites, like Hambledon Hill (**44-46**), overlook rich grass grazing country (the Vale of Blackmore), and Roger Mercer, the excavator, has suggested (1980, 29) that the 50ha. within the enclosures could have been used for protecting the valuable stock (over 70 per cent of the bones were from cattle) in times of unrest. Likewise, 60 per cent of the bones at Windmill Hill were cattle (see fig **19**, chapter 2), and over 40 per cent at Etton. In tribal societies — which are typically unstable and politically dislocated — the theft of stock, crops and even people is a continuous threat (Sahlins 1968). In such a world of instability, the protection of stock animals, which represented one of the main sources of wealth, was a matter deserving massive investment in building and in signalling ownership. This ownership would have been effectively broadcast across the landscape to neighbouring communities from the prominent stock enclosures, with their bare banks and palisades. The evidence from sites suggests that the palisade constructions were often built quite late in the development of the enclosures, as cattle rearing became increasingly important. Across Neolithic Europe similar enclosures had been in use for almost two millennia before they developed in Britain. Stock control seems to have been one of the motivations underlying the building of the great enclosures of southern Italy, France, Denmark and Germany (Whittle in Burgess *et al.* 1988 and others in that volume), and is still a feature in contemporary tribal societies in Africa.

41 *Causewayed and other enclosures recorded in Britain*
    have a largely southern distribution, although new sites
    are being located through survey. Hem=Hembury,
    WH=Windmill Hill, Whi=Whitehawk Hill,
    MC=Maiden Castle, HH=Hambledon Hill,
    CC=Crickley Hill, LH = Lyles Hill,
    DH=Doneygore Hill. After Oswald and others

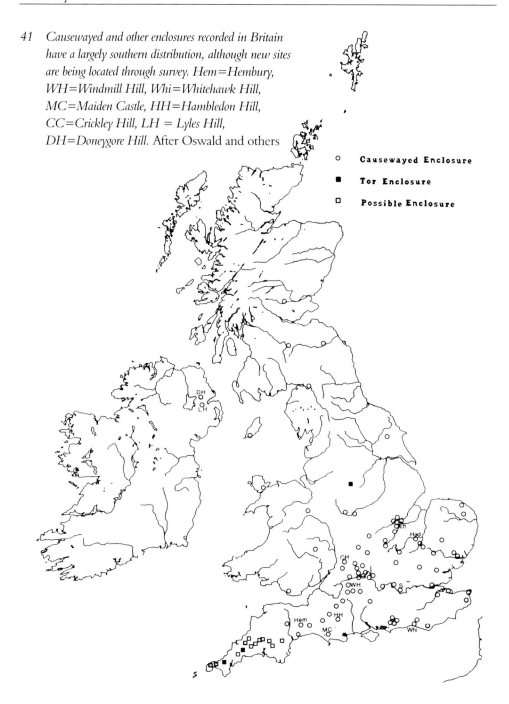

○   **Causewayed Enclosure**

■   **Tor Enclosure**

□   **Possible Enclosure**

Topographical interpretations are best supported by the western enclosure examples. These are located in dramatic natural situations and concerns for defence might have favoured prominent hills such as Haldon (Willock 1936, 1937), Hembury (Devon), Whitesheet Hill and Knap Hill (Wiltshire). Such concern for prominent position was not replicated in the south and east of England where the natural topography is less dramatic.

42   Roger Palmer's regional enclosure groups

Sites like Haddenham and Etton (Cambridgeshire) were located on the edge of flat fenland, and at Staines (Surrey) (Robertson-MacKay 1987) and Abingdon (Oxfordshire) (Whittle and Case 1982) at a river confluence. They were subtler in appearance and had other visual devices to attract attention. The use of banks, ditches, hillsides, reflective water, palisades and the construction of impressive exterior façades are now much discussed as some of the devices used (Evans 1988). The surrounding landscape and the viewshed of other contemporary sites — the sacred geography — from major monuments is potentially significant in the interpretation of how sites functioned within their territory.

Some sites were situated in almost impregnable defensive positions, like Crickley Hill (Dixon 1981; 1988b), Hambledon Hill (Mercer 1980), Hembury (Liddell 1930, 1931, 1932, 1935) and Carn Brea (Mercer 1981a). The earthworks and palisades further emphasised defence, and their surprisingly dense scatters of arrowheads are stark reminders that furious life and death battles once raged around the sites. At Hambledon, there is evidence for the burning of the once 2m high palisades and the subsequent collapse of the banks. The remains of an individual shot in the chest by an arrow were found in the ditch, covered with chalk rubble and burnt soil — a graphic illustration of at least one tragic assault. Excavations at Hembury recorded high numbers of arrowheads, and similar densities of arrowheads (some 400 from a small area around the eastern entrance, **55**) demonstrate that Crickley Hill was also attacked. The skeletal remains of individuals in tombs and ditches include embedded arrowheads and testify to combat and violence in the Neolithic.

Research since the 1980s, especially within a Post-processual framework, has emphasised social, ideological and ritual interpretations of causewayed sites. Such ideas stress the nature of the interrupted ditches as symbolic, and the 'structured' association of materials and deposits (for example, human or animal bone in association with axes, flint tools, pots and antlers) in them. The theme of structured deposition now occupies much discussion, with the aim of differentiating the symbolic from the random materials. For instance, the

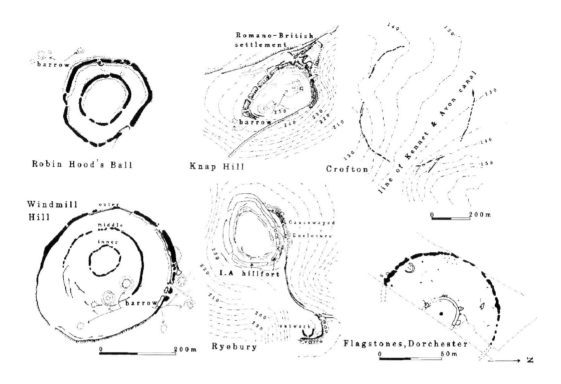

43 *Wiltshire and Dorset enclosures are known from earthworks and crop-marks, and vary immensely in size and complexity (Windmill Hill, Crofton, Knap Hill, Ryebury and Robin Hood's Ball, Wilts, Flagstones, Dorset). (Note: Crofton and Flagstones are planned at different scales.)* After Oswald *et al.*, Woodward *et al.*

apparently careful placement of antlers at the terminal ends of ditches, or the position of human remains and associated material in ditches or pits, seem to be intentional and meaningful, especially when similar finds are repeated on other sites. The high concentrations of exotic goods, such as axes and pottery, have been seen as evidence for high status and show the ability of the occupants to engage in a widespread network of social interaction and exchange. Some researchers, such as Pryor, following his work at Etton, see the role of the enclosures as providing a liminal place, between one world and another. The remains of the dead associated with the careful placement of potentially symbolic objects in particular locations could suggest that the enclosures represented an entry point to the afterlife. The location of so many enclosures close to rivers might represent a parallel to the River Styx in Classical mythology — the crossing or entry point between the worlds of the living and the dead. The ditches too, may have symbolised the conceptual divisions between a domestic world inside the enclosures, and the wild world of nature beyond, between a human world versus a spiritual world, or have acted as metaphorical rivers. The offerings in the ditches, conceivably seen as entry points to other worlds, may have represented magical charms seeking protection against real or imagined threats and curses. A preoccupation with

44   *Aerial view of Hambledon Hill, Dorset showing the northern spur with its Iron Age earthworks. Neolithic earthworks are visible as the bank barrow along the main spur, and as the outworks demarcating the main enclosure and the Shroton Spur on the top left of the picture.* Photo CUCAP — AY21

superstitious beliefs may explain the curious deposits of worn deer antlers (used to excavate the ditches, in the terminals of ditches, the caches of axes and tools hidden in banks, ditches or bedrock and the skeletal remains accompanied by food-filled vessels and animals remains. There seem to be patterns of deposition that imply the Neolithic people felt the need to return bodies, spirits and wealth to the earth, perhaps as part of the rituals of regeneration that regulated their world.

Evidence from enclosures

The variety of landscapes and cultural adaptations in Britain resulted in considerable regional variation in enclosed sites. They range from boulder-enclosed upland sites in the South-west (Carn Brea, Helman's Tor, Dewarstone) and the Peak District (Gardom's Edge) (**56**), to the multiple ditched enclosures of the chalk, limestone and lowlands. Few of the truly upland sites, which are loosely classified as causewayed enclosures, are similar to the multiple-ditched lowland and chalkland sites, and careful survey is required to locate them. Recent work by the RCHM(E) has located four surprisingly large sites enclosed by interrupted stone banks in the high uplands of Cumbria, including Carrock Fell and Aughertree Fell. They await investigation to confirm their Neolithic date and details of construction (Topping pers com). The distribution map (**41**) shows there to be few confirmed sites north of a line between Gloucester and the Wash, and no ditched sites west of Exeter. The site of Duggleby Howe (**49**), surrounding a late Neolithic burial mound, is the only causewayed enclosure in Yorkshire, and a similar arrangement of a later

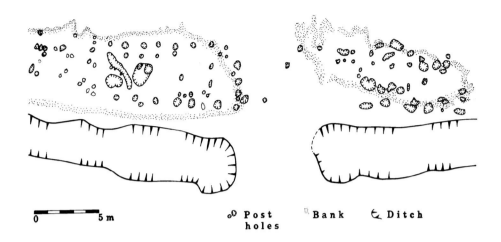

0   5 m   **Post holes**   **Bank**   **Ditch**

45   *Hambledon Hill, Dorset. Plan of post-holes from the timber revetment set within the banks of the Stepleton Enclosure.* After Mercer

tomb within a ditched enclosure has been identified in Anglesey at Bryn Celli Wen. Wales has only one other enclosure, in Glamorgan, with other sites in the Welsh borders. The single ditched site of Leadketty (**56**) in Scotland is one of only three enclosures north of the border. Recent excavations at Billown on the Isle of Man have confirmed an enclosure site, and two examples in Northern Ireland — Donegore Hill (**56**) and Lyles Hill — indicate that similar monuments were constructed in Ireland. The greatest concentrations of sites have come to light through aerial research on the lowland gravels, with dense groups along the Fenland-Wash rivers, the Thames valley and its tributaries, the Cotswolds, and the Wessex and Sussex chalklands. Many areas outside these well-flown regions still require preliminary prospecting.

The site of Hembury, Devon (**56**) underlies a later Iron Age hillfort. It was excavated by Dorothy Liddell in the 1930s and was important in bringing causewayed sites to general recognition. The site lies on a prominent 270m high greensand hill, and was defined by two lines of enclosure ditches stretching over 120m across the promontory and enclosing an area over 200m in length. These appear to have been reinforced by a timber palisade of upright posts along the outside of the ditch. There was also post-hole evidence for a timber gateway. Besides the typical evidence of structured deposits in the ditches, Hembury contained a number of structures, which may have been domestic houses and their pits, and had been under attack, with some 146 arrowheads left across a burnt area (Liddell 1930, 1931, 1932, 1935).

Further west some 11 Cornish sites known as Tor enclosures are typified by boulder walls set between rock outcrops. Helman's Tor had rough lines of walls, and a larger example is Carn Brea (Mercer 1981) (**27, 56**), which is better preserved within an Iron Age fort. Houses had been built up against the surrounding boulder walls, and excavation revealed burnt levels, arrowhead scatters, post-holes, industrial sites and domestic material from a large settlement. In Devon, three further Tor sites include Hound's Tor enclosure

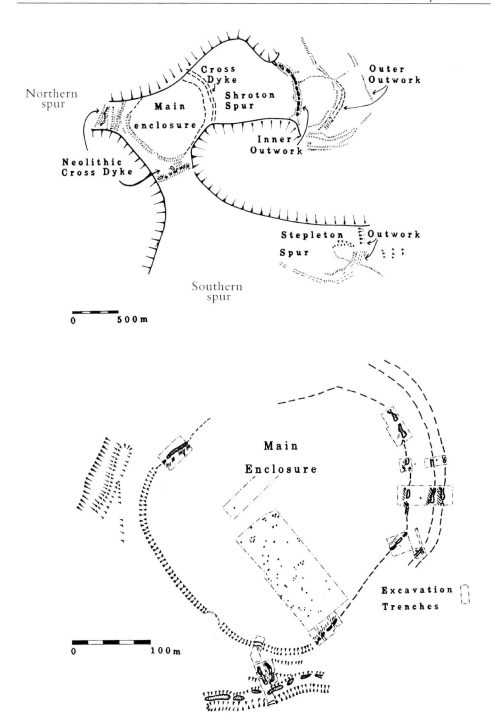

46 *Hambledon Hill, Dorset. (Top) General plan of the Main and Stepleton enclosures and
outworks. (Lower) Detailed plan of the Main enclosure showing the excavation trenches and
the scattered structural postholes within the enclosure.* After Mercer

47   Knap Hill causewayed enclosure overlooking the Vale of Pewsey, Wiltshire, commands an impressive view. Photo C. Malone

between the two Tor outcrops. A similar type of site has been identified at Gardom's Edge in the Derbyshire Peak District. This enclosure commands an extensive view over the gritstone scarp, the Derwent valley and its communication routes to the east. The enclosure is defined by a bank of boulders about 625m long with several entrances through it on one side, and is demarcated by a 500m length of steep scarp on the other (Edmonds 1999) The classic enclosures are those on the Wessex chalkland. Not only has their preservation been relatively good but the early excavations ensured that later research was compared with them as the type-sites (**56**).

Windmill Hill, Wiltshire is one of the largest enclosures yet recorded in Britain. The largest is the 28ha. *Crofton* enclosure (Wilts) (**43**). Windmill Hill had three widely spaced, irregular causewayed ditches and banks, with a small early inner ditch enclosing at the centre an area of only 0.50ha across a diameter of 150m. The outer ditch enclosed a total of 8.45ha, across a diameter of 360m. The ditch sections were constructed in lengths of 50-120m, but appear to have had a continuous bank on the inner edge, with a modified entrance on the east side. They became filled with slumped bank material, domestic residues and animal and human remains. The location, on a knoll over 190m OD, is prominent in the local landscape, and now with extensive views over the surrounding valleys and hills, but in its early stages it was enclosed by woodland which would have interrupted such views (R. Smith 1984) (**10**). The enclosure was placed towards the north side of the summit, making it visually prominent from the north, east and west, but not in the least impregnable as a defence from the gentle slope on the south.

Excavations and research in the 1920s (Smith 1965) and again 1987-93 (Whittle et al. 1999) make Windmill Hill the most extensively studied of any causewayed enclosure. Within the ditched enclosure, a number of features such as pits and gullies were traced through excavations, and through recent geophysical survey. These features may relate to several episodes of pre-enclosure occupation from before 3700 cal. BC. Carbon 14 dating

*48   Excavations at Haddenham causewayed enclosure (Cambridgeshire) in 1981 show the flat
fenland landscape.* Photo S. Stoddart

places the construction and use of the enclosures between *c*.3600-3000 cal. BC. The dates
provide a secure chronology for a sequence of ditch building — with the inner and middle
ditches probably a century earlier than the outer ditch and bank, which overlay earlier
occupation and shallow graves. In one area, a line of post-holes and hearth debris may
represent a hut of 7 x 3m from an earlier settlement at the site (**21**). Later occupation in
the late Neolithic (Peterborough pottery), Beaker and early Bronze Age periods left
pottery, features and occupation debris on the ditch surfaces, and in the form of several
large round barrows.

The primary ditch fills have been of great interest to researchers because, as suggested
above, groups of material seem to have been deposited intentionally on the ditch bottom or
at the terminals of the ditch sections. Some contained Windmill Hill pottery, worked bone
and antler, querns, flint and stone tools and waste, as well as scatters of animal and human
bone. One example included a child's skull against the frontal bones of an ox skull and
selected cattle bones. Other symbolic deposits included carved stone balls, chalk cups,
weights, phalli and crude chalk figurines, imported stone fragments and shells. Some
patterns of deposition have been discerned, with the outer and middle ditches having greater
numbers of articulated human and animal deposits. The surrounding landscape of Windmill
Hill contains over 20 early-middle Neolithic long barrows within 10km, and the site is also
geographically close to several Wessex enclosures, suggesting that the area was intensively
occupied in the earlier Neolithic. One of these is Whitesheet Hill which lies on a prominent
chalk escarpment to the south-west. It had a single ditch which enclosed a sloping area of
2.39ha. (5.9 acres). Small-scale excavations identified animal remains in the ditches, and
scatters of artefacts. Further east, also on the chalk escarpment, Knap Hill (Connah 1965,

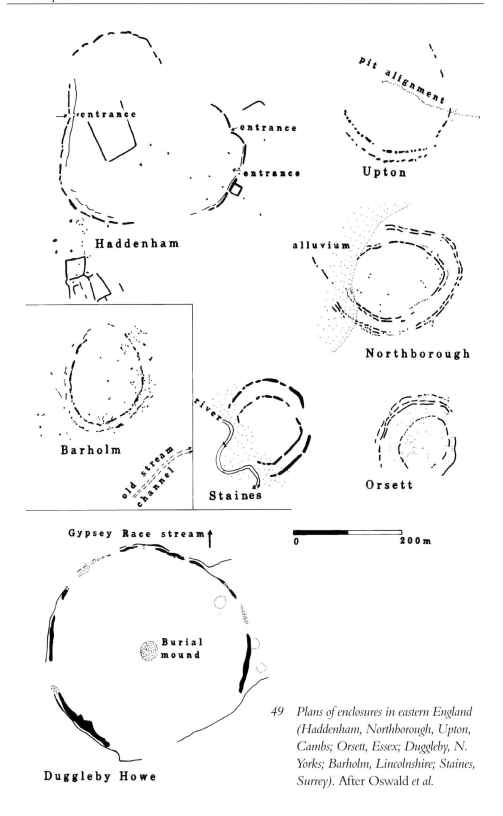

49 Plans of enclosures in eastern England
(Haddenham, Northborough, Upton,
Cambs; Orsett, Essex; Duggleby, N.
Yorks; Barholm, Lincolnshire; Staines,
Surrey). After Oswald *et al.*

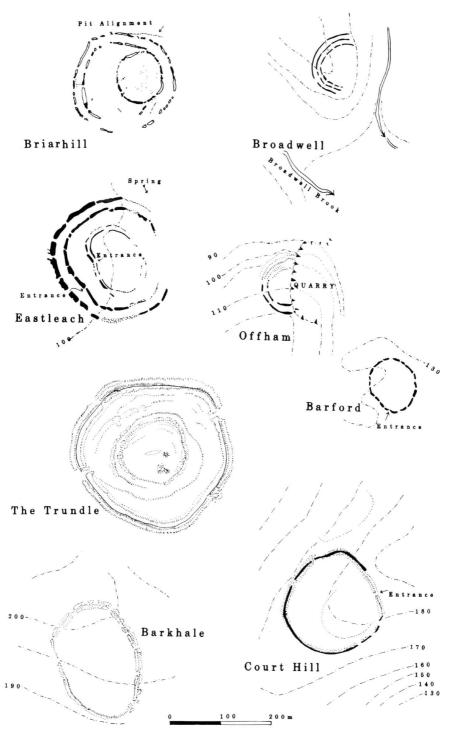

50 *Plans of enclosures in Northamptonshire, Gloucestershire and Sussex. (Briar Hill, Northants; Broadwell, Oxfordshire; Eastleach, Glos, the others East & West Sussex). After Oswald et al.*

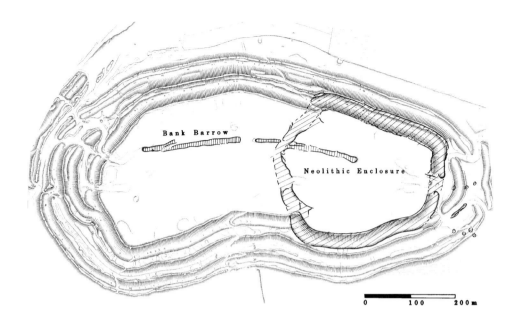

51   Plan of Maiden Castle, Dorset, showing the Neolithic enclosure and Bank Barrow within the Iron Age fort. After Sharples, RCHM and others

1969, Cunnington 1911) (**43, 47**) is dramatically situated at 261m on a knoll of the escarpment overlooking the Vale of Pewsey where later Neolithic monuments were built. It had a single oval ring of ditches just below the summit of the hill, and two lines of ditches extended the site to the east. Excavations in the 1960s gave dates of *c*.3640-3360 cal. BC and there were traces of interior features and flint mining which had disturbed the interior. To the south on the northern edge of Salisbury Plain the site of Robin Hood's Ball (J. Richards 1990), lying 5km to the north of Stonehenge, had two irregular ditches and banks. Environmental material suggests the site, like several others, was constructed in a woodland clearing which became open grassland during the site's period of use (see chapter 2, **6**). The inner ditch enclosed an site of about 100x130m, and the outer ditch a total area of 250x200m. Excavation and survey of the immediate surroundings have located dense flint scatters, charcoal, pits, post-holes, pottery and bone indicating the area was settled before the construction of the enclosure between 3770-3194 cal. BC.

Hambledon Hill Dorset (**44-46**) is located on a many-spurred isolated hilltop, forming a dramatic landmark on the chalk of Cranborne Chase. It overlooks the fertile Blackmore Vale to the west. The enclosures cover 60ha, and includes four distinct enclosed areas, with cross-dykes and outworks linking them securely together. At the summit is a 4.5ha. unexplored enclosure (now beneath the Iron Age hillfort), which was perhaps the main focus of the site, with a long barrow along the spine of the hill. The 'main' enclosure covers 9ha on the saddle between the three spurs. It was excavated, together with the two smaller enclosures, between 1974-84. It is thought that the hilltop surface soil and rock have been eroded and reduced by at least 70cm, through millennia of agriculture and erosion, and

52 Maiden Castle, Dorset — aerial view showing the immense Iron Age fort which in turn encloses the Neolithic enclosure, visible only as the slight earthworks dividing the centre of the fort and the faint bank barrow running across the it. Photo CUCAP 70K EN 56

only deeper pits and post-holes survived for archaeological investigation. Pit fills showed they had been left open for long periods, and had filled with deposits of pottery and axes from distant places. The surrounding ditch segments had been carefully re-cut in order to support an impressive timber-laced rampart of chalk and soil. This structure was then burnt and left to rot and collapse into the ditches. The ditches, as at other excavated sites, had formed the repository for human remains. At Hambledon many bones were gnawed and scattered by dogs, and, importantly, children's bones represented at least 60 per cent of the total, a section of the population normally poorly represented in Neolithic tombs. The occupation of Hambledon Hill has been extensively dated by C14 into seven phases:

(1-2) Construction — occupation 3720-3460 cal. BC.
(3) Episode of silting and bank collapse.
(4) Deep pits cut through it and refilled (suspicious dates 3640-3010).
(5) Later silting above ditch.
(6) Ditch re-cut as many as four times, maintaining the line of the once impressive ditch. The excavator interprets this re-cutting and the deposits in it as acts of veneration or commemoration until about 3340-3210 cal. BC.
(7) Enclosure ditch covered by a linear cairn, and beyond it, additional and unique cross-banks were constructed, protecting the east and south flanks, and designed to keep animals out of the enclosure. To the south a long barrow of 20m length was orientated north-south, facing a much larger (66m long) barrow placed on the spine of the northern spur of the hill. These turf and chalk-built tombs offer an intriguing answer to the exposed bones from the enclosure ditches, and reinforce the theme, noted at other enclosure sites, of death and ancestors. Dates for this earthwork were *c.*3700-3510 cal.BC and for the fill

53 Crickley Hill, Gloucestershire — aerial view of the promontory overlooking the Cotswold escarpment , and showing the massive Iron Age ramparts, and the slighter Neolithic earthworks beyond. Photo CUCAP — AJN56

*c.*3630-3000BC To the north-east, beyond the cross dykes, lay another enclosure — the Shroton Spur, which was contemporary with the main enclosure. The ditch was larger and had wider causeways, but no obvious symbolic deposits. Behind this was a further outwork bank containing post pits which had flint nodules rammed in to hold the timber posts fast. There was at least one gateway through the bank and the structure was a massive and sophisticated barrier abandoned after 3360-3090 BC.

The south-eastern extremity of Hambledon Hill was marked by another ditched area — the Stepleton Enclosure (**46**). In its first phase this small 1ha. enclosure, on the end of a lower spur, had slight banks and a substantial fence (similar to Hembury and Crickley); its entrance faced the main site 800m away. The initial occupation involved flint knapping, potting and the deposition of antler picks along with food debris, including the remains of cattle feasts. The bank was then covered by the linking outworks and cross-dykes that secured the entire hilltop (phase 2b). The bank was box-framed with oak timbers set every metre and braced across to the other side of the bank. The excavator estimated that over a distance of 3000m some 10,000 massive oak beams were required, together with hurdles of ash, hazel and alder. Its three gateways were 2.5m wide, and had gateposts and timber-lined gate-passages. Some time later, two further impressive timber framed outworks were added to protect the spur to the edge of the escarpment. Then catastrophe struck — at least 200m of the outwork was burnt, which led to the collapse of the rampart, and the killing of at least six individuals — some buried under the collapse, others hastily buried where they lay, and all young males, presumably protecting the site from this fatal attack.

Whilst the final report of Hambledon is awaited (Mercer & Healy, forthcoming), it is clear that the site fulfils many of the criteria of a multiple use enclosure. It had contemporaneous mortuary, domestic, economic and industrial functions, which later

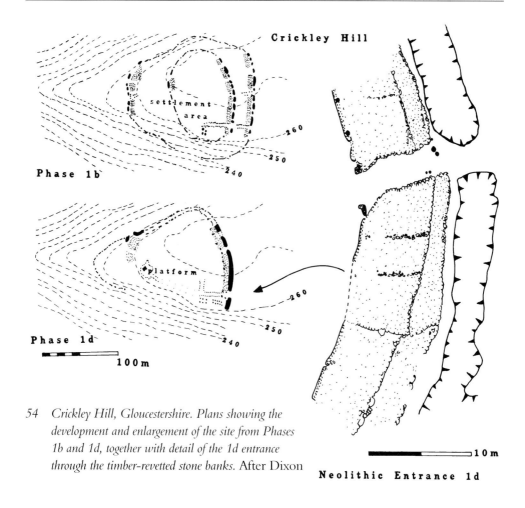

54 Crickley Hill, Gloucestershire. Plans showing the development and enlargement of the site from Phases 1b and 1d, together with detail of the 1d entrance through the timber-revetted stone banks. After Dixon

became dominated by concerns for defence with the enclosures and cross-dykes that protected the site. Enormous demands were placed on labour, planning and local resources for this vast enterprise. It tells us much about Neolithic concerns and social organisation and the immense numbers of hours it was necessary to work to satisfy them (Mercer 1980, 1988, Oswald et al. 2001).

Maiden Castle, Dorset (**51, 52**) causewayed enclosure is similarly located beneath a massive Iron Age Hillfort and was excavated in the 1930s by Sir Mortimer Wheeler and more recently by Niall Sharples (1991). The Neolithic enclosure was formed from two closely spaced (only 14-15m apart) ditch circuits, with a bank between them constructed at a later stage. The enclosure was probably about 350 x 250m across, covering an area of about 8ha., and construction took place between 3900-3700 cal. BC. The inner ditch, of 3-4m width and 1.2-1.6m depth, was intentionally filled with rich midden deposits after *c*.3700 BC. The outer ditch (1.7-2.4m wide and 1.3-1.8m deep) was filled from naturally derived deposits, and indicated very different practices (dating *c*.3700-3360 cal. BC for the secondary fills).

Later (around 3350 BC) a bank barrow (546 x 17.5m wide) was built across the enclosure. It is a unique feature in Britain, and its function is difficult to interpret. It was

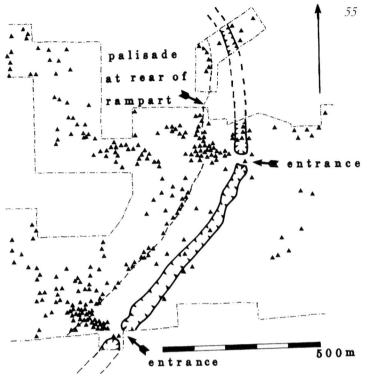

55 Crickley Hill, Gloucestershire — detail of the arrowhead distribution recorded around the main entrances in the enclosure. The hatched line indicates the edge of the timber-revetted bank, against which many arrowheads fell. After Dixon

flanked by two parallel ditches 5.5m wide and 1.5m deep and is constructed in three segments, each slightly different in orientation. The central segment is 65m long and sited at the head of a dry coombe, the eastern mound (155m long) and the western mound (225m long) were located on a false crest giving the monument a dramatic appearance. Bradley has suggested the barrow started life as a single barrow at the edge of the enclosure and was integral to the site's rituals, as seen at Hambledon. The east and west ends were added afterwards. Several post-holes suggest there may have been a timber façade at the west end, and there were several skulls and cattle bones at the terminals of the long ditches. The phasing of the bank barrow construction, between moments of occupation and at a time when other causewayed sites were destroyed and burnt, could, as suggested by Niall Sharples, represent a symbolic barrier between different sectors of the enclosure. Activities at the enclosure ceased for a while during the bank barrow building, but occurred again between 3350-3100 cal. BC when the site was reoccupied. Various pits and gullies probably relate to the Neolithic occupation, but because of the later disturbance are difficult to relate to precise phases. As in many causewayed enclosures, numerous human remains were found in pits, ditches and under the bank barrow.

The Neolithic occupants seem to have engaged in several of the typical enclosure activities listed above. Principally the site served a domestic community, and on-site animal butchery (cattle represented 52 per cent of the bones) flint tool and axe production all testify to this. Since very little of the ditch segments has been excavated due to the Iron Age constructions above, the nature of any human remains or cult deposits remains

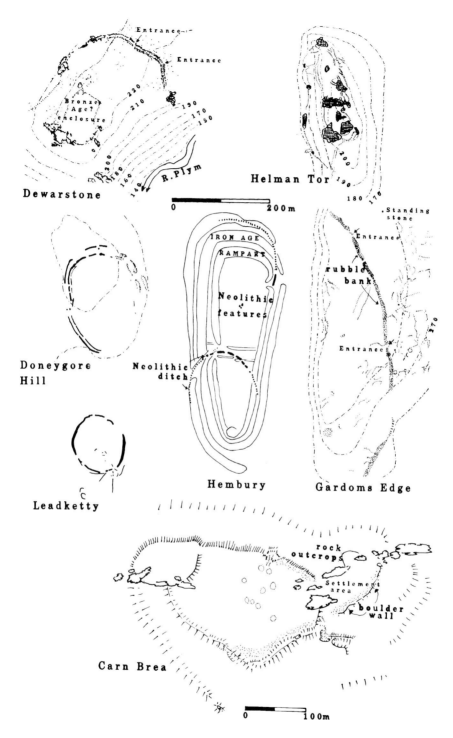

56 *Plan of enclosures and tor in the uplands of the North, the West and Ireland: Helman Tor and Carn Brea — Cornwall; Dewarstone and Hembury — Devon; Doneygore Hill — Antrim; Leadketty — Perthshire; Gardom's Edge — Derbyshire.* After Oswald *et al.*

57 *Aerial View of
Hembury Hill,
Devon, showing the
Iron Age ramparts
that enclose the
Neolithic enclosure.*
Photo CUCAP

sparsely known. The situation on a prominent plateau overlooking the surrounding country might argue for social prominence and ritual significance.

Cecil Curwen began work on the Sussex enclosures in the 1920s and recognised several of the seven to eight known sites along the chalk Downs. There seems to have been a close relationship between the location of the enclosures and the early flint mines in the South Downs. The pattern suggests that the middle block of the Downs where the flint mines were located was 'protected' on the east and west by groups of enclosure sites over a distance of about 80km.

Whitehawk Hill, Sussex (Curwen 1934; 1936) lies on a chalk saddle at a height of 118m between two high points, and consists of four concentric rings of ditches, which have additional tangential and radial projections. The ditches were widely spaced and enclosed an area of 0.67ha. although the outer ditches collectively cover a much larger area, with the fourth ditch alone enclosing 5.5ha. Within the ditches, human burials were found, and in one instance a child's skeleton had been placed in a deep narrow hole at the edge of a causeway. The outer (and incomplete) ditch was later than the interior constructions and contained later Neolithic Peterborough pottery, whereas the inner ditches contained the characteristic earlier Neolithic Whitehawk pottery style. Close by, on the north face of the South Downs, the small causewayed site of Offham Hill, Sussex (**50**) (Drewett 1977) formed a two-ditched enclosure of about 80m diameter; it was excavated in 1976. The bank/ditches once ran to edge of the scarp (now a quarry), and may have been semi-defensive. The ditches at Offham had been dug in short sections or as individual pits, later joined together, with entrance causeways into the interior, although no trace of gateways was found. The inner ditch contained environmental evidence showing the earliest site was constructed in woodland, and careful study of the surrounding area suggests that there were no field systems; the other ditch was built slightly later in a more open, treeless landscape. Several instances of the formal deposition of human remains, symbolically arranged artefacts and animal bones were found at Offham Hill. In one pit at the base of the outer ditch a leaf-shaped arrowhead, waste flint flakes, a pot and bones from deer, cattle, beaver and pig were placed together. The interior was badly damaged and only a couple of pits were of Neolithic date, although many other gullies could have been contemporary. Other Sussex sites include the Trundle with two concentric banks and ditches, and Barkhale with its simple ditch.

The limestones of central England

Enclosures located on the limestones of the Cotswolds and Midlands were often impressively sited, and none more so than Crickley Hill, Gloucestershire, overlooking the Vale of Gloucester (**53-55**). The site also had Iron Age fortifications overlying the Neolithic levels. The enclosure had two main circuits of ditches, and was constructed, according to its excavator Philip Dixon (1988b), over five main phases with periods of abandonment followed by rebuilding and modification. The functions of the site changed between ritual-domestic and strategic defence like Hambledon Hill over several phases:

1a) There was an early pre-enclosure phase of occupation, with at least four huts and various sterile pits arranged around an oval space of 10 x 4m, together with post-holes and stake-holes. The huts were small (from 3 x 2m to 1 x 2m) and had no traces of domestic artefacts or hearths.
1b) The outer interrupted ditch was dug (1bi) followed by re-cutting and realignment together with the building of the inner ditch (1bii). The outer ditch probably had five entrances and the three inner entrances, which seem to have led, via established roads, into the enclosure.
1c) Both ditches were further re-cut in phase 1ci, and then the inner ditch was modified, recut and timbers were placed in the outer ditch (1cii), with further recutting of the inner ditch and the abandonment of the outer ditch (1ciii).
1d) New enclosure ditches were cut, this time in longer lengths on the east side following just outside the line of the previous inner ditch (1d) and some entrances were abandoned. This enclosure was larger than the previous one, and extended over the western end of the plateau. The ditch was located on the outside of the substantial 2m-high stone bank parallel to it. A palisade of timbers was then set into the inner edge of the bank, some 8m from the ditch edge. By phase 1d the wall was a honeycomb of intersecting cells, using the same drystone construction as local Severn Cotswold tombs, and it was during this phase that an assault on the palisade and entrance left upwards of 400 arrows scattered as evidence of the vicious attack (**55**). Within the enclosure, fenced roads led from the entrances to the interior, with at least three rectangular buildings aligned to them, and towards the centre, a dense scatter of artefacts and occupation evidence indicated that in this phase the site was used as a settlement. Pits, post-holes and a stone platform were built in phase 1d, which was then covered by cairn 1.
1e) This cairn phase saw the construction of a formal fenced pathway from the road leading

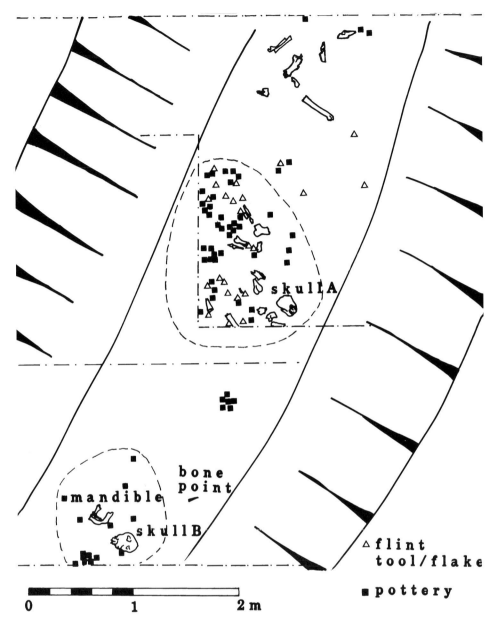

skull A

bone
point

mandible

skull B

△ flint
tool/flake

■ pottery

0   1   2 m

*58   Structured deposits of human and animals bones and artefacts from the causewayed enclosure
ditch at Staines and similar sites are important for reconstructing Neolithic economies. After
Robertson Mackay*

from the east entrance, via a natural gully, through a gateway running over 70m in length to
the cairn. The path was wider as it approached the cairn, which was partly blocked by a small
standing stone, and the area was enclosed by the fence. A small open-sided rectangular
building stood on the west edge of the mound. At its base two troughs contained Windmill

Hill style pottery and bone, and on the mound surface there was evidence for burning and bone, perhaps representing a domestic shrine at the centre of the settlement. Following destruction by burning, the cairn was partially covered and the western end was then cut away for the construction of a stone circle on a cobbled platform (1eii) with burnt areas at its centre, almost directly above the early shrine hearth. Finally, (phase 1eiii) the circle was rebuilt, with a large burnt stone replacing the hearth, and this was covered in bone fragments. The cairn was then covered by a turf mound (nearly 100m long) with large stone slabs set into its sides, like the kerbs around Severn Cotswold tombs. A large post stood at its east end, associated with trampled animal bones, probably from animal sacrifices. Dixon concludes that the centuries of ritual practiced at the site became fossilised in memory, with the long succession of rebuilding and later the cluster of round barrows on the same spot.

Briar Hill, Northamptonshire is located on the northern limits of the oolitic limestone, above the town of Northampton on a distinct low hill (**50**). It was fully excavated in the 1970-80s before the building of a housing development, and is one of few extensively excavated enclosures (Bamford 1985). It had an inner ditch enclosing an artefact-rich area of 0.71ha and apparently predating the outer two ditches. An indented ditch line on the eastern side suggests an early entranceway. Two closely spaced outer ditches enclose a further 3.15ha.

Lowland, fenland and riverine locations were particularly important for enclosure sites in southern and eastern England (**49**). The largest group of all falls into this category, and recent excavations at Etton, Haddenham, Staines, Abingdon, and Orsett provide important details. Invariably, the sites were located close to streams, rivers and open water, and it has been argued that there may have been special visual effects from reflection in water that added to the ritual and atmospheric character of the sites. Pryor (1988) has suggested that in flat landscapes enclosures were less visible and were not monumental territorial markers as the upland sites were, but had other functions. In many cases, the lowland sites were short-lived in comparison to the western examples, and may sometimes have been abandoned for environmental reasons as well as for social or political ones.

The site of Abingdon, Oxfordshire (Case and Whittle 1982) was first excavated in the 1900s, followed by more recent work, which has made Abingdon one of the type-sites for the earlier-middle Neolithic in central southern Britain. The site lies on a gravel terrace about 1km north of the river Thames between two streams, and was partially destroyed by gravel digging before its full extent was recorded. It had two series of interrupted ditches, in places over 200m apart, which curved around the gravel spur with the centre of the enclosure covering the highest ground (61m OD) and descended to the river on the south side. Three phases of building were identified as follows:

1. Inner ditch excavated and low bank reinforced with timber enclosed area of about 1.2ha.
2. The ditch silted and was then re-cut and refilled when the outer ditch was excavated and a bank formed. This enclosed an area of 3-4ha.
3. Occupation of area within the outer ditch consisted of pits, gullies and post-holes. Human burials, deposits of domestic/ritual material in ditches and the form of the site provide evidence of non-domestic material, but research has nevertheless suggested the site was used as a settlement. Dates range from *c.*3920-2920 cal. BC.

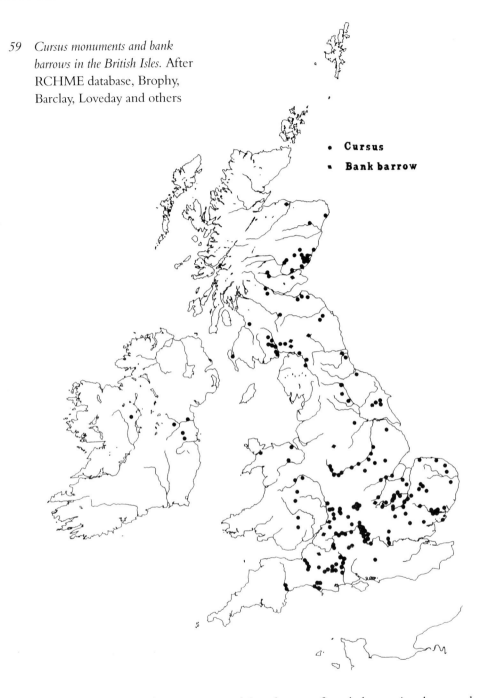

59 *Cursus monuments and bank barrows in the British Isles.* After RCHME database, Brophy, Barclay, Loveday and others

• **Cursus**

▪ **Bank barrow**

Staines (Surrey) (**49 & 58**) was excavated in advance of total destruction by gravel quarrying in the 1960s (Robertson MacKay 1987). The site was lowlying, between 15-16.5m OD, and was located on a gravel island between streams running into the river Thames less than 1km away. The local habitat was probably a rich wetland, full of different resources suitable for subsistence. The site had two concentric ditches forming a half circle some 174 x 151m, with a stream forming one edge of the site, and the site enclosed 2.4ha. There were probably banks following the inside edge of the ditches. The site had particularly interesting primary ditch deposits, which have been interpreted as ritually 'structured'. They included groups of selected pottery, tools and human and animal bone which had been arranged (**58**) in apparently symbolic ways. The site had been intensively used and partitioned with pits, fences, palisades and perhaps buildings, leaving quantities of domestic/industrial waste material. As at most other causewayed sites, cattle were the dominant animal in the economy, although the excavator argues that the location may have seen considerable seasonality in the economy, and also a greater emphasis on wild resources such as fish.

Excavated a quarter of a century after Staines, the causewayed enclosure at Etton, Cambridgeshire was rediscovered through aerial photography following a very dry summer. A dense Neolithic and later prehistoric ceremonial landscape surrounded the enclosure (Pryor 1999) and included a contemporary enclosure across the stream (Etton Woodgate), a cursus complex (**60**), a later Neolithic henge complex, settlement enclosures, barrows and field systems. The causewayed enclosure dated from 3775-2900 cal. BC, and its excavation has been particularly important for the organic survival of material in wet conditions which were unavailable to earlier excavators. The site was located on a knoll that frequently flooded the enclosure ditches. The water may have been intended, as part of the visual effect, and may have played an important symbolic role in the way the site was seen and used. The landscape around had been cleared of woodland before the site was constructed, which was then surrounded by open grassland and cultivation areas during its occupation. The surviving enclosure ditch measured 180 x 140m, but originally may have enclosed 2.5ha. Several phases of construction and occupation chart the development of the site:

1a. Initial ditch cut.
1b. Recutting and gateway construction, and division of interior into two parts.
1c. Narrowing of causeway and enlargement of internal division.
2. Later Neolithic use and construction of cursus cut diagonally across enclosure.
3. Bronze Age.

The main earlier-middle Neolithic use of the site lasted only two to three centuries before it was semi-abandoned (phase 1c). Within the interior, a building just inside the entrance formed the only interpretable structure; the rest was a mass of random pits and post-holes that might have been structures associated with the ritual activities of the site. The pits contained various types of deposit, which the excavator has divided into different classes and phases. Some pits contained flints and waste, others cremation-type material of burnt bone and charcoal, others had rubbish or carefully placed high status material, suggesting an intentional pattern of excavation and filling that may have been linked with individual events and people. The interior division was aligned on pits at each end. Evidence from the ditch segments indicated bonfires or perhaps pyres to incinerate animal remains; and rare human remains. Although the surrounding area was cultivated with cereals, and the Etton enclosure was almost equivalent to another 'field', the excavators argue against a mainly settlement use at

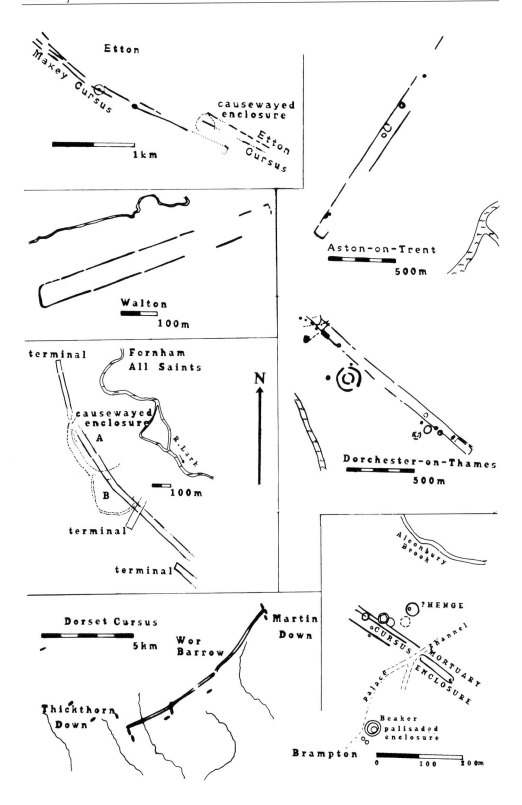

*60 (left) Cursus monuments in England are often part of complexes involving enclosures and
            mortuary structures and are frequently associated with rivers and springs. Maxey-Etton,
            Brampton — Cambridgeshire; Aston — Derbyshire; Dorchester — Oxfordshire; Fornham
            — Suffolk. After Barret and Bradley, Malim, Gibson, Pryor, Last and others*

Etton. Instead, they interpret its occupation as seasonal, used for rituals of a liminal
nature, which were played out in a location on the periphery of more populated zones.
Death, with all its symbolic significance, is suggested as a major theme at Etton. Such
ideas are supported by the structural division of the site into an east and west half by
the fence-line. In addition the intentional cremation of animals, the deposition in the
ditches of valuable objects like exotic axes, and the curious arrangement of
skeuomorphic stones and pots, perhaps symbolising human body parts, in the ditches
and pits all signify Neolithic belief systems.

Further south in the Cambridgeshire fenland, the enormous D-shaped site of
Haddenham is located, like Etton, on a gravel peninsula close to a major river, and semi-
covered in alluvial deposits. It is a single ditched oval enclosure, covering 8.5ha with an
impressive internal palisade. Traces of a bank were absent: it may be that on gravel soils
banks were replaced by wood palisades and timber gateways. Entranceways were
identified at one or two points, and appear to have been impressive, perhaps forming a
façade rather similar to some Neolithic burial monuments (Evans 1988). It is many times
larger than other local enclosures, for example the 2.5ha Great Wilbraham
(Cambridgeshire), Melbourn (0.95ha) (Cambridgeshire), Orsett (Essex) (2.7ha) or
Roughton (Norfolk) (1.22ha). The average size of enclosures in Midlands and east is
between 1-4.5ha, so Haddenham may have been functionally different than these, perhaps
as the focus of a particularly large local population. The chronology of the site is also
longer than found at the others, and continues to the mid-third millennium BC, as
confirmed by Peterborough pottery. The theme of death is well represented at
Haddenham, with human remains in the ditches and mortuary sites (the Haddenham
long barrow of the mid-fourth millennium BC) close by.

Beyond the enclosures

Southern British causewayed enclosures were major ceremonial foci in the emerging
'ritual' landscape. They are related to similar structures found across central and northern
Europe, which may indicate close contact or a shared tradition between communities
across the English Channel. An important observation based on soil and geological studies
is that many causewayed enclosures are located in countryside which contains, according
to Barker and Webley (1978) (**37**), the essential range of soils and economic resources to
support a self-sufficient site territory. These territories were defined by an enclosure, a
large number of barrows and tombs and other monuments, such as cursuses. This idea
has been developed and accepted, although in fact it still needs to be demonstrated
(Cunliffe 1993; Renfrew 1973).

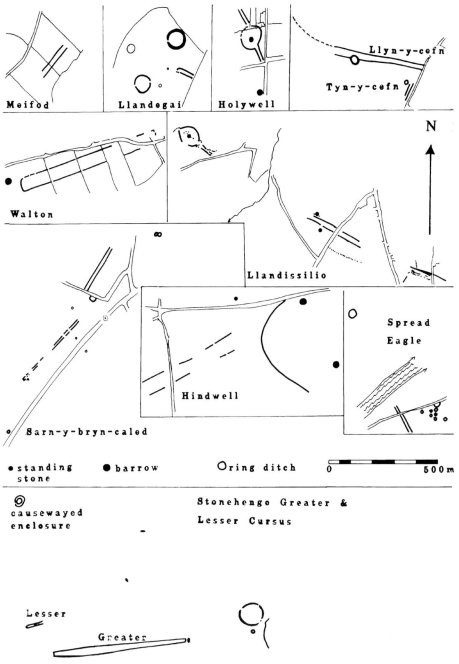

Meifod

Llandegai

Holywell

Llyn-y-cefn

Tyn-y-cefn

N

Walton

Llandissilio

Spread
Eagle

Hindwell

Sarn-y-bryn-caled

● standing   ● barrow   ○ ring ditch   0   500 m
stone

◎
causewayed   Stonehenge Greater &
enclosure   Lesser Cursus

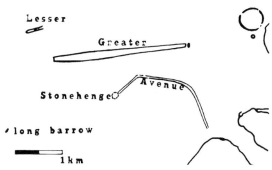

Lesser

Greater

Avenue

Stonehenge

∕ long barrow

1 km

*61 (left) Top: Welsh cursus monuments. After Gibson.
Bottom: the Stonehenge greater and lesser cursus monuments predate most of the Neolithic building
works on Salisbury Plain, and their position clearly influenced the arrangement of the later
monuments. After Darvill and others*

Neolithic sites in the north and west

Once we move outside the relatively lowlying landscape of southern and eastern Britain,
very different landscapes and resources were available to Neolithic communities, and the
development of enclosures was similarly diverse. Lynch argues (Lynch *et al.* 2000, 53-4)
that the more marginal agricultural zones of the north and west supported much lower
levels of population, which probably meant that the social pressures for central places in
which to congregate were less intense, and instead family-focused tombs were the main
monumental constructions.

There are, however, several varieties of enclosure in these western and upland areas
suggesting a regional response to the apparent need to build spaces, even though they
tended to develop much later than in the south. Later Neolithic enclosure sites have been
identified in the Welsh borders, where some elements of the English causewayed
enclosure seem to have been adopted. These are discussed in chapter 7 as part of later
Neolithic monumental landscapes, which develops the idea of enclosures and other
modified spaces created from pit alignments, timber palisades and various ditched
arrangements, including henges. Gibson (1998) has traced a sequence of types of wood
enclosures, starting with fenced sites from *c.*4000-2800 BC, followed by spaced post-holes
from 3300-2200 BC, then closely set post-holes 2800-2400 BC, and finally, contiguous
palisades dating from 2700 BC to the early centuries of the Bronze Age.

At all stages in the Neolithic it seems clear that the creation of artifical open space was
a preoccupation that engaged local populations in vast collective building projects lasting
centuries. One of the most distinctive types of monuments of the earlier Neolithic are the
cursuses. These mysterious linear constructions are usually found in close association
with Neolithic monumental landscapes, where they seem to be contemporary with long
barrows and causewayed enclosures. Many of the later henges are located close to them,
showing continuity of ceremonial use over a millenium and more.

Cursus monuments

The curious term 'cursus' was coined by William Stukeley in 1740 in his highly speculative
account of Stonehenge. He identified the Stonehenge cursus, with its parallel banks, as an
ancient linear course for chariot races by Ancient Britons, and drew heavily on Classical texts
and ideas to support this notion. With the increase in aerial survey from the 1920s onwards,
many more cursus and related pit-alignment monuments have been identified and examined
from southern Britain to Scotland. In total there are now at least 110 cursus monuments
identified in the British Isles and Ireland, of which some 8-11 are in Wales, 43 in Scotland, and

62   (right) Cursus monuments in Scotland consist of several pit alignments as well as bank-ditch structures. (Bennybeg, Balneaves, Douglasmuir; Inchbare, Kinalty, Milton of Guthrie Angus; Cleaven Dyke, Blairhall, Perthshire). After Barclay, Brophy and others

at least 3 in Ireland. Interestingly, like several other classes of Neolithic monument, cursuses are not known outside Britain and Ireland, although some linear enclosures in France may be parallel developments. Most cursus sites are located in lowland areas, on gravel terraces and rolling chalkland of the Yorkshire Wolds, Salisbury Plain and Cranborne Chase. Cursuses have been defined as 'elongated, parallel-sided sites, normally totally enclosed by their defining ditch or pits, but on rare occasions having one open end' (Loveday 1985). Very often the sites are lined up on a linear mound or long barrow, and the association of mortuary monuments with the rectilinear enclosure suggests they may be linear mortuary enclosures. The size of cursus-type sites varies enormously from 170m to 4km, and the Gussage and Pentridge cursuses of Dorset combine to cover 9.9km in length (the 'Dorset Cursus') (**60**). Most are much shorter and 2km is a good length for major cursus sites, whereas between 170-480m long typifies the minor ones. Width is highly variable, not apparently conforming to the length of the monument and can range from 20m to a maximum 128m at the Greater Stonehenge cursus. Some of the longest cursus sites are also the narrowest, as at Stanwell (London) and Scorton (N.Yorkshire). The shape of the ditch terminals that define the ends of the cursus-type monument vary from convex to square and usually both ends of the site can be identified, although in several cases, shallow ditches or open ends result in no obvious terminal structures. The ditches are usually continuous, although some seem to have segmented ditches or pits, or even double ditches. The ditch was excavated to provide material for the internal bank that seems to have been the most visible feature of cursuses, and defined an inner enclosed area for the activities which were played out. Quite what these were is open to speculation. However, the general consensus at present is that cursuses were associated with mortuary ritual and funerary activities, lined up at they often are, on long barrows, and in sight of a variety of burial sites and monuments, especially enclosures. Many scholars have speculated about their precise use or symbolic meaning (see Barclay and Harding 1999, 3-6) but it is still unclear whether the actual process of building the sites was the primary function, or whether the enclosures themselves were used to contain burial mounds, buildings and structures. Some scholars have suggested that the linear earth enclosure of the cursus reflects in many ways the stone rows of the uplands and Brittany, which similarly link together different sites, locales and often a long succession of separate communal building projects.

Other ancient projects include less easily defined monuments, which because of their inconclusive character or function, have been considered as 'ritual'. Pit alignments, enclosures, linear enclosures, standing stones and doubtless also organic constructions of timber or even living trees and hedges must have functioned as means to define areas and territories, marked by a physical structure symbolising an idea. The difficulties of recognizing the function of monuments like cursuses are considerable; however, the concentrations of various types of burials, beaker burials and cremations do point to a funerary role. The Dorchester-on-Thames cursus, for example, contains evidence for more Neolithic cremation burials than any other site. The complex there was one of the

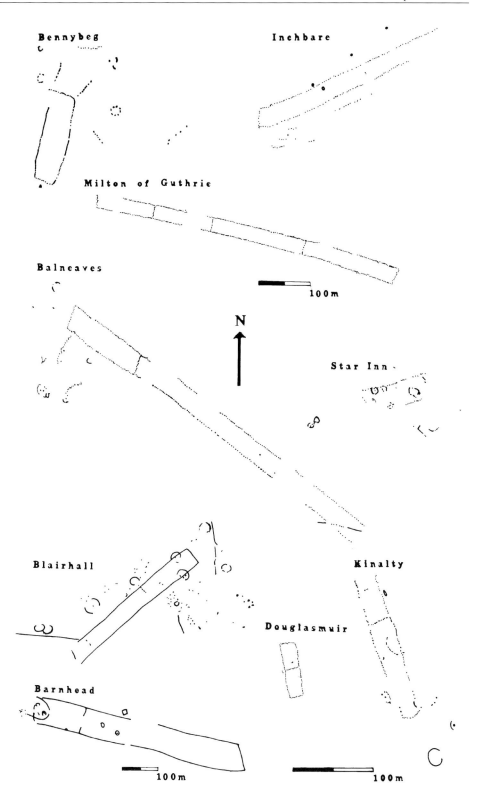

Bennybeg

Inchbare

Milton of Guthrie

Balneaves

100m

N

Star Inn

Blairhall

Kinalty

Douglasmuir

Barnhead

100m

100m

first sites of its class to be recognised through aerial photography, and it remains one of the most complex. It was the first major complex of the type to be excavated from the 1950s and to be systematically dated. There is a great range of monument types and ritual complexes over the gravel landscape, and all appear to focus upon the cursus, which runs over a length of 1600m. The cursus is dated between 3510 and 2920 cal. BC. (**60**)

There are many cursus monuments in Scotland, especially in the areas occupied by recumbent stone circles in eastern Scotland, including 16 in Tayside. A recently studied example is the 2km-long Cleaven Dyke in Tayside north of Perth (**63**). This site is preserved mostly as banks, ditches and cropmarks (Barclay and Maxwell 1998). It was begun early, and charcoal buried beneath the banks suggests dates for the moment of woodland clearance from 4750-4000 cal. BC. The ditches of the cursus are between 38-50m apart, broadening at the north-west end, and between 1.5 and 5m wide. A bank was raised between the ditches some 7-15m across and about 1.7m high which survives for a length of about 1800m, and the ditches survive as cropmarks for a further 380m. It was focused at the north-west end or terminal on a mound, which seemed to have been attached to a long barrow and, subsequently, the Dyke. There may a third barrow in the south-east section, which may have mimicked the north-east mound. Careful study of the possible astronomical alignment of the Dyke showed that there seemed to be little likelihood of it having any specific orientation. Close by a later structure, the Littleour timber enclosure, formed from posts laid out in a round-ended parallelogram shape, has been interpreted as a possible mortuary site. It dates from the later Grooved Ware Neolithic 2350-2030 cal. BC, and so is unlikely to have any relationship with the Dyke, other than as a continuation in a 'mortuary' inspired landscape feature.

In the uplands and Scotland, where soil was less easily excavated, cursuses were often formed from alignments of pits and posts. Bennybeg and Douglasmuir (**62**) represent small rectangular enclosures, whereas sites like Milton of Guthrie and Batneaves extended over hundreds of metres, punctuated by divisions or sections. Several sites appear to be associated with other pit/post structures and enclosures. At the smallest scale, there are close similarities between cursuses, longhouses and mortuary enclosures, again implying a close functional and symbolic relationship. For example, the association of a cursus beside the passage tomb of Newgrange (Ireland) provides a graphic illustration which is borne out by many other cursus sites.

5 Burials and tombs
in Neolithic Britain and Ireland

The burial of the dead was an important ritual amongst the Neolithic communities of Britain, and it contrasted markedly with the Mesolithic peoples' apparent lack of concern with their ancestors. Only a few burials are known from before about 4000 BC, and these are usually random, placed in caves or middens with little apparent ritual, such as at Cheddar in Somerset and Oronsay in the Hebrides. It seems that the role of ancestors in Neolithic society was much more important than in the world of hunter-gatherers. Clans and forebears began to have symbolic importance to the settled farming communities of the Neolithic. Dead ancestors were celebrated through funerals, feasts and grave goods, and their carefully selected body-parts were housed in specially built monuments, often symbolising 'houses' of the dead. Similar to the prominent burial mausolea of recent land-owning families, Neolithic tombs were often used for centuries, elaborated and extended, and echo similar sentiments about land ownership 6000 years ago. The tombs provide the earliest and most tangible evidence of Neolithic people and their customs, and are some of the most impressive and aesthetically distinctive constructions of prehistoric Britain. As the Neolithic world developed and societies became increasingly populous, sophisticated and competitive, burial practices turned more towards the interment of individuals in single graves, accompanied by their own ornaments, food and weapons. Thus earlier collective rites incorporating whole communities were replaced by evident social hierarchies which emphasised the important individuals. It seems likely, however, in spite of collective tombs or later cemeteries, that large sections of society were never buried in the formal graves or tombs of elite ancestors, and instead were placed in settlements or in the open countryside, leaving no lasting remains.

European background

The formal burial of individuals was rarely practised in the earlier Neolithic, and instead the phenomenon of collective burial predominated. This was where the remains from several corpses (often following excarnation and dismemberment elsewhere) were buried together, and were frequently represented by selected parts of their skeletons. The traditions for the collective rite, and for monumental (often megalithic) tomb architecture, developed centuries before they were adopted in Britain. The Atlantic façade of Europe (**2**), from southern Spain to Ireland, Scotland and Scandinavia, has fifth-fourth millennium BC monumental tombs which seem to have been the inspiration of the many

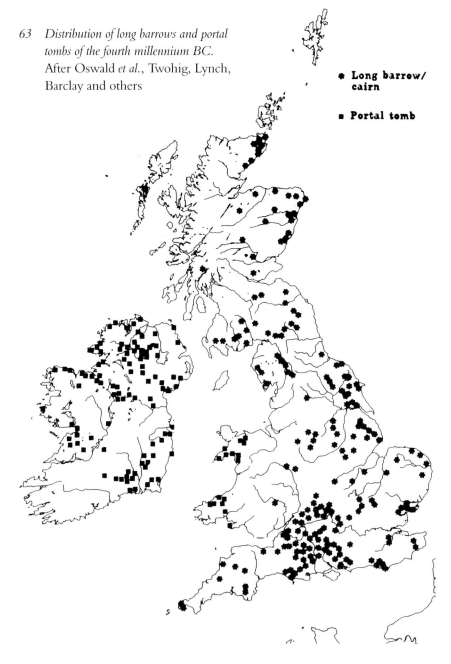

63   *Distribution of long barrows and portal*
      tombs of the fourth millennium BC.
      After Oswald *et al.*, Twohig, Lynch,
      Barclay and others

● **Long barrow/**
   cairn

■ **Portal tomb**

varieties of monument that developed in Britain. The coastal regions of western Europe
(especially Portugal and Brittany) were home to populous Mesolithic communities, and
the building of impressive stone tombs seems to have been triggered by the arrival of
agriculturalists from central and southern Europe. Both indigenous communities and the
agricultural colonists participated in tomb building, perhaps intent on claiming territory
in an increasingly crowded environment. Certainly, the large, prominent and immovable

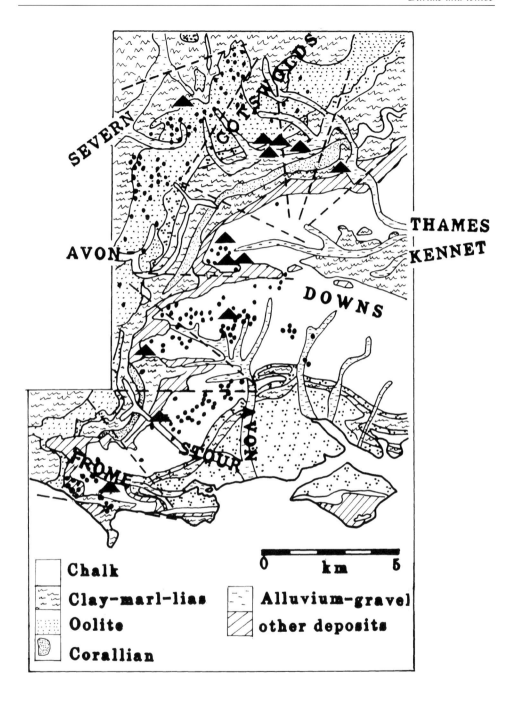

SEVERN

COTSWOLDS

THAMES

KENNET

AVON

DOWNS

STOUR

AVON

FROME

	Chalk			
	Clay-marl-lias		Alluvium-gravel	
	Oolite		other deposits	
	Corallian			

0   km   5

64   *Barker and Webley/Cunliffe. Territories and tombs*

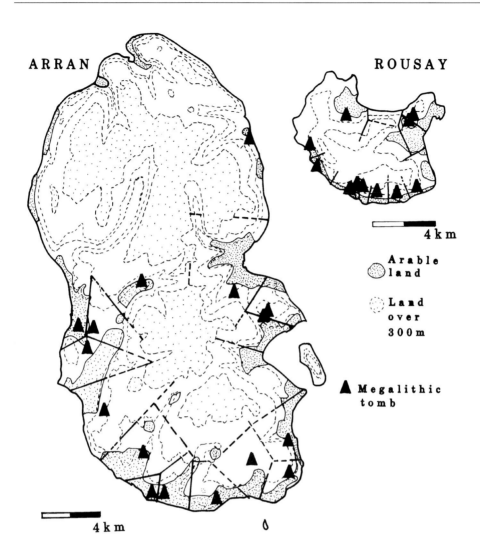

65 *Islands with limited fertile soils such as Rousay in the Orkneys and Arran on the west coast of Scotland
seem to show territorial spacing of chambered tombs around the coast, suggesting that each family group
had equal access to farmland, coast and upland.* After Renfrew, Henshall and Childe

man-made structures presented very clear messages of ownership, and impressive sites
such as Barnenez in Brittany are still effective signals.

Locations

The location chosen for these early tombs was often on prominent hills and slopes, at the
junction between different territories. Favoured places were above rivers and inlets or

overlooking fertile farmland and valleys. In southern Britain the tombs were important focal points in the man-made landscapes centred on causewayed enclosures. Studies of the territories of enclosures (Barker and Webley 1978; Cunliffe 1993; Renfrew 1973) (**64**) have suggested that the enclosures were surrounded by an unusually high density of barrows and tombs, each 'tomb-territory' having access to a range of soils and landscape types within the larger territory of the enclosure. This pattern suggests that each tomb might have represented a viable and self-contained territory. The distributions of tombs on some Scottish islands (Henshall 1963, 1972; Renfrew 1973) have shown similar patterns closely mirroring the modern land division of farms and crofts. Tombs on Rousay (Orkney) and Arran (**65**) are spaced at regular intervals around the islands and also seem to relate to land parcels containing the essential natural resources for self-contained subsistence. The tombs remain now as the only surviving markers in what may have been a complex array of physical and symbolic signals concerning territory, political alliegiance, ownership, and ancestors.

Regional patterns and types

The regional diversity of tombs, grave goods and body disposal practices represents a large and important body of data about the people of the Neolithic. There is a bewildering variety of shape, size, materials, location, orientation, contents, ritual and longevity of use that defies an easy definition of typical Neolithic burial. Less obvious, non-monumental burials are known from pits, ditches and wooden funerary structures but, in essence, there are two main varieties of surviving monumental tomb: earth and stone structures. Most formal tombs combined many materials, incorporating earth, turf, wood, rubble and stone. Tombs were generally built from local stone where it was plentiful, in the north and west of Britain and monumentality was clearly a major preoccupation (Kinnes 1976). In the east, where stone was scarce, earth, turf and timber formed the building materials together with flint rubble and chalk. Many tombs started as simple cairns and mounds (such as Wayland's Smithy, Oxfordshire), but were reused and remodelled over centuries, so that the final structures and their muddled contents combined many episodes. Where large stones were used to form the chambers, passage and façade, the tombs are known as 'Megalithic'. Simple classification over past decades of scholarship attempted to present logical regional sequences of development and style, but following excavation it has become clear that many Neolithic tombs and barrows spanned immense periods of time in use, and were progressively changed and restyled sometimes for well over a millennium, thus defying simple categorisation.

Dating and the landscape of the burials

Barrows and tombs (like the banks of causewayed enclosures discussed in chapter 4) often buried the existing ground surface, sealing important information about the local environment and its changes in the earlier Neolithic. Pollen evidence, land molluscs, charcoal fragments, peat in northern and western areas, micro-fauna and soil types from recently studied sites suggest that many earlier Neolithic tombs may have been constructed in wooded landscapes, often just outside the areas of prime soils chosen by early farmers for cultivation. The South Street long barrow at Avebury was placed directly over land that had been broken by the plough with a criss-cross pattern of ard movements, but then covered by the barrow (**9**), sealing in important information about the local landscape changes (Evans 1971).

The dating of tombs can be complicated, for different components may be very widely spaced in time. The bones placed in the tombs were sometimes antique before they were finally deposited, and occasionally have radiocarbon ages many centuries older than the charcoal within the soil that covered them, or in the post sockets of the wooden structures that formed the burial monument. Sometimes corpses were deposited in graves over many centuries. For example, the Beaker burial within the earlier Neolithic tomb of West Kennet (Wiltshire) suggests closure of the tomb in the final centuries of the third millennium BC, while the earlier burials and deposits have been radiocarbon-dated to the early to mid-fourth millennium BC, suggesting the tomb saw intermittent use over some 1500 years. Pottery styles and the forms of other grave goods changed relatively slowly over the course of the earlier Neolithic and are difficult to assign to precise dates, although thermoluminescence may indicate when pottery was fired. Finding reliable dates that relate directly to the construction of the tombs, whether of earth or stone, is particularly difficult. Buried organic materials, such as charcoal or bone in the covering mound, or in the subsoil beneath the structure, can date from entirely different periods that the built structure. Ultimately, precise dates are of less importance that the overall sequence of building, and the burials contained within the tomb.

Populations and bones

Studies of bones are especially important for understanding the composition and health of Neolithic populations, and their role should not be underestimated. However, few earlier excavations recorded or kept bones, and only a very partial picture is available, especially for attempts to reconstruct the population structure of the buried communities represented in the tombs. Since the middle of the twentieth century routine records of archaeological human remains have been made, and specialist researchers have studied them, thus enabling an understanding of the populations in the tombs, as well as the architecture in which they were placed. Recent analysis of the location of different bones in tombs has shown that body parts and the age and sex of the buried individual sometimes determined their precise placement in the chambers. Thomas' study of Notgrove and West Kennet Severn Cotswold tombs (Thomas 1988) produced a pattern of age and sex division between different chambers of the tombs (**84**). However, such patterning does not seem to be universal, since Shanks and Tilley (1982) showed that proportions of body parts varied, both between similar types of tomb (Fussell's Lodge, Lanhill and Luckington) and between their individual chambers (**66**).

The practice of 'collective' burial often involved the muddling, breakage or partial removal of earlier interments, and some carefully excavated tombs have revealed extraordinary arrangements of selected bones. Excavators at West Kennet found smaller

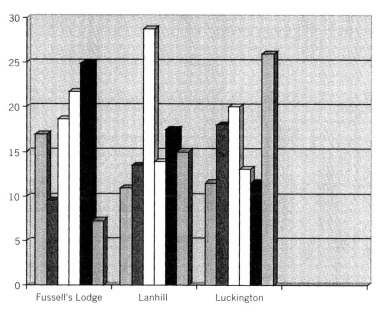

66 *Relative percentage of body parts in three long barrows.* After Shanks and Tilley 1982

67 *The arrangements of bones found in the West Kennet long barrow.* After Piggott

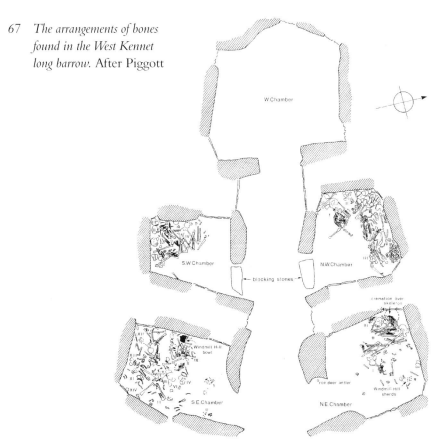

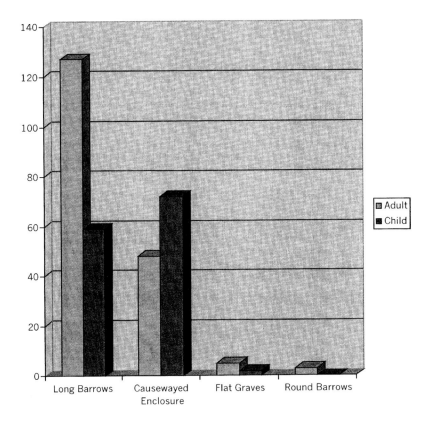

68   Contents of burials in Wessex, for children and adults. After Thorpe 1996

bones such as vertebrae stuffed into crevices between stones, and skulls or long bones heaped together in an orderly fashion. The age and gender of bones and their selection and placement in the tombs may also have been deliberate (see discussions in Shanks and Tilley 1982, Thomas and Whittle 1986, Thorpe 1984). Some excavations, such as Hazelton North in Gloucestershire (Saville 1990), recorded the precise location of the bones in situ and showed the extent that bones were moved between chambers. Other sites such as Skendleby and Lankill contained discrete 'bone bundles' which represented the collected remains of people (**69**).

A simple quantification of the different body parts deposited in barrows and the graves in ditches of causewayed enclosures suggests that different ritual activities and cults were practised at different types of site. Thorpe (1984) showed that skulls amounted to over 40 per cent of the bones from Wessex causewayed enclosures, and nearly 30 per cent were long bones; other body parts were poorly represented. The reverse was true of Wessex long barrows, where skulls represented only about 8 per cent of the total, long bones over 40 per cent, and other body parts about 50 per cent. Another distinction is in the overwhelming number of cattle bones accompanying the dead in long barrows compared with the many other animal species found associated with the burials within causewayed

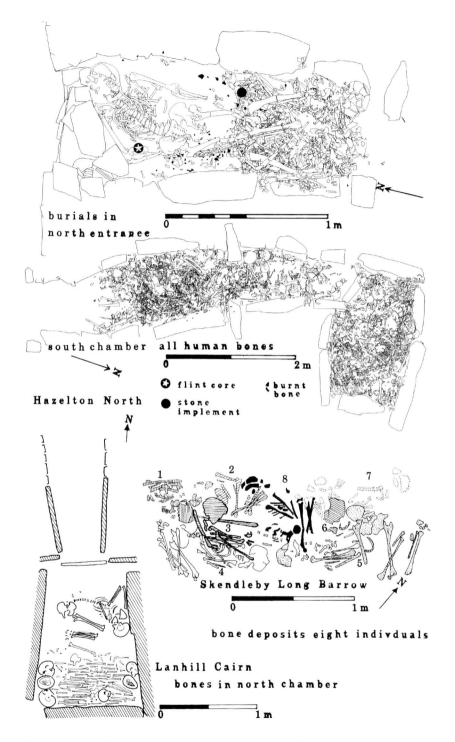

burials in
north entrance

0   1 m

south chamber   all **human bones**

0   2 m

✪ flint core   burnt bone

● stone implement

Hazelton North

N

1   2   8   7

3   6

4   5

Skendleby Long Barrow

0   1 m

bone deposits eight indivduals

Lanhill Cairn

bones in north chamber

0   1 m

69   *The arrangement of human remains in many Severn-Cotswold tombs and long barrows shows haphazard heaps together with articulated skeletons, as at Hazelton North, and carefully arranged bone bundles at Lanhill and (Giant's Grave) Skendleby.* After Saville, Piggott and Phillips

enclosures. Thorpe's work also revealed that in long barrows twice as many bones were disarticulated and muddled as opposed to articulated burials.

Ethnographic studies of ancestor cults and bone veneration, still practised by societies like the Merina of Madagascar, show that collective burial practices often involve the frequent removal of bones for cleaning and veneration when new corpses are added to the family tomb. The jumbled, broken, selected body parts that survive in Neolithic tombs are extremely difficult to interpret in terms of total populations, since only certain bones are informative about age and sex. Fingers, toes, ribs and vertebrae are of relatively little use in determining the number of people in a tomb, or informing about their gender and age. The population estimates are surprisingly low in the tombs that have been studied, often between 10-50 people over many centuries, but sometimes far fewer. The Orkney cairns appear to contain the largest numbers of people, perhaps several hundred, whilst the great passage graves of the middle-later Neolithic appear to have specialised in the cremated remains of very few people. The different types of body treatment — from scorching, burning, excarnating (leaving the corpse in the open to rot before collecting the clean, dry bones) and defleshing, to burying whole — leave different types of remains and proportions of body parts. Where tombs combined several rites over centuries, it is not surprising that the total population of each tomb can only be estimated. In some conditions, such as acid soils, bones do not even survive, so the tomb must be assessed simply as a receptacle for the dead, where structure, grave-goods, orientation and size are, at best, broad indicators of the burial practices. Assessing the health and cause of death amongst the buried population is difficult from the fragmentary remains, and in particular, the vulnerable bones of children are usually poorly represented or preserved. Where they do survive, they are valuable for showing deficiencies in diet and disease that are less obvious in adult skeletons. Indications are that most people died quite young, between birth and their twenties. Relatively few individuals survived, it seems, into middle or old age, and those that did were frequently plagued with arthritis and poor teeth. The disarticulated nature of most Neolithic human bone means that it is very difficult to build up a clear picture of individuals and their health and stature. The recent report on Hazelton (Saville 1990) offers some of the most recent and systematic research on the subject, and the mixed nature of the deposits (**69**).

Early tombs — long barrows

The term barrow refers to an earthern — often turf covered — mound over an ancient tomb. Neolithic barrows are normally long, trapezoidal structures, but in Yorkshire they are sometimes round, and in Scotland and the west they may have long curved or horned entrances. The earliest sites have radiocarbon dates from the early centuries of the fourth millennium BC, (between 3900 and 3500 BC). Late dates show some long barrows remained in sporadic use until the later Neolithic, in the final centuries of the third millennium BC. There are clear regional patterns of distribution of earth barrows across the British Isles that relate to the parent rock. Barrows are generally found in eastern and southern Britain, with some 230 long barrows of the earlier Neolithic known from southern England, concentrated on the Wessex chalklands (**63**). The other main barrow concentrations (at least 54) are in Yorkshire and Lincolnshire, centred on the chalk Wolds.

Other barrows are thinly distributed in Derbyshire and Cumbria. The Scottish equivalents of long barrows are long cairns, which unlike most northerly cairns have no obvious inner stone structure, although timber and some stone formed small chambers. They are concentrated in north -east (28-plus cairns) and southern (21-plus) Scotland, and may well be the ancestral form of the cairns and passage graves of the region. They have been called the Balnagowan group by Henshall (1963) and are especially frequent in Aberdeenshire.

Many barrows were built around a timber, hurdle, turf and chalk-flint rubble framework, perhaps symbolic of the longhouses of north-western Europe, and later covered with rubble, turf and soil. Occasionally the structure was deliberately destroyed or burnt before a mound was raised over the site, perhaps as part of a rite of purification and closure. A few sites have been subjected to very thorough study and excavation in recent years and they are described below. This work has shown that the apparently simply sausage-shaped mounds contain much more complex components such as mortuary houses, timber-built structures, pits, cairns of stone, ditches, façades and turf or stone revetments along the sides. The mounds were mostly trapezoidal in shape — wider and higher at the entrance end than the 'tail' — or parallel-sided, and some had a straight (in Wessex) or curved (in Yorkshire-Lincolnshire) convex entrance façade. Most long barrows were constructed from the material dug from quarry ditches excavated along each side of the mound. Some barrows in Yorkshire and Cranborne Chase had ditches on three sides or all around them.

Barrows, as seen today, give little impression of their original appearance. The structures were impressive, with high wood plank façades, avenues of posts leading to the entrance, and well-defined 'kerbs' formed of cut turves, wood or stone. They were buildings which were accessible, yet they were closed to most people, except when people entered to place the remains of the dead inside. The earth cover was simply the final stage of closure (for a broad discussion see Kinnes 1992).

Long barrows range from *c.*20m to over 125m long. About half the known total are between 30 and 60m long. Longer barrows are much rarer — seven measure between 80-95m, twelve between *c.*95-120m, and two between *c.*120-140m. Only five are longer, including the 545m long Maiden Castle bank barrow, Long Bredy, Dorset (197m), Broadmayne, Dorset (182m), Pen Hill, Somerset (228m) and Lowther, Cumbria (274m). These long bank-barrows seem to have a close affinity with cursus monuments, and perhaps they shared similar functions in special funerary rituals.

The original height of barrows is difficult to estimate now, but many must have been well over 5m high. Adam's Grave in Wiltshire is still over 7m high, but others have been ploughed flat, and only their lateral ditches and soil marks distinguish the location. The greatest proportion — over 80 per cent — of barrow entrances are orientated within 45 degrees of east-west. The remainder includes a significant number of north-south orientations, and on Cranbourne Chase barrows respect the local orientation of the ridges (NNW-SSE) plus the existence of cursus monuments, which seem to have influenced barrow orientation.

Burials were placed either on the floor of barrows, in burial pits, on paved platforms, within cairns of chalk, stone and flint in bundles, or in wooden mortuary chambers formed from hurdles or stakes. Most burials were located at the entrance end of the tomb where these structures were concentrated around a passage of timber or hurdle, and which has now, of course, collapsed or been intentionally in-filled.

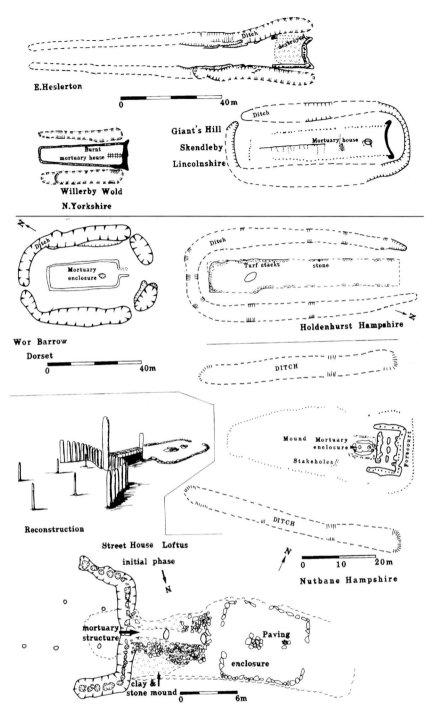

70   *Long barrows with mortuary enclosures and associated structures have been identified following excavation
at several sites. Earth mounds were the final phase of complex mortuary buildings with forecourts and
impressive entrance facades of tall wood posts. (Willerby Wold, East Heslerton — N. Yorkshire; Giant's
Hill, Skendlby — Lincolnshire; Holdenhurst, Nutbane — Hampshire; Wor Barrow — Dorset; Street
House — Cleveland).* After Manby, Piggott, Pitt Rivers, Phillips, Vatcher Vyner

The simplest earthen long barrows consisted of a burial mound and side ditches, and were not subjected to drastic rebuilding or enlargement. They were mostly constructed of earth and timber. The site of Holdenhurst, Hampshire (Piggott 1937) was located on a lowland gravel site. The mound was 91m long, 27m wide and 1.2m high, bounded by parallel turf revetments 10m apart, which defined the burial area. Within this was found a large stone, a small pit containing burnt flints and an area of human burial, although the acid soil had destroyed the bones, leaving only stains in the gravel. (**70**)

Not all Neolithic barrows are long in shape (Kinnes 1979), as was demonstrated by the excavation of the Alfriston (East Sussex) oval barrow in 1974 (Drewett 1975). This small, oval-shaped mound was flanked by lateral ditches, and contained a burial pit (1.8x1.2m) and the crouched and articulated skeleton of a woman. An additional pit close by contained no other burial, but post-holes at each end of the mound suggested that there may have been some sort of wooden structure, façade or entrance.

The Haddenham long barrow, Cambridgeshire (Hodder and Shand 1988, Evans and Hodder 2002) represents another lowland site, in this case on the Fenland edge. The trapezoidal mound was located on gravels, and buried in later peat formations. It was about 50m long, 15m wide at the north-east end and 10m wide at the south west, with ditches (2.5m wide, 1.5m deep) encircling all but the north east entrance façade. The façade and burial chamber of the site had been constructed of wood, some of which was preserved through burning and peat cover. The burial area was a rectangular chamber with a flat roof of oak planks 4m long and 1.3m wide. This wooden chamber had walls 1.3m high, axial posts supporting the roof, and was encased in clay banks. The chamber faced the north-east and was entered through a 12m long continuous façade formed from split-oak trunks each 60cm diameter. The façade had curved 'arms' returning along the north and south flanks of the chamber for 3.5 and 4m, with right-angled posts at the butt ends. Like the cairn at Street House, the Haddenham façade (see below) was probably a freestanding structure before the mound covered it. There were five burials within the wooden chamber and two secondary ones within the earth mound, and it seems that the bodies were inserted whole but later disturbed by the additions of burials. The date for the construction of Haddenham is 3500-3600 cal. BC (**70b**), and the wood chamber was then filled and closed. The barrow was constructed over the structure, sealing it from further use and access.

Barrows not only covered wooden burials chambers and burial pits, but also wooden buildings, special enclosures or mortuary houses elaborated with façades, passages and open areas, within which funerary activities and perhaps the exposure of corpses took place. The mortuary areas were defined by trenches dug into the subsoil, which sometimes formed the bedding trenches for posts, and within these areas there were pits, paved areas, burnt areas and deposits of bones. They were then intentionally covered over to form barrows. The stylistic and functional link between longhouses and the European tradition of mortuary houses is represented at several sites, especially in the east-north-east of England.

Nutbane long barrow, Hampshire (Morgan 1959) (**70**) is a rare southern example of mortuary enclosure. The structure was found beneath a trapezoidal mound measuring 51x22m wide at its east and 7m at its west end, and flanked by parallel ditches. The mound overlay a series of unusual structures interpreted as a mortuary enclosure. The building sequence began with a forecourt building (4.8x3.5m), attached to an embanked burial

71a   *The Haddenham (Cambridgeshire) long barrow during excavation in 1987, showing the timber burial chamber.*
Photo C. Malone

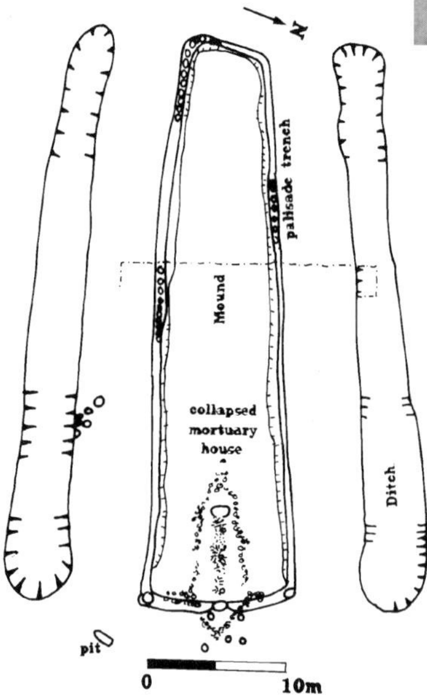

71b   *Fussell's Lodge (Wiltshire) formed a similar timber mortuary house, with walls made up of upright posts, entered through a porch at the east end. Burials were placed on the floor in four distinct groups.*
After Manby and Ashby

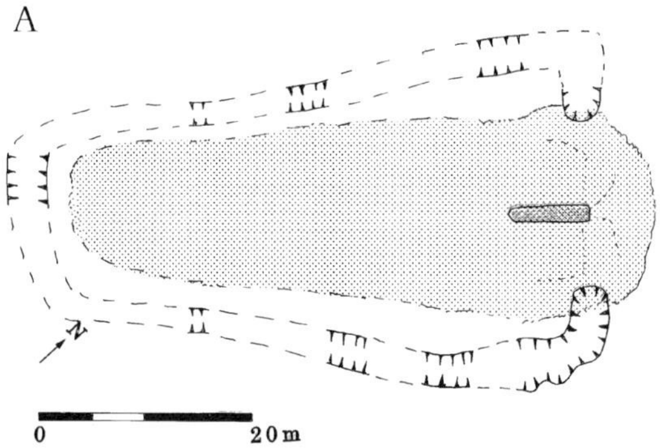

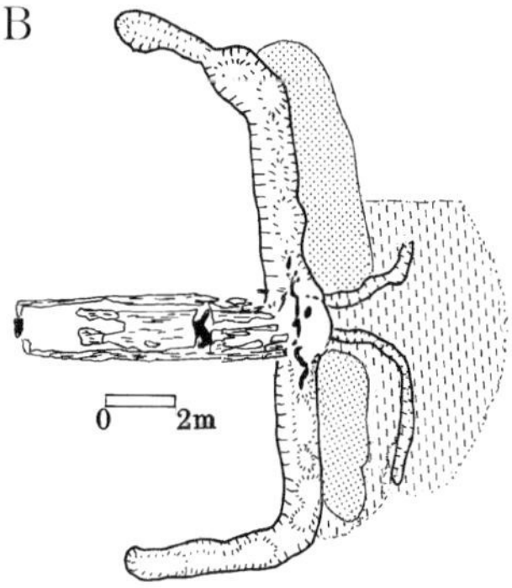

A

B

71c   *The Haddenham long barrow in plan. A: the three-sided surrounding ditch, the gravel-earth mound and the location of the timber mortuary structure. B: the timber mortuary structure formed a rectangular box, set against the entrance of upright posts, which in turn were supported by a gravel bank*

enclosure with entrance posts and three burials. The entrance forecourt was replaced by a larger building (12 x 5.4m) with a flanking façade of posts set in a trench, and then the banked enclosure was replaced with a fenced enclosure (c.6 x 5.5m) and another burial, with a covering cairn of chalk and soil. The entrance to the enclosure was then blocked by posts, and the enclosure and forecourt filled with soil and chalk dug from the quarry ditches. Finally the forecourt was burnt, and a secondary mound was constructed over the whole structure.

The immense barrows of Yorkshire (Manby 1988) and Lincolnshire have been explored for over a century and a half, when Bateman, Greenwell and others sought to understand the ancient tombs. Several sites (Willerby Wold, East Heslerton and the Giants' Hill (Skendleby)) contained complex mortuary structures (**70**). These barrows had palisade trenches and entrance façades of posts set in impressive convex or concave arrangements opening onto arenas for funerary rituals. The Giant's Hill barrow was 64m long x 22m wide, and was defined along its perimeter by lines of posts, within which was an enclosure of between 10-13m wide. East Heslerton was of tremendous length (c.110m) with discontinous bedding trenches 40m long at either side forming a rectangular enclosure with a crescent-shaped façade of 60cm wide posts set in a trench, and bounded by lateral ditches (Vatcher and Vatcher 1965).

The Giant's Hill (Ashbee 1984, 37-8) dated from c.3300-2870 BC, had a slightly tapering plan under an extensive mound c.64x22-10m, and the enclosure was closed by a massive façade of split logs set in a palisade trench. The side trenches held smaller posts that probably decreased in height from the façade. Willerby Wold, North Yorkshire (Manby 1963) was excavated by Canon Greenwell in the nineteenth century, and by Manby in 1958-60. The barrow measured 37m long x 10.6m wide and was 2.1m high at the east end and 1.6m at the west when Greenwell explored it. The three-phase sequence of construction, from enclosure to barrow:

1. Construction of trapezoidal mortuary enclosure, defined by roughly parallel post-bedding trenches 6 to 8.2m apart which extended along each side for c.35m. A bedding trench 11.8m long formed the front of the tomb and supported a curved timber-built façade.
2. The wooden post-built enclosure was then burnt in situ, and a central trench and adjoining pit 1.6m in diameter were dug, together with two further pits, into which cremated bones, three skulls and sooty deposits were placed.
3. The whole structure was covered by soil, turf and chalk to form the barrow (**70**).

Kilham long barrow, North Yorkshire (Manby 1976) dated from 3700-3500 BC, also had three main phases of construction:

1. Parallel quarry pits 7m apart were excavated, possible enclosing a small temporary mound within a long enclosure.
2. Side ditches were extended from the quarry pits to enclose a trapezoidal mortuary enclosure which may have been a roofed structure connected to a wall of end posts. It contained five crouched inhumations and Grimston pottery.
3. A massive trapeziform mortuary enclosure 58m long, and between 8.5 and 10.7m wide, aligned to the earlier ditches and post slots, was constructed. The burial chamber

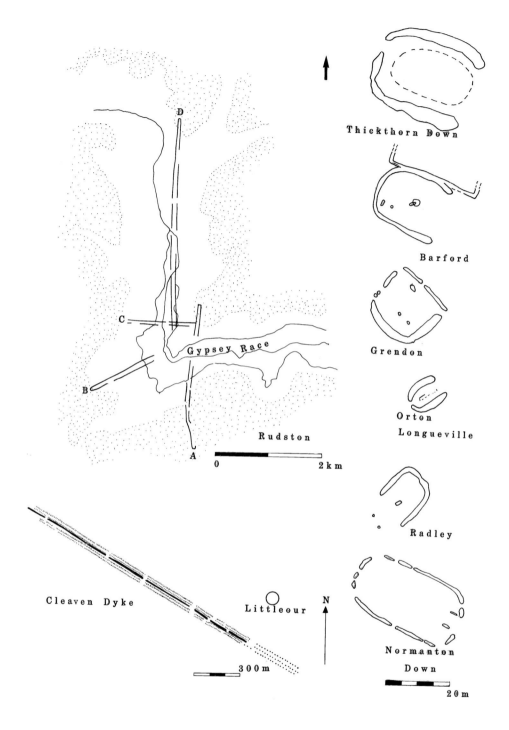

72 *The Rudston cursuses form the densest group of cursus monuments in Britain, and two line up on the great Rudston Monolith standing stone at the curve of the Gypsey Race River.*
Sources — various

was approached via an avenue of posts. The mound was then built in two stages, over the western two-thirds of the enclosure, leaving the eastern burial area of parallel banks and wall structure accessible, and much of it was burnt in situ.

The mortuary house at Street House, Cleveland (Vyner 1984, 1988) was constructed over several phases at the interface between long barrow and later cairn traditions, and includes characteristics of both. It first consisted of a double row of upright timbers set up as an avenue, leading to a curved timber façade. Behind this was an embanked area supporting a wooden burial chamber, embanked with five large timbers in trenches on each side, deliberately burnt in situ. Behind the burial chamber (which contained two burial pits and a clay mound), a rectangular enclosure was formed from a kerb of stones, which was added to in successive remodellings of the site. The whole structure was then enveloped in a stone cairn of the later tradition. Interestingly, the separate components did not interconnect via passages, and appear to contain three quite separate functional structures. Carbon 14 Dates cluster around 3700-3600 BC and a TL date corresponds closely at 3575 BC ± 850 (**70**).

Long barrow enclosures with entrances

A different if parallel tradition prevailed in Wessex, where several long barrows were constructed over earlier enclosures, similar in character to the northern mortuary houses, but without the elaborate superstructures and façades. Some enclosures seem to be developments in parallel to cursus monuments and current thinking about mortuary enclosures, bank barrows and long barrows of this group identifies similar forms and likely function.

Wor Barrow, Dorset (Pitt Rivers 1898) (**70**) began life as a rectangular enclosure (27 x 10.5m) with its walls formed from upright tree trunks set into a bedding trench, packed with flint, entered by a restricted passage at the east end. Early dates associated with pottery were *c*.3650-3300 BC, contemporary with two crouched male burials — one mature, one immature — inserted into the terminal of the entrance ditch. The timber structure was then buried under a 4m-high mound, with a discontinuous ditch encircling it, and associated with later Neolithic Peterborough pottery (Ebbsfleet-Mortlake styles). The mound formed an impressive monument in the local landscape of Cranborne Chase, closely associated with the Dorset Cursus and with numerous barrows, especially two later Neolithic round barrows (Handley 26 and 27), which were close by and were associated with Mortlake pottery. It seems that they were contemporary with the closure of the long barrow, and offer an intriguing insight into the local burial sequence (Barrett et al. 1991, 84-7) . At the west end of the Dorset Cursus, the site of Thickthorn long barrow (**72**) (excavated by Drew and Piggott 1936) offers a parallel to Wor barrow (dated *c*.4000-3940 BC). The barrow covered an enclosure which had been defined by two U-shaped ditches, with the turf walls of a mortuary structure and internal bays of stakes. No human burials were found, although animal bones, artefacts and pottery were buried in the ditches. The distribution of these deposits seems to have been intentionally patterned (Thomas in Barrett et al. 1991, fig. 2.11). Animal bone was clustered around the ditch terminals, earlier pottery only at the north-eastern terminal, later Peterborough pottery at both terminals, Beaker pottery at the west end of the ditch and at the

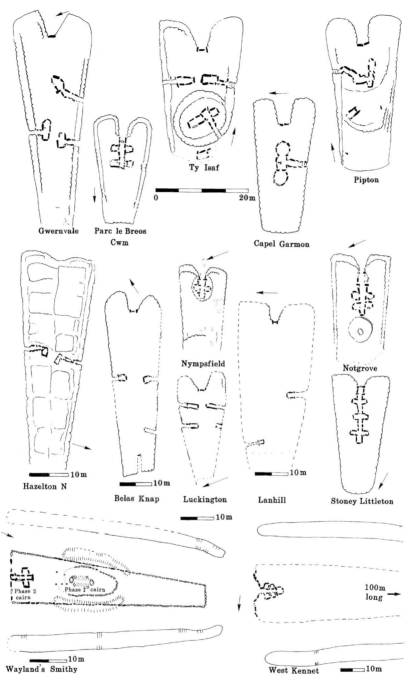

73 *Severn-Cotswold tombs form a distinctive group of monuments, with impressive long cairns, often
edged in stone kerbs and incorporating burial chambers, either at the ends or along the sides. Many
tombs have 'horned' entrances (often facing east) which formed areas for funeral rituals. West Kennet,
Lanhill, Luckington — Wiltshire; Stoney Littleton — Somerset; Notgrove, Belas Knap, Hazelton
North — Gloucestershire; Wayland's Smithy — Oxfordshire; Parc le Breos — Glamorgan; Ty Isaf,
Gwernvale, Pipton — Breconshire; Capel Garmon — Denbeigh).*
After Cocoran, Lynch, Saville, and others

southern terminal, and burials at the centre of the enclosure. There had also been some type of entrance porch at the south-east end between the ditch terminals.

The timber mortuary house of Fussell's Lodge long barrow in Wiltshire (Ashbee 1966) measured about 4m long, 3m wide, and the structure, supported by three large axial posts, and was accessed through a four-post porch-entrance fronted by a timber palisade façade. The mortuary house was encircled by a trench that held a stake revetment some 40m long and between 6-12m wide. The 'house' was probably roofed in turf on timbers supported by a flint rubble bank/wall, which later collapsed inwards over the burials when the mortuary house was partly burnt in situ. It covered three distinct piles of skeletal remains amounting to at least 51 individuals. An inner box held the remains of 13 adults and 4 children represented by selected body-parts (rarely skulls or long bones — see above) and animal bones were strategically placed with the burials (**71b**).

Wayland's Smithy 1, Oxfordshire (Atkinson 1965; Whittle 1991) represents an earlier Neolithic stone-built enclosure burial site that had become increasingly monumental by the time of structure 2 (see below). Following clearance and early occupation, the first building phase probably began with an ovoid enclosure defined by post structures and delimited by a sarsen stone kerb. Over this a wooden mortuary house was erected supported by two upright posts 4.6m apart — perhaps supporting a pitched and ridged mortuary 'tent' similar to Fussell's Lodge (an idea promoted by the excavator Richard Atkinson), or an embanked box structure (a view that assumes the mound was later). A paved area between the posts was covered in burial remains 20cm thick, and flanked by linear sarsen stone cairns and two pits. At least 14 individuals (mostly adults) were deposited as disarticulated body parts, although one complete individual was placed separately from the bone heaps, at the north end of the paved area. At the entrance two rows of post-holes supported a trapezoidal entrance porch or platform. A modest primary barrow 14m long x 7m wide of chalk and soil/turf covered the structure around 3700-3390 cal. BC. The second structural phase (also dating from 3700-3390 BC) saw the construction of a trapezoidal mound and stone structure covering the mortuary house, typical of Severn Cotswold chambered tombs (see below). Two curved lateral ditches were excavated and found to enclose an area of 20x11m, in which the low mound was defined by a sarsen stone kerb. A stone-capped passage and three small rectangular transepted chambers formed the new burial area, and were entered at the south end through a façade of six large upright stones. Human remains from old excavations numbered at least eight individuals. Outside and to the west, another (probably Beaker) burial was located in a small pit. Grave goods were all but absent, with three leaf arrowheads found in the burial area (**73**).

Later Neolithic burials

Round barrows (from the later fourth to the early third millennium BC) continued to be constructed around supporting wooden structures, and relate broadly to a northern cairn tradition. Late barrows are generally rare, but were a feature of Yorkshire (some 40 are known) with rare outliers in the south Midlands. Several barrows show evidence for wooden structures similar to those beneath some long barrows — entrance enclosures and mortuary houses. There is evidence for circular kerbs set around the base, reflecting the linear kerbs around some long mounds and the passage graves (see below). The C14 dates suggest that the round barrows were constructed at about the same time that many long barrows went out of use in the later fourth-earlier third millennium BC. Grave goods, such as those from Duggleby Howe, indicate that the tradition was associated with high status individuals and splendid artefacts. Interestingly, the northern barrows seem to be associated with males, whereas those in the south are associated with women. The shift from collective ancestors and burial traditions in long barrows, to lavish individual burials under round barrows, anticipates the trends of the third-second millennia BC Copper and Early Bronze Ages, which focused on articulated individual burials and distinctive grave goods. For most of the later Neolithic population there was no formal burial, as traditions shifted from collective ancestral tombs and ritual deposits in enclosures. Instead corpses seem to have been randomly placed as disarticulated body parts in the ditches of henge monuments, pits, and across the countryside and in rivers. Unfortunately too little is known of how later Neolithic populations disposed of their dead because of the rarity of known sites. Up to 40 round barrows of Neolithic date are known, especially in north-east/central Britain. Some are early, but the trend seems to be that many were constructed in the later Neolithic. For example, in 1892 Callis Wold 275, North Yorkshire (Coombs 1976), was a mound 3.7m high, 27m in diameter and enclosed by a ditch. It is one of a group of Neolithic and Bronze Age barrows on the western edge of the Yorkshire Wolds. Body parts were scattered throughout the mound, and 10 contracted inhumations were located on a 3.6 x 3m platform of lias stones. Pits at either end supported a mortuary structure, and contained cremated human and animals bones. The straight east end façade and the curved west end both had lines of wood posts bedded into trenches. Turf and chalk soil were then heaped over the structure within the encircling ditch, forming the impressive mound (**74**).

Duggleby Howe, North Yorkshire, is a very impressive mound, and particularly significant, since it is located at the centre of a rare earlier (?)Neolithic ditched enclosure. It contained richly furnished individual (and mostly male) burials. The grave goods included a flint adze, arrowheads, boars' tusks and bone pins as well as pottery (**175**). The predominance of males under these northern round barrows contrasts with the southern round barrows which tend to cover the burials of women. All these round barrows date from the later fourth and third millennia BC, demonstrating a new preoccupation with the burial of individuals instead of collective groups.

Whitleaf (Lincolnshire) (Childe and Smith 1954) was located on a low hill on the false crest. A circular ditch enclosed the kidney-shaped earth/chalk, flint/clay mound, and post-holes defined a central chamber-cove. The inner chamber was probably constructed of horizontal logs which formed a chamber (2.4 x 1.6m) defined by four corner posts. Within the chamber area a large pit 2.5 x 1.5m in diameter and 60cm deep was surrounded by stake holes and, the remains of one (?male) corpse were accompanied by 15 or more ceramic vessels (of Ebbsfleet, Abingdon and Mildenhall styles) and a large number of flints. Linch Hill Corner, Stanton Harcourt, Oxon, is an example of late Neolithic female burials. The large round barrow had a double ditch and contained a single female inhumation, accompanied by a polished edge flint knife and a jet belt fitting. A round barrow at Dunstable (Beds) may also be Neolithic (**74**).

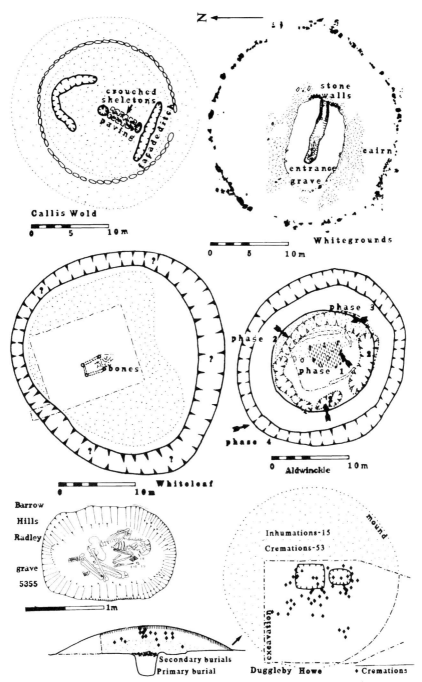

74 *Round barrows replaced the earlier long barrows as burial monuments in the later Neolithic. Some are impressive mounds, such as Duggleby Howe, but generally they contained relatively few richly furnished burials. Most burials were less formal, as shown by the pit grave from Barrow Hills at Radley which usually contained one or two individuals. (Duggleby Howe, Whitegrounds — N. Yorks; Callis Wold — Humberside; Whiteleaf — Bucks; Aldwinckle — Northants; Barrow Hills, Radley — Oxon).* After Kinnes, Brewster, Vyner, Childe and Smith and others

75 *The huge late Neolithic
burial mound of
Duggleby Howe in the
Yorkshire Wolds.*
Photo Mick Sharp

The round cairn of Pitnacree, Perthshire, has some similarities with the Yorkshire round barrows and late Neolithic sites in Northern Ireland and Scotland. It was located amongst 20 other similar mounds in the Tay valley, and is the only example to have been excavated. The first phase of construction involved two pits containing large upright timbers. Then a rectangular stone walled enclosure (some 5x1.3m) formed a burial passage, with capstones over each end. It was soon enclosed in a turf and stone mound surrounded by a dry-stone revetment some 22m in diameter. A smaller four-sided stone cist was built within the turf mound and at the summit a tall standing stone marked the site; beneath this were the cremated remains of a female (dated at 2910-2660 BC). In total only five cremated individuals were identified from the partial excavation of the site (Coles, and Simpson 1965) (**76**).

The Derbyshire cairns may also fall into the later Neolithic and indeed, subsequent Bronze Age. There are many sites, mostly badly damaged, which consist of central stone settings and cists, covered by earth and stone mounds. Minninglow began life as a long mound some 35m long, which was then remodelled into a more circular structure 45m in diameter and about 2m high incorporating three separate chambers. Others, like Fivewells, incorporate two or more chambers within the mound. Many of the chamber tombs and mounds, such as Pea Low, Gib Hill and Green Low, are probably also of later Neolithic date, though like many tombs were used again by Beaker and Bronze Age people (**77 & 78**).

Scottish long cairns

A northern variant of the long barrow tradition is the Scottish long cairn. At least 28 long cairns from north-east Scotland and 21 from southern Scotland appear to have no evidence of internal stone structures. Few have been excavated, so the construction sequences and dating are still little understood. The Slewcairn, Wigtownshire, Lochill

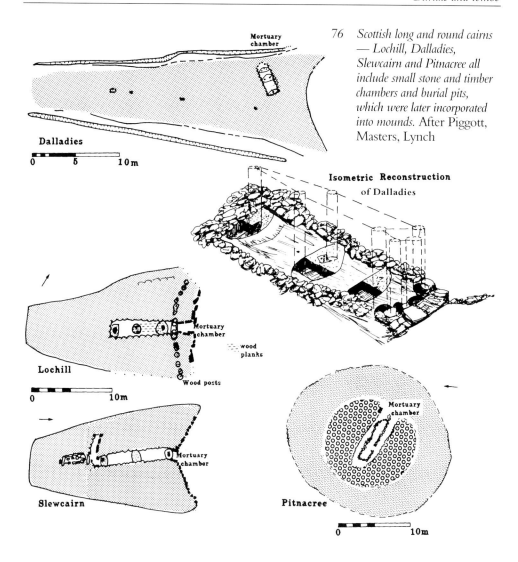

76 Scottish long and round cairns — Lochill, Dalladies, Slewcairn and Pitnacree all include small stone and timber chambers and burial pits, which were later incorporated into mounds. After Piggott, Masters, Lynch

cairn, Kirkudbrightshire (Masters 1973) and Dalladies long cairn near Montrose (Piggott 1973) had later stone cairns and chambers built over earlier narrow rectangular post-built wood burial chambers. The links between timber and stone on these sites offers an interesting link between earlier and later tomb-building traditions and also parallels to earthen mounds in England (**76**).

Slewcairn is a trapezoidal cairn with a V-shaped forecourt formed by its two horns reminiscent of the Yorkshire long barrows. Originally, three wooden post structures were aligned north-south, and were built over by the stone-lined passage that was orientated north-south, and led to an L-shaped chamber. South of the passage and incorporated into the cairn was a rectangular stone structure that formed additional areas for burial.

Lochill seems to be a hybrid between long cairns and Clyde tombs (see below). It began as a structure made of birch bark and oak planks supported on three axial posts, with granite boulders and soil thrown up between them. The north-east entrance area held 16 vertical

77 *Minninglow chambered tomb in Derbyshire, with the capstones of its various chambers visible.* Photo Mick Sharp

posts forming a curving façade, but this was burnt before the stone phase of building began. The stone cairn measured 25 x 14m and was orientated north-east and enveloped the earlier wooden structure. A stone façade replaced the wood version, and a stone passage led to a stone-lined rectangular box of 7.5 x 1.4m. Burial fragments and cremations were found on the floor of the earlier tomb and the date from wood in the deposit was 3120 ± 105 BC (**76**).

The excavated Dalladies long cairn (Fettercairn, Kincardinshire) was located on a gravel terrace (Piggott 1971-2). The final cairn was 65m long and 9-18m wide and orientated east to west. The mound was built from turf and soil, with dry stone revetments and a shallow crescent façade at the west end, and was constructed over three distinct phases. The first phase was a post built structure, with massive timber uprights and an entrance at the north-west end. This layout was respected by the next phase (2), a turf built mound around a stone and timber structure some 9m long and 3m wide which formed a three-sided enclosure 6x2.5m open to the north-west. This had been roofed in timber, birch bark and large flat stone 'tiles' (3240 ± 105bc) and included burials, a flint knife and a cup-marked stone. The final phase (3) saw massive mound construction over the earlier structures, but orientated on a different angle and incorporating four additional Beaker period cists along the spine of the mound axis. An estimate by Piggott of the turf used in the tomb suggested that 7300m square (1.5 acres) of grassland was required for the mound (**76**). A kilometre away, the Capo long barrow is even larger than Dallachies (80m long, 28m wide, 2.5m high) and remains unexcavated. It appears to contain a stone mortuary structure close to its horned entrance, but probably had as complex a sequence of development as Dalladies.

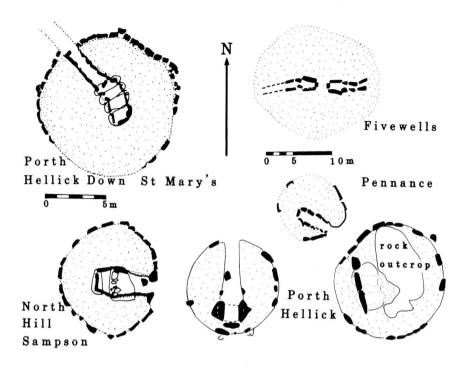

78   Passage graves in the Scilly Isles, Cornwall and Derbyshire were modest constructions, often with kerbs, and crude megalithic passages which formed the burial chambers. After Ashbee, Lynch

Megalithic and stone-built tombs

Across the British Isles, a great variety of stone built tombs were constructed as burial monuments. In the same way that earth barrows were elaborated, the stone monuments, many of them megalithic in scale, were also modified and extended. However, because stone is durable, these structures survive better, and can be more readily sorted into separate categories and types, resulting in a long tradition of research. Yet many tombs were looted and emptied of their contents long ago, and the lack of buried remains often makes accurate dating difficult. Surprisingly few have been fully excavated, although work over the last 50 years has ensured that representative examples are known from each main type. The geographical spread of these tombs is across the rockier north and west of Britain, with relatively few examples in the east, where building stone was in short supply. Some areas are particularly well studied, such as the Orkneys, where an entire landscape of tombs, settlements and other monuments can be appreciated, enabling our ideas about the social role as well as the chronological development of tombs to be set in context. Elsewhere, a subtle mix of different architectural styles, materials and traditions existed side-by-side in Wales and Ireland, or developed into its own particular tradition, as in Derbyshire (see Barnatt & Collis 1996), Cornwall and the Scilly Isles. Where earth barrow and stone tomb traditions mixed, as in the Cotswolds, an interesting combination of both

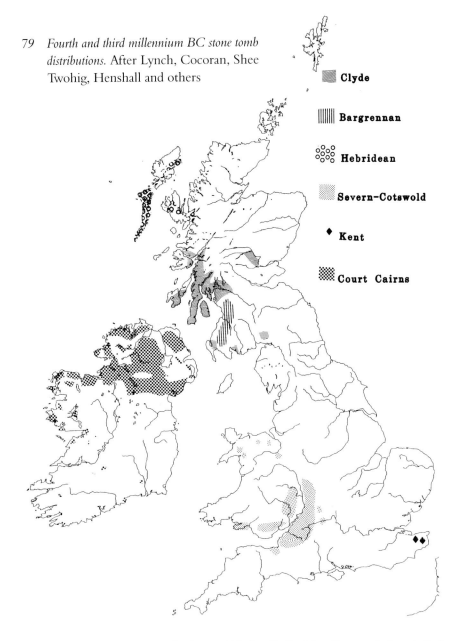

79 *Fourth and third millennium BC stone tomb distributions.* After Lynch, Cocoran, Shee Twohig, Henshall and others

Clyde

Bargrennan

Hebridean

Severn-Cotswold

♦ Kent

Court Cairns

building styles sometimes resulted (as at Wayland's Smithy discussed above). Ireland has been the subject of careful megalithic tomb surveys for 40 years, and this allows a full appreciation of the range and problems of distribution of tombs (de Valera & O'Nuaillain 1961, 1964, 1972, 1982).

In south-east England stone tombs are rare because of the lack of stone, and the stong local tradition for long barrows. Examples exist in Kent distributed along the Medway valley, and at least five stone tombs have been identified, and include Kit's Coty House, Addington, and Coldrum. The tombs are mostly badly eroded, but are characterised by large east-facing chambers. Addington contained the remains of 22 individuals.

Severn Cotswold tombs

In the south and west of England and south Wales, the dominant stone tomb tradition is the Severn Cotswold style, which is characterized by a trapezoidal cairn plan, carefully constructed stone and earth mounds, fine external walling (kerbs) and massively built stone chambers. Three main chamber types are distinguished from the 120-30 tombs of the group, which are centred around the Cotswolds, with outliers around Avebury, Somerset, and in south Wales from Gower to Chepstow. Changing theories about

80 *Belas Knap Severn-Cotswold chambered cairn (Gloucestershire). The aerial view shows the entrance between the hornworks and the side and end entrances.* Photo CUCAP GX0010

the development of the tombs over past decades have suggested a progression from simple to complex. In general, it is supposed that the tombs with chambers set into the long sides (lateral chambers) may be earlier, and transepted chambers (chambers opening from a main passage and entrance) are a little later, along with the decorated pottery found in them. Alternative views show that concurrent styles existed independently (Corcoran 1969). Severn Cotswold tombs appear to date from the early fourth millennium cal. BC (3800-3500 BC). Saville suggests the long duration of use implied at sites such as West Kennet, where later Neolithic activity connected to tomb blocking and ritual use is evident, is not typical of the main tomb tradition (Saville 1990). Although one or two significant examples replaced earlier mounds and cairns, as at Wayland's Smithy and Notgrove, all the chambered tombs seem to have been constructed on a defined trapezoidal ground plan. In number the chamber types are as follows, with a much greater number of sites too damaged to enable categorization:

(a) transepted chambers with antechamber and passage (14 sites);
(b) single terminal chamber (20 sites);
(c) lateral chambers within cairn, entered from the side, with false portal and forecourt (*c.*20 sites in Cotswolds).

West Kennet long barrow, Wiltshire (Piggott 1962) is one of the longest of the group, some 100m long, with the stone chambers at the east end only forming a small part of the total length. The rest of the barrow is a chalk, sarsen and flint mound, apparently containing no other chambers or cists, although no work has been undertaken to explore this

*81   The entrance hornworks at Parc le Breos Severn-Cotswold chambered cairn (Gower, Wales)
are finished in fine stone walling. The larger megaliths in the chamber are just visible.*
Photo Mick Sharp

possibility. The mound material was derived from two deep linear ditches either side of the barrow. The tomb is a typical transepted example, with a large end chamber and two small chambers on either side of the passage. Originally the passage opened to a concave forecourt, which was marked by sarsen kerbs and drystone walling (**82 & 83**). However, at closure, the tomb was symbolically blocked by huge sarsens, which formed a straight barrier across the forecourt. When the tomb was systematically excavated by Stuart Piggott and Richard Atkinson in 1955-6, prior to restoration, the side chambers proved to be still intact, even though excavations by Thurnam in the nineteenth century had thoroughly cleaned the end chamber. The material was important, because it enabled a detailed study of the human remains and their location within the tomb (see above) which could suggest that age and gender may have been a consideration in the placement of the body parts in the these tombs (Thomas & Whittle 1986) (**84**).

Stoney Littleton (Somerset) is more typical of the transepted terminal chamber type of Severn Cotswold tomb which is found in the southern Cotswolds and south Wales. It has a more pronounced trapezoidal plan and the longest passage (over 14m) of any of the group. A curved forecourt opens to the south-east, and the passage then connects the six lateral chambers and end chamber encased within a carefully constructed stone kerb or wall around the entrance hornwork and sides. Other examples include the very simple terminal-chambered tomb of Randwick (Glos), Tinkinswood, St Lythans, and the transepted Parc le Broes Cwm (Glamorgan) and Nympsfield (Glos) which both have marked hornworks and terminal chambers. Park le Broes Cwm was excavated in the last century, but its disarticulated bones have been restudied (Wysocki & Whittle 2000) showing the complex patterns of discard in these tombs. Carbon 14 dates suggest they were in use from 3700-3300 BC (**73 & 81**).

82 *The sarsen stone façade and closure stones at West Kennet (Severn-Cotswold) long barrow, Wiltshire.* Photo C. Malone

83   *The interior of West Kennet shown by Stuart Piggott's classic isometric drawing.* After Piggott

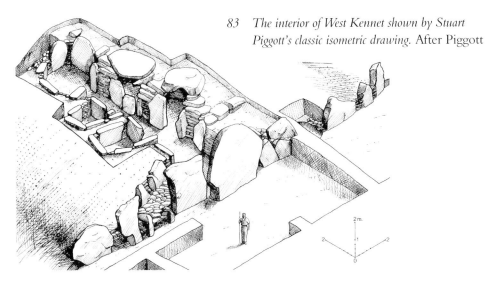

84 *Representation of different ages and sexes in chambers of two Severn-Cotswold tombs.* After Thomas 1988

		Adult			Old	
Adult				NOTGROVE		
Male						
		Young		Young & Female		

		Adult		Old		
Adult				WEST KENNET		
Male						
		Young & Adult		Young		

At Hazelton North (Gloucestershire) (Saville 1990) is a stone cairn of the lateral chamber type. It is 53m long x 8m wide, trapezoidal in shape with lateral L-shaped stone chambers opening to the north and south, and revetted with stone around the whole, with a recessed forecourt at the west end but no façade. Rather than lateral ditches, there were two quarries to the north and south, excavated with red deer antler. The south chamber contained the disarticulated remains of 14 adults and 6-11 pre-adults scattered throughout the tomb. The remains in the north chamber were concentrated in the chamber (four adults and four to six pre-adults) and entrance (adult male with grave-goods, plus the remains of three plus adult males, two children and a pre-adult. (The tomb total was 21 adults, 12-19 pre-adults, plus one adult cremation and one pre-adult cremation.) Apart from the male's grave goods, only a pottery cup, bone beads, stone tools and flints were found. The landscape around suggested small-scale clearance and cultivation. (**69 & 73**)

The Breconshire tombs of the Severn Cotswold group are distinctive through their very variability and eccentricity of form, although they have much in common with Hazelton North. They have the same trapezoidal plan and walled sides, but the forecourts lead to blind entrances, and instead lateral chambers provide the burial places. Several examples include earlier cairns deep within the later trapezoidal cairn, and this may partly explain the rather random nature of the plan in these tombs, as at Luckington (Wiltshire), Ty Isaf and Pipton (Breconshire) and Capel Garmon (Conwy). Although it was argued in the past that these strange tombs must be late, new C14 dates show that in fact they are amongst the earliest of tombs in Britain dating from 3900 BC. In particular, Gwernvale (Breconshire) (Britnell and Savory 1984, Britnell 1979; 1980) was subjected to thorough and modern study. Its three lateral chambers, two opening from the west and one from the east side of the mound, contained human remains, that, as at West Kennet and Ty Isaf, may well have been symbolically placed in special areas of the tomb. Several tombs in Wales and in Gloucestershire are built around earlier cairns, and appear to envelope them in the more structured and formal plan of the typical Severn Cotswold tomb. Notgrove, Gloucestershire (Clifford 1936) is a typical example of this type. It was located on high ground, and consisted of a long mound with an east facing entrance and forecourt, leading via a passage and antechamber to four polygonal transepted chambers. The structure is formed from orthostats and drystone walling and extends about 10m from the entrance. Immediately beyond the stone structures, a primary mound 7m in diameter, edged with a kerb and containing a polygonal stone line cist, formed what the excavator interpreted as a constructional feature. However, like Wayland's Smithy, Pipton and Ty Isaf (Breconshire) there is the strong possibility there are earlier burial structures beneath later mounds. (**14**)

Portal dolmens or tombs

Portal dolmens are a widely spread tomb group, from Ireland, Wales, Scotland and south-west England. They are some of the most impressive tombs, with high megalithic stone uprights supporting huge capstones. They were single chambered with narrow, high entrances or portals and formed a typically H-shaped arrangement of slabs. High façades are rare, but forecourts are known, and the tombs were frequently covered by a rectangular or round cairn.

85   *The portal grave of Lanyon Quoit, Morvah, Cornwall is the dramatic remains of a former burial chamber which formed the core of a mound of earth and stone.* Photo Mick Sharp

Welsh and western portal dolmens (**63**)

In north and west Wales the dominant Neolithic stone tomb type is the single-chambered Portal tomb (up to 50 survive in Wales and the west) and other rectangular shaped structures. These are close relations to the Irish portal tombs (see below) and form the classic simple dolmen or stone box, where a capstone is supported by uprights at the side and back, and forms an open fronted structure. It seems likely that the stone box was the western equivalent of wooden boxes as found at Haddenham and probably under many earth barrows. The structures were encapsulated within a small round or rectangular cairn, which in most cases have now disappeared through erosion, robbery and agricultural activity. Many of these sites were on good farmland, and often faced east and uphill. Impressive examples such as Dyffryn Ardudwy (Merioneth) survive, and show that in many cases a forecourt fronted the tomb. Dyffryn Ardudwy was excavated in 1960-2 and demonstrated at least two phases of construction. The first was the western portal dolmen, which was then blocked from its forecourt; in the second, an eastern chamber was constructed as a simple low chamber. Pentre Ifan (Pembrokeshire) is similarly impressive, and had remnants of a horned cairn and an orthostatic façade. The remains of bones are almost unknown from these sites, and it may be that individual bones were inserted into the structure, but have long since eroded away (**101**).

86   The remains of the burial chamber at Chun Quoit, Morvah in Cornwall. Photo Mick Sharp

Cornwall and the Isles of Scilly

In Cornwall the portal tombs were much smaller and less impressive, and formed rectangular stone boxes with stones at the entrance set forward of the portal. The type is best represented at Trethevy Quoit, which consists of six large upright stones supporting a massive capstone. At the higher south end, two stones once formed the pillars of a forecourt. The whole structure stood on a stone platform, and was closely associated with the Bearah Common tomb. Similar sites include Mulfra Quoit, Chun Quoit, and Lanyon Quoit which all had stone chambers sited on stone mounds and support capstones. Zennor portal tomb (the best preserved) had two massive front stones forming a flat façade and a small square chamber behind formed from two side slabs and a front and back stone, under a massive capstone (**75, 85 & 86**).

Irish portal tombs

The Irish portal tomb tradition is closely related to portal tombs in western Britain (Shee Twohig 1990). Secure dating evidence for both regions is lacking, but pottery and other affinities suggest they developed from the earlier part of the fourth millennium BC, alongside local court tombs, and contemporary with the barrow traditions of eastern Britain (**63, 87, 88**).

Typical portal tombs had a single chamber formed by two tall stones, with side stones set wider at the front than the back, supporting an often disproportionately large capstone. Ireland has several regional styles of portal tomb, incorporating one or two side stones (Poultnabrone, Co Clare), inturned side stones (Crannagh, Co Galway), out-turned portal

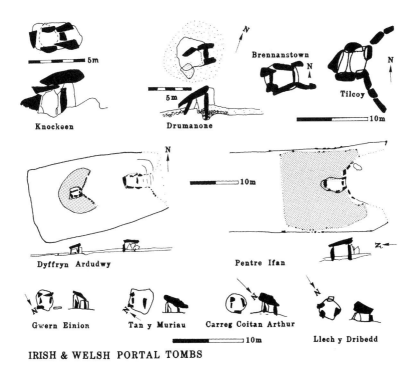

IRISH & WELSH PORTAL TOMBS

87a   Irish and Welsh portal tombs. Portal tombs with their heavy capstone supported on upright megaliths were originally encased within earth/stone cairns, as the remnant mounds at Drumanone, Dyrrfyn Ardudwy and Pentre Ifan show. Most Portal tombs survive as dramatic stones, such as Knockeen. (Knockeen, Waterford; Drumanone, Roscommon; Brennanstown, Dublin; Tilcoy, Antrim; Dyffryn Ardudwy, Merioneth; Pentre Idan, Pembrokeshire; Gwern Einion, Merioneth; Tan y Muriau, Gwynned; Careg Coitan Arthur, Dyfed; Llech y Dribed, Pembrokeshire)

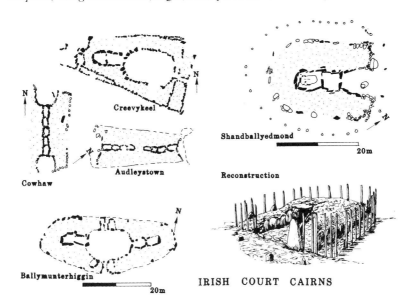

IRISH COURT CAIRNS

87b   Irish court tombs are a distinctive local tradition, with 'courts' located at the end or within the cairn structure, and may have been the arena for funeral rituals. (Creevykeel, Sligo; Cowhaw, Co. Cavan; Audleystown, Co. Down; Shandballyendomon, Co. Tipperary; Ballymunterhiggin, Co. Donegal). Sources — various

88   Portal tomb at Knockeen, Co. Waterford. Photo C. Malone

stones (Gaulstown, Co Waterford), tilted capstones, no sidestones tripod tombs (such as Proleek in Co Louth), elongated chambers made up of several side stones (Haroldstown, Co Carlow), and yet others with subsidiary capstones (such as Knockeen Co Waterford). Portal tombs were almost certainly covered by a mound or cairn, but in most cases this has been eroded or quarried away. Ballykeel in Co Armagh had traces of walling around the burial area, rather similar to Pentre Ifan in south Wales. Some 26 examples still retain traces of a long cairn over the portal tomb, and Ballykeel revealed a dry stone kerb around the edge and other lines of stone within the cairn. Excavation of portal tombs has been limited, since so many have been emptied of their contents in the past. Work at Poultnabrone in Co Clare in 1986 showed that the site had contained at least 16-22 adults and six juveniles, but as disarticulated body parts, not articulated burials. The site produced grave goods including a polished axe, stone beads, a bone pin, pottery, flint arrowheads and scrapers. Comparable deposits from other sites include decorated pottery, polished axes, flint tools and personal ornaments. Eight sites suggest that cremation rather than inhumation was the favoured burial rite, and possibly that several individuals were deposited together. Some 174 tombs are known with a northerly distribution, with a scatter of tombs in the south-east, Clare and Galway. Like the Welsh and Cornish portal tombs, the locations of Irish sites seem to be close to the coast or river valleys, and most are on level land and below 122m asl (**63**) (Cooney 2000).

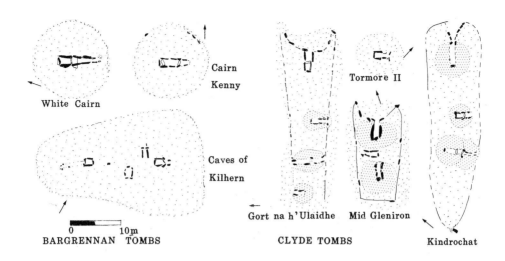

89   *Clyde and Bargrennan tombs form two distinct groups in western Scotland. Bargrennan tombs had roundish cairns and small stone burial chambers; Clyde tombs incorporated small round cairns within impressive long horned cairns with concave façades. (White Cairn, Kirkubrightshire; Cairn Kenny, Caves of Kilhern, Mid Gleniron, Wigtownshire; Gort na h'Ulaidhe, Argyll; Kindrochat, Perthshire).* After Henshall

Clyde Tombs (79)

This distinctive group of about a hundred tombs is distributed around the Clyde estuary in west Scotland from the Hebrides to Kintyre (Henshall 1972). Clyde tombs range greatly in size and complexity, and in some respects are rather similar in shape to Cotswold-Severn tombs. At their simplest they consist of a single stone cist or box, and at their most complex include impressive façades and several stone-built chambers, linked together. Roof slabs sealed the chambers and may have had to be raised to allow entry on each occasion. Stylistically the Clyde tombs are also related to the portal tombs, if on a modest scale. Some tombs developed piecemeal, with separate cist/box graves constructed and later united through the long cairn that covered the structures and the façade, as at Mid Geniron 1. Several examples suggest that the original stone box was lengthened and a portal area of high stones added. Later tombs were located in more marginal land, and incorporated concave forecourts as well as impressive façades such as Carn Ban on Arran, with its semi-circular forecourt, four main chambers and additional cist. The tombs contain, where soil conditions allow, disarticulated bones, cremations and some inhumations. The almost complete incineration of the cremated bones shows they were burnt elsewhere, with the charred remains then stored in the tombs. A local tradition for depositing whole pots in tombs differs from the fragmentary pottery from tombs in other parts of Britain where domestic rubbish and broken material seem to dominate the grave goods (**89**).

To the south-west of the Clyde tombs, the Bargrennan group of tombs, located in Galloway and Ayrshire, consists of only a dozen or so sites. These have circular cairns over rectangular chambers with entrance passages, and reflect a close link between passage graves in the Irish Sea area and the Clyde tombs (**89**).

90   Creevykeel court tomb, Sligo. Photo C. Malone

Irish court tombs

Irish court tombs developed alongside several other related classes of tomb in Britain and western Europe. In particular, the Clyde tombs, Severn Cotswold and Irish portal tombs form parallel developments and share various features. Court cairns or tombs form one of the four main tomb types in Ireland, and some 400 have been recorded, with the highest densities in the north and west (Sligo and Galway), and few in the south, and they share similarities with the Scottish horned cairns. Traditionally they were known as horned cairns because of the distinctive projections either side of the entrance to the tomb which enclosed the court. Normally they consist of a trapezoidal stone cairn between 25 and 35m long, opening onto an internal court. This was an unroofed area perhaps used for special funeral rituals, with access to the burial chambers. The cairns were frequently orientated to the east, and most were located on land below 213m, often close to fertile farmland. The dating of the court tombs ranges from as early as *c.*3900-3400 cal BC to as late as 2900 BC, with cremation deposits forming the earlier burials and inhumations the later ones. The most common form of court tombs had two burial chambers constructed of stone and separated by pairs of stone door jambs and a sill stone. More rarely, three and four chambers are recorded, for example at Creggandevesky in Co Tyrone and several, especially in the west, have cruciform chambers (transepted) as at Carrowkeel in Co Sligo similar to the passage graves. Often the chambers were corbelled with three-four rows of stones, sometimes topped by a large lintel stone. The cairn was often bounded by a kerb or revetment around the outer edge, the inner court and the horn-like projections. The courts ranged from curved semi-circular and open forms to almost closed oval shapes. One or two examples were more angular, almost V-shaped, their horns formed from tall standing stones infilled between with drystone walling. Occasional standing stones were located within the court. With some excavated examples, such as Shandballyedmond (Co Tipperary), post-holes and paving around the entire outer edge of the tomb indicate that there may have been timber structures incorporated.

The full court tomb type is exemplified at Creevykeel (Sligo) which was excavated by Henken in the 1930s as one of the first systematic studies of these tombs. The site was seriously damaged in the past yet is still about 40m long, and consisted of a straight façade of stone with a small opening into a large oval court, which in turn gave access to a passage containing two chambers. Beyond the chambers, additional chambers opened from either side of the cairn, and in the destroyed western end, a second court and chambers had once backed onto the surviving part (Henken 1939).

Numerous variations show the broad interpretation of the court cairn idea such as the double-ended court cairn at Audleystown in Co Down, where two cairns shared a central court, or the side entrance types such as Deerpark (Co Sligo) where there were passages with chambers opening at each end. Court cairns were used principally for cremated remains, and there is evidence for fires within the court areas on paved areas, later sealed by stone slabs. Due to the haphazard collection of bones from cremation pyres and the subsequent weathering of the cremated material, the total number of people buried in court tombs is unknown, although the highest number recorded is 21 from Creggandevsky (Co Tyrone). Grave goods from the court cairns include flint leaf arrowheads, scrapers and knives, beads and pottery.

The survey and excavation work in north Mayo at the Ceide Fields (**14a**) suggests that court tombs were intimately linked with the patchwork of fields and settlements in the local landscape. Fieldwork at Ballyglass in Mayo (adjacent to the Ceide Fields) has demonstrated that two court cairns covered earlier houses which dated from the early fourth millennium BC, and the link between mortuary house and later tomb is repeated in Northern Ireland where the cairn at Ballybreist in Derry covered some sort of mortuary house or pyre, and also dated from the early fourth millennium BC. The lack of C14 dates in some areas, such as Galway, means that an evolution from simple to complex and from small to large cairns is unproven, although likely.

Passage graves

The passage graves are an important tomb group and contain the extraordinary megalithic art that has been seen as characteristic of Neolithic Britain and Ireland. They emerged early (first half of the fourth millennium BC) in the Neolithic in areas bounding the Irish Sea, but continued into the third millennium BC in several areas. In Ireland cemeteries are especially numerous around the Boyne valley and in Sligo, and in Britain isolated tombs are common in the Orkneys, Lancashire and Anglesey (**91**). Various models for passage grave development have been proposed, suggesting that the tradition was introduced from Brittany, that it developed from the court tomb tradition, or that, in the west of Ireland, the tombs were an indigenous Mesolithic development. Studies in Ireland show that passage graves, court tombs and portal tombs cross over in chronology and in distribution, suggesting that the various traditions were cultural, and

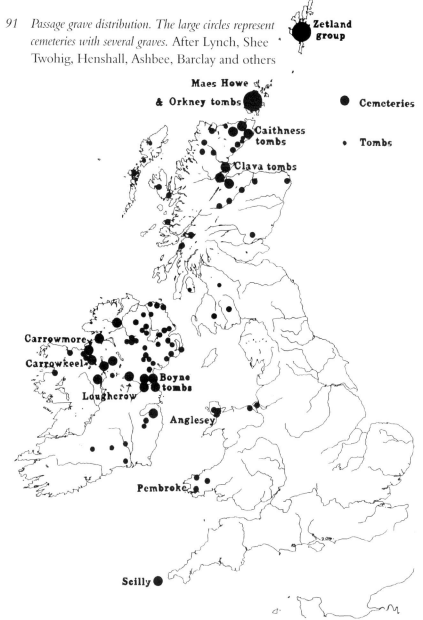

91 *Passage grave distribution. The large circles represent cemeteries with several graves.* After Lynch, Shee Twohig, Henshall, Ashbee, Barclay and others

perhaps as much related to identity, status and wealth as to chronology, local tradition and materials. There are several forms of passage grave, and if grouped loosely, they include the stalled cairns of the Orkadian tradition, and other regional variations. Burials in passage graves were furnished with distinctive grave goods, and human remains were frequently cremated. Sheridan (1985-6) has suggested that the passage graves were made large and prominent as the status of ancestors and ownership became increasingly significant in the mid-later Neolithic, especially after *c.*3200 BC.

92   The walled 'terraces' of Wideford Hill chambered cairn, Orkney command a fine view over the surrounding land. Photo C. Malone

Tombs and cairns on Caithness and Orkney

In Caithness and the Orkney islands the tomb traditions of the Neolithic specialised in stalled cairns and passage graves and their variations. Great numbers of tombs, in comparison to elsewhere in Britain, still survive and continued to be discovered — at a rough count (see Davidson and Henshall 1989) there are some 77 tombs on Orkney:

19 stalled cairns and 9 other possible stalled-tripartite cairns.
6 long cairns
7 Bookan-type chambered cairns
9 Maes Howe cellular chambered tombs-passage graves
19 Stalled chambered tombs and 8 further possible stalled cairns

In Caithness, Davidson & Henshall (1991) have recorded 78 chambered cairns, and others across Northern Scotland. Several scholars have seen a connection between tombs and houses (Hodder 1984; Richards 1988; Ritchie 1995) suggesting that the two different tomb styles related to the two main forms of house design that prevail in the islands. These were cellular or rounded Skara Brae types which may be reflected in the rounded plans of the passage graves, and the Knap of Howar longhouses (3690-3370 cal BC — 3200-2490 cal BC) (Papa Westray type) that closely resemble the plans of the stalled cairns. Radiocarbon dates imply that the stalled cairns, like the Knap of Howar houses, are generally earlier (from *c*.3600-3000 cal BC) than the passage graves (which seem to date from the end of the fourth millennium BC to mid-second millennium BC) and compare with dates from cellular houses such as Skara Brae 1 (3100-3000 cal BC), Skara Brae 2 (2900 BC onwards) and Barnhouse (*c*.3100 BC). There has been much debate about how the different tombs functioned and how they related to the changing society of the Orkneys. Indeed, a disproportionate amount of research has been done on the Orkneys compared with most areas of the British Isles, and thus a rich record of data and ideas is available (see for example: Davidson and Henshall 1989, Renfrew 1985, Ritchie 2001).

93 The chambers at Unstan chambered cairn, Orkney.
Photo C. Malone

Changes in ritual, beliefs about the afterlife and the status of ancestors, seem to be reflected in changes in tomb design. The stalled cairns, with their many internal divisions, provide a combination of individual — perhaps family — units and identities, within the greater communal context of the tomb and the society that used it. Ancestors probably remained identifiable for a long time and were venerated individually. Funerary ritual would have had to be conducted outside the tomb, whereas the internal space within the passage graves might have been designed for small scale and private funerary activities.

Stalled tombs (**93-4**) are a particular development in Orkney and Caithness, and seem to have evolved from simple bipartite, tripartite and Bookan forms (**96**), to long and elaborate tombs such as Midhowe on Rousay, and, indirectly, the cellular passage graves. The stalled tombs consisted of a long passage that provided access to a series of stone compartments. These were formed from vertical stone jambs and slabs, which provided separate burial areas with stone shelves for the corpses. Collective burial ritual seems to have involved the careful arrangement of corpses in a crouched or sitting position on the

94 *Large sandstone slabs were built into the passage structures of Orkney stalled cairns to provide individual burial compartments of stalls. (Blackhammer, Holme of Papa Westray, Calf of Eday, Unstan, Knowe of Ramsay, Midhow, Keifa Hill, Point of Cott, Sandhill Smithy). After Davidson and Henshall*

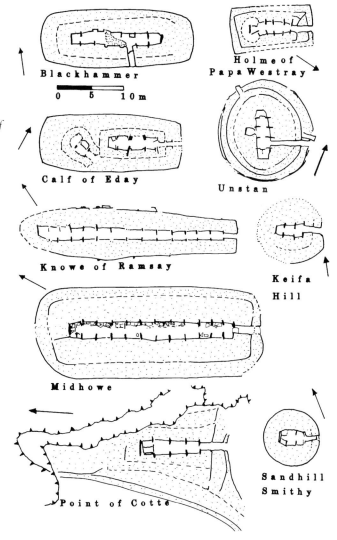

stone shelves. At Midhowe (**95**), there were 12 stone compartments on each side of the central passage plus an end compartment. When excavated, nine skeletons were still crouched or sitting in position on the shelves, but in general, the bones (of 17 other individuals) appear to have been moved about and pushed to the back, as new occupants were inserted into the tomb.

The impressive stalled cairn of Blackhammer on Rousay has a rectangular plan, entered from a side passage, and a single chamber with five pairs of stalls and two end chambers. Only two adult male skeletons were found, as the tomb had been badly damaged, but there was a mass of burnt animal bone (cattle, deer, cormorant and goose) from funeral feasts (**94**).

The Holm of Papa Westray is one of the largest (38 x 19.5m) and most impressive cairns surviving, and its location on a small, virtually uninhabitable island is particularly

95   *The cells divided by sandstone slabs at Midhowe Stalled Cairn on Rousay, Orkney.*
Photo C. Malone

striking. Inside, it conforms to the Maes Howe type of chamber, with 12 distinct cells opening from it. Dates of 3340-2910 cal. BC — 2960-2470 cal. BC show that is was in use over the middle-later Neolithic.

The recently excavated site of Isbister (**97**) on Mainland is an oval stalled cairn with three side and two end chambers, and some of the burial ritual is suggested by the cramming together of body parts in small niches to provide space for new arrivals (Hedges 1984). The final count of buried individuals is some 341 and dates ranging from 3349-2910 cal. BC to 2590-2060 cal. BC suggest long, if intermittent, use. Other sites reveal other rituals, and the burials in the stalled cairn at Knowe of Yarso had been much reorganised with far too many skulls (22 crania and no mandibles) relative to the other skeletal parts, suggesting they may have been assembled from other sites. This evidence could represent a sequence of burial and veneration that progressed from the initial crouched burial of an individual in the tomb compartment, its subsequent disturbance and, finally, movement of bones to other areas in the tomb or even to different tombs, as new occupants filled the space. The veneration of ancestral skulls and bones, in cults that presumably manipulated the power of ancestors, may well have been a widespread practice amongst the Orkadian Neolithic communities, with skulls found in the Knap of Howar houses, and the jumble of disassociated body-parts found throughout many tombs (see Richards 1988).

An important chronological distinction is that the stalled cairns were associated with Unstan ware pottery, which predated the Grooved ware of the later Neolithic, which also characterises the cellular passage graves and the rounded, cellular Skara-Brae type houses.

Alongside the human burials, it appears that animals, fish and birds were also the

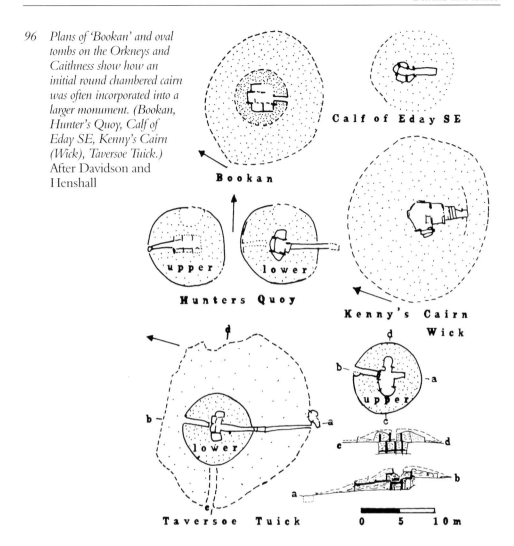

96 Plans of 'Bookan' and oval tombs on the Orkneys and Caithness show how an initial round chambered cairn was often incorporated into a larger monument. (Bookan, Hunter's Quoy, Calf of Eday SE, Kenny's Cairn (Wick), Taversoe Tuick.) After Davidson and Henshall

subject of burial, although some of the remains found in tombs may be the consequences of nesting otters, roosting birds, owl droppings and suchlike. At Isbister, the remains of white-tailed or sea eagles made up 88 per cent of the bird remains in the tomb, and the tomb has been renamed the Tomb of the Eagles (Hedges 1984). Other animal remains in the tomb included seal, 17 taxa of fish and 21 species of bird, together with domestic farm animals. Some tombs appear to contain a disproportionate number of specific animals, for example Yarso and Knowe of Ramsay had red deer, and other tombs suggest an emphasis on pig, fish, and dog deposits. Point of Cott (Westray) contained large quantities of human and animal bone (especially large birds) which have encouraged the excavator to consider natural agents as responsible for their presence (animal nests?) rather than human action. This long horned cairn, located on eroding sea cliffs, was once over 30m long, and has early dates (3620-3350 cal. BC to 2950-2740 cal. BC). There is, however, continuing debate about whether the animal remains were simply accidental material in the tombs or whether they were used symbolically as emblematic of a group's identity –the tribe of the

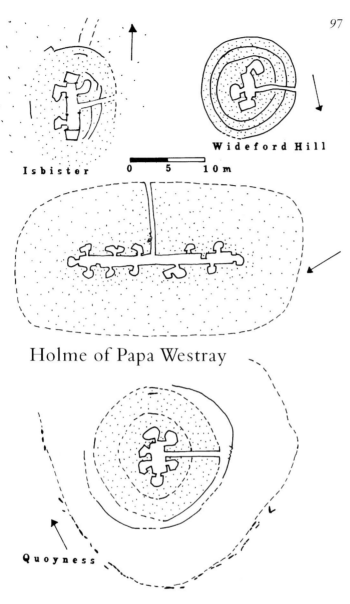

97 *Maes Howe type cairns showing the burial cells opening from passage, and forming both circular and linear arrangements. (Isbister, Wideford Hill, Holme of Papa Westray North, Quoyness.)* After Davidson and Henshall

Sea Eagles, or the Red Deer troop for instance. Certainly, native North Americans identified strongly with animals and animal deities, as is seen so graphically on Totem Poles and carvings from British Columbia. It is tempting to see the bones in Orcadian tombs as a prehistoric parallel.

More modest but related passage graves of the Orkney-Cromarty-Hebridian group are found across Caithness (Davidson & Henshall 1991), Argyll, Sutherland-Rossshire and the Western Isles. Dating evidence is not conclusive, but several large and early sites appear to have been constructed from *c.*3600 BC. The Caithness examples (**98-9, 101**) are particularly fine because of the good building stone — sandstones similar to Orkney. This

98 *Long and horned cairns on the Orkneys and Caithness often incorporated earlier round cairns within the final impressive structure. (Knowe of Lairo, Camster Long, Cambster Round, Tulloch of Asssery, Tulach an T'Sionnaich, South Yarrows, N.) After Davidson and Henshall*

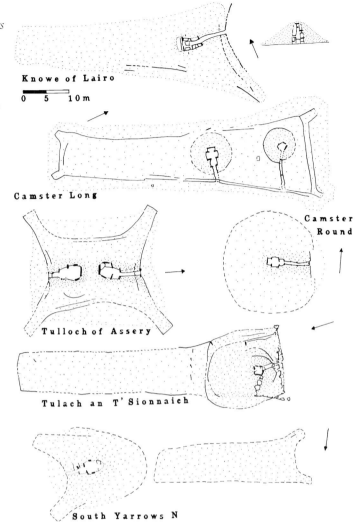

Knowe of Lairo

0   5   10 m

Camster Long

Camster Round

Tulloch of Assery

Tulach an T' Sionnaich

South Yarrows N

enabled refined chambers of bi- and tri-partite form, and there seems to be a development over time from simple to more complex plans, culminating in the stalled versions of Caithness-Orkney type. In some cases the cairns are round, in others they are incorporated into later long cairns such as Camster Long. This massive long cairn 60.5m long, 17m wide and 4.5m high contains two modest round cairns, with passages opening to the sides, that were presumably precursors to the expanded site with its concave ends and impressive hornworks. Similar tombs formed around a primary cairn are known at Ormiegill (Caithness) where the early central cairn and the chambers are enclosed within a four-horned outer cairn. The forecourt between the horns on the south-east side was 15.4m across and some 20m in length. The 62m long Tulach an t'Sionnaich (Caithness) is another example where the primary cairn forms just one end of the long cairn. It contained a small square chamber separated by a stone sill from a short passage opening to the south-facing

99 *The immense long cairn with its hornworks and two separate burial chambers at Camster Long, Caithness.* Photo C. Malone

100 *The stone passage of Camster Round passage grave in Caithness. The massive stone jambs support the roof slabs.* Photo Mick Sharp

façade (**98**). The South Yarrows (north and south = 73m long) tombs are of similar scale, but had stalled cairns opening to the east-facing curved façade. Balvraid (Inverness), Torboll and Embo (Sutherland), with their short, covered passages and two-period cairn structures may be the precursors of the grander Orkney stalled tombs. In the Shetlands,

*101   The roofless but regularly shaped chambers of the short-horned Cairn O'Get, Ulbster,
Caithness.* Photo C. Malone

tombs were more modest in scale, reflecting the less competitive social and economic
world of the remote north. Heel-shaped cairns around a concave entrance façade and a
three-chamber trefoil plan seem to have been the principal tomb type, and probably date
from the end of the fourth and earlier third millennia BC. Craw Knowe measured between
7-8m long, with massive stones forming the outer walls/kerb and a small oval burial
chamber about 3m across. A smaller heel-shaped version at Mangaster has a concave façade
only 5m long, providing the entrance to a short passage and oval chamber (1.5 x 2m). An
impressive heel-shaped tomb on the island of Vementry contains a primary circular cairn
and its cruciform chamber, which was then encased in the later 10m-long cairn. The
façade's two projections link to natural rock outcrops. Other tombs are square in plan, such
as the 10 x 10m square March cairn, which is edged in large stones. A short passage opens
directly to a modest cruciform chamber 2.4m in length (**102-3**).

Architecturally, the most important passage grave on the Orkneys is Maes Howe on
Mainland. This vast tomb is enclosed by a ditch (*c*.85-95m in diameter and up to 2m deep),
and protected by a mound 35m in diameter and 7.3m high. A long stone-lined passage (6.8m)
connects the inner cruciform tripartite chambers to the entrance. The fine local sandstone
was used to great effect in the almost ashlar finish of the walls, and the fine corbelling of the
high roof. Three burial chambers open from the main central chamber, forming clearly
defined boxes with additional small chambers for burial. Sacked in ancient times, no human
remains have been found (due to centuries of looting and use by Vikings and others), but it
is assumed that cremated remains were placed in the individual chambers (**104-6**).

The passage grave of Quanterness was excavated in recent times (Renfrew 1979) and thus
provides an indication of the population buried in the tomb, and the ritual activity that
prevailed. The main chamber had three primary cist burials in the floor. Above this were layers

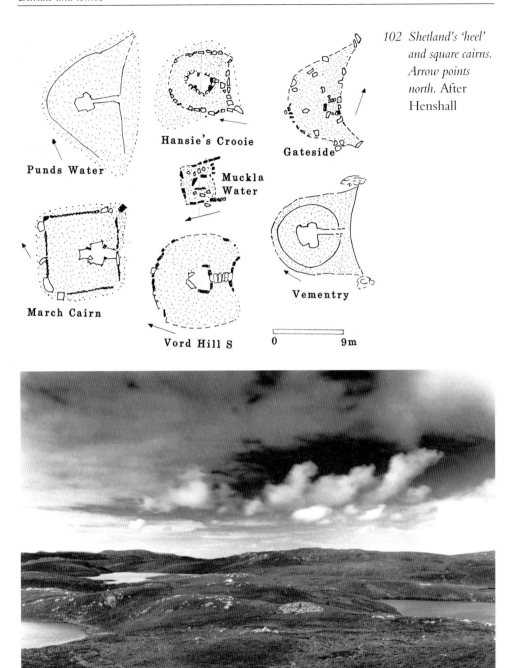

102 Shetland's 'heel' and square cairns. Arrow points north. After Henshall

Punds Water

Hansie's Crooie

Gateside

Muckla Water

March Cairn

Vementry

Vord Hill S

0   9m

103 The Neolithic heel cairn of Punds Water, Shetland. Photo Mick Sharp

104 *The great passage grave of Maes Howe on Orkney not only has a large mound, but is surrounded by a deep rock-cut ditch.*
Photo CUCAP
— GR0038

105 *Plans of the Orcadian passage graves of Maes Howe and Quanterness.*
After Davidson and Henshall

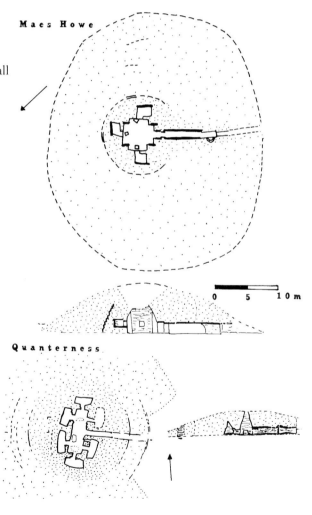

Maes Howe

0   5   10 m

Quanterness

151

of disarticulated bone, with at least 150 individuals recorded, and later a crouched burial was placed in a pit dug through the bony layers. In total, although the tomb was not completely excavated, a hypothetical population of 394 individuals was proposed, showing that the passage graves were places for huge numbers of communal burials, rather than of a few individuals as suggested by the disturbed evidence from Maes Howe. The change in burial practice evident from the stalled cairns to the passage graves has been interpreted as one where the individual identities became irrelevant. Instead, the massed jumble of body parts in the passage graves focused on the collective and non-hierarchial identity of the larger group. Some archaeologists see this as a reversal of the true state of affairs, where is seems likely that status and power increasingly separated members of the community from each other. However, in death, they were reincorporated under a single ancestral and communal identity. (**78**)

106 Maes Howe — interior of the passage grave, showing the precise stonework

Clava Cairns (107-9)

In north-west Scotland, clustered around northern Inverness-shire on the Moray Firth at the head of the Great Glen, another distinctive group of passage graves surrounded by 'kerbs' and stone circles is known as the Clava Cairns. Most of the tombs (Henshall counted 37 in 1963) are located on the gravels close to good farmland, and unlike other chambered cairns in more upland locations, they favour the flood plain. Two types form the group — simple passage graves, and ring cairns without an obvious passage but an open central area.

Passage graves, such as Balnuaran of Clava and Corrimony, had circular cairns some 3m high formed of large river cobbles and stone and quartz fragments. They were bounded by kerbs 10-17m in diameter, with the entrance facing between south and west. An entrance passage up to 1m wide and roofed by slabs led to the central chamber. This is always circular-oval, between 3 and 4m in diameter and constructed of large stones forming, in some cases, a corbelled vault up to perhaps 2.5m high, and occasionally completed with a huge roof slab as at Corrimony with its cupmarks. Circles of often tall (up to 3m) standing stones were set up between 2-6m from the cairns to complete the monuments, carefully graduated in height from entrance to rear. At Corrimony, an area

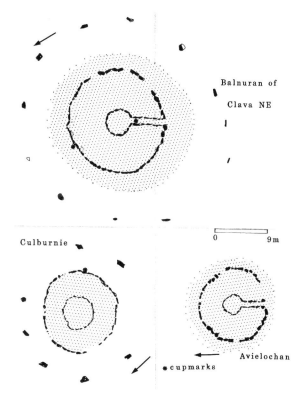

107 *Clava Cairn plans (Balnuran of Clava NE, Culbirnie and Avielochan).* After Henshall

Balnuran of Clava NE

Culburnie

Avielochan

0   9m

＊cupmarks

108 *The cemetery of Balnuaran of Clava, Inverness has three cairns aligned to the south-west and the midwinter sunset. This photo shows the circle of standing stones located around the south cairn, which in turn has a marked kerb and slight mound.* Photo C. Malone

109   Cemetery of Balnuaran of Clava, Inverness: the cup and ring stone on the outer kerb of the northern cairn (left); the interior burial chamber. Photos C. Malone

between the stones was cobbled, rather as at Knowth, and suggests that some structure and activity was similarly associated with funerary rites (see chapter 7). Ring Cairns seem to be closely associated with the Clava passage graves, and form a separate facet of the same cultural tradition present at 13 sites. They have larger diameters enclosing central chambers from 4.5-10.5m in diameter. Very large stones were involved in the construction and similar expertise employed, and the cairns also had similar kerbs; at Grenish granite blocks up to 1.3m high were used. The chamber at the centre was also similar to the passage graves, but it is unclear whether they were roofed either by corbelling or slabs, since the size was so large, and no post-holes to support a roof have been found. The cairns similarly had a surrounding circle of standing stones; at Culburnie there were nine stones, and other sites had ten to twelve, often with a tall slab located on the south-west side, for example at Gask, of 3.5m height. The orientation of the tombs is consistently towards the south-west, which is the opposite of most passage graves elsewhere. Burial ritual is difficult to assess, but inhumation was practiced at Corrimony, and scraps of charcoal at several sites suggest cremation. Bone pins are known, and are typical of passage grave ritual elsewhere.

Passage graves in Wales (91)

There are two groups of passage grave in Wales: a scattered group of seven small tombs in west Wales, and the impressive later Neolithic monuments of Anglesey. The western examples seem to be similar to ones found in Brittany, western Ireland and Scotland, and dates suggests that they come early in the Neolithic sequence (although they continue longest in the western isles of Scotland). The Welsh graves are not typical passage graves, and include characteristics of other tomb forms, such as portal stones, horned forecourts and suchlike, indicating a good mixing of ideas and styles. The west Wales tomb chambers are polygonal, and connected to the outside by short passages. Carreg Samson (Pembrokeshire) and a similar site at Broadsands (Devon) both contain early Neolithic pottery, which places the use of the tombs in the earlier fourth millennium BC. Other examples include Hanging Stone, Burton (Pembrokeshire), a small, almost round chamber made up of four standing stones and one fallen, and a passage, and Bodowyn (Anglesey) which is similarly round, but with most of the passage now removed. Other possible early passage-type tombs (Trefignath and Din Dryfol) on Anglesey have similarities to Clyde tombs. Trefignath had an early, small passage grave with high portal stones leading into an east facing passage and chamber. The tomb was then enlarged and incorporated with two further box chambers and passages, the middle one forming a horned east facing chamber, and the west box and chamber facing laterally to the side of the tomb to the north. Din Dryfol had a second chamber formed by a wooden portal; if broader comparisons are made with Scottish and other examples, it seems clear that these early passage graves had the potential to be adapted and modified over time with very different styles of tomb architecture.

The larger and later true passage graves of Wales (and probably too some now lost examples in Lancashire — for example the decorated slab from Calderstones) are important sites containing some of the megalithic art of the British Isles, and closely related to the sites of the Boyne Valley in Ireland (**110-11**). The sites are Bryn Celli Ddu and Barclodiad y Gawres, both of which appear to date from the later Neolithic in the early third millennium BC. Bryn Celli Ddu is an impressive mound, which incorporates a henge, a long passage and a small round cairn. Lynch (1991) argues that although the association of destroyed henge and passage grave is secure, it does suggest a revival of earlier traditions through the slighting of the later Neolithic henge. (**25**)

Barclodiad y Gawres (Powell & Daniel 1956) has much in common with Irish passage graves; its chamber is cruciform and decorated in an almost identical fashion to the Boyne sites (see below). It has a large round cairn, a long passage leading to the corbelled central chamber and three side chambers. These contained cremated bone, and the remains of cremation fires were found in the central area. Five stones are decorated in lightly pecked abstract patterns, less well defined than the Boyne examples.

Irish passage graves

The passage graves of Ireland are amongst the most spectacular of Neolithic tombs in Europe, and since they occur in sizeable cemeteries, together with the finest art of the western Neolithic, they deserve detailed discussion. At their simplest, Irish passage graves are stone chambers linked to the outside world by a stone built passage. However, the examples of Knowth, Dowth, Newgrange, Fourknocks, and Loughcrew are on a massive scale and of remarkable architectural complexity and subtlety. Of the recorded *c*.230 tombs, the major concentration of passage graves is in the north and east of Ireland, bordering the Irish Sea. Many were sited on hilltops, the most spectacular of these being Queen Maeve's tomb above Carrowmore in Sligo, and Fourknocks I in Meath, although the bulk were actually sited below 100m asl. Generally the tombs occur in cemeteries that can number from just a few to the 50-60 of Carrowmore, or the 25 of Carrowkeel (**110,**

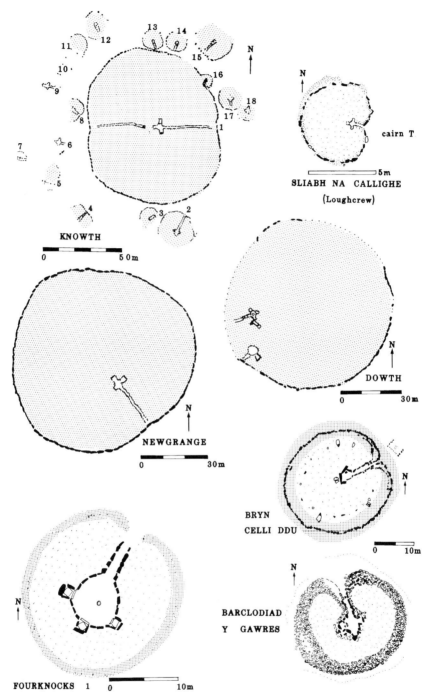

110 Passage graves in Ireland and Wales form a distinctive class of monument, incorporating large mounds edged with stone kerbs, and stone-lined passages with cruciform or circular burial chambers. (Newgrange, Knowth, Dowth and Fourknocks, Sliobh na Callighe-Loughcrew, Co Meath; Bryn Celli Ddu and Barclodiad y Gawres, Anglesey.) After Eogan, Lynch, and others

111   The Bryn Celli Ddu passage grave on Anglesey has a marked ditch and a stone kerb, and close by an enclosure has also been located. Photo Mick Sharp

112-13). In an area of 16km² around the Boyne there are at least 40 tombs (20 sites at Knowth, 5 at Newgrange, Dowth, and some 17 other cairns), 25 at Loughcrew (**23**) and, usually, one tomb dominates the group. Irish passage graves have been quite extensively excavated over the last century, and much new data has come to light, enabling broader interpretation of the British tombs. Newgrange was extensively explored by O'Kelly from 1962, Knowth by Eogan from the same time until the present, Carrowmore since the 1980s by Burenhuilt (Burenhuilt 1980, 1984, 1995) and Berg (Berg 1995), and Fourknocks by Harnett in the 1950s (Hartnett 1957) (**113-18**). This work has provided a long and secure C14 chronology, and information on construction methods, phases, materials and art, and on the cremation burial rites and grave goods. Related research has provided understanding of the broader Neolithic context, landscape change and economy.

Carrowmore cemetery and tombs

Cremation was the main rite, and cremated material has been found on several sites around the chambers or just outside the tomb. Inhumation was also practiced and sometimes both burnt and unburnt bone is found sealed beneath paving, as at Fourknocks I, with additional remains in a crematorium at a neighbouring site, Fourknocks II. The numbers of individuals buried in the tombs range from just one in each of the chambers of Knowth, to 65-plus at Fourknocks, and 100-plus at Tara. Grave goods include Carrowkeel ware, a distinctive decorated funerary pottery found in at least 20 passage graves, and various personal ornaments, such as bone and stone beads and pendants. Stone balls and bone or antler pins are particular features, often with carved decoration. The most impressive objects found include the wonderful spiral-decorated flint mace from Knowth, maces and a carved phallus (**175**).

The earliest passage graves in Ireland date from soon after 4000 BC, if the dates from post-hole fills beneath Carrowkeel are to be trusted. The majority of dates from the larger

*112a The cemetery of
Carrowmore
(Sligo) kerbed
cairns, with the
prominent cairn of
Queen Maeve on
the horizon.
Photo C.
Malone*

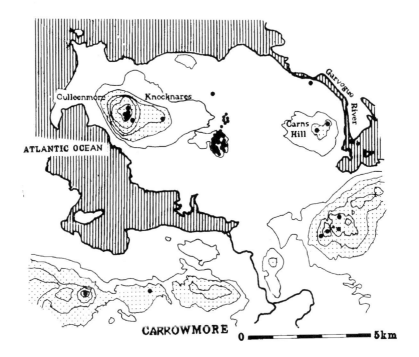

*112b Plan of the cemetery of Carrowmore, Sligo. The circles denote passage graves.
After Berg*

tombs, such as Knowth, place the building phase in the later fourth millennium and into
the third millennium BC. Dated contexts for Carrowkeel ware are found in tombs as late
as the early third millennium BC, and at present the chronology suggests that the western
and smaller passage tombs were early — in the early-mid-fourth millennium — and that
the vast Boyne valley tombs represent the florescence in the late fourth-early third
millennia BC. The tombs seem to have remained in use for up to half a millennium.

113 The passage grave of Newgrange as restored with white quartz walls and a new 'visitor' entrance. Photo C. Malone

Knowth Newgrange Dowth and the Boyne cemetery

The Boyne valley offered Neolithic farmers, as it does the dairy farmers of modern times, a rich and particularly productive landscape, ideally suited to cattle raising, and the wealth that a stock economy could provide. The climate is amongst the driest and most sheltered in Ireland, and must have always offered the best economic returns. The landscape is comparatively gentle, with rolling terraces, a variety of local soils and rocks and good communications. The wealth is reflected in the extraordinary density of vast tombs — over 40 in a small 16km² area. (Eogan 1984, 1986; Eogan & Roch 1997)

Knowth has been extensively excavated and is currently under restoration as a public site. It is the most complex of the passage graves with a huge central mound 80-95m in diameter and 9.9m high, covering an area of 0.6ha. and surrounded by satellite cairns (at least 18 survive) which are mostly miniature passage graves, with their passages facing towards the great mound at the centre. The whole complex was built over an earlier settlement site. The central mound has two passages entered from opposite sides, with a cruciform chamber and 40m plus long passage opening to the east and a simple linear chamber and passage to the west. The alignment of the passages appears to have been quite deliberate: the rising sun penetrates the 40m long eastern passage and chamber on the equinoxes of 21 March and 21 September, and the setting sun enters the 34m long western chamber on the same days. Some of the satellite tombs clearly predated the building of the great mound, and cairn number 16 was partly incorporated into the final structure (**112**).

There is much that is highly symbolic at Knowth (see chapter 7), revealed by the excavations. Different stones were used in specific areas of the tombs and their surroudings — some brought in from considerable distances. The alignment of features from the tombs to the landscape beyond which included standing stones, henges, and other monuments may also have had significance, and so too did the placement of particular artistic motifs.

Knowth has the greatest number of decorated surfaces of any of the Irish passage tombs, over 200 having been recorded, and these are located around the kerb of the main mound, and several of the smaller cairns and within the passages and chambers. The most significant decorated slabs are located in the passages and the burial chambers of the main mound, and careful analysis by Eogan has shown how different art styles are clustered and

114   *The passage grave at Newgrange in the Boyne valley, Co. Meath, under excavation in 1963, with its encircling standing stones. A cursus is visible as a crop mark to the right of the mound.* Photo CUCAP — ALK65

115   *Satellite tombs, Knowth surrounding the main mound.* Photo C. Malone

associated (**177**). Some slabs were decorated with hammered pick marks and others are scratched and gouged. The art divides into several types of patterns — curvilinear, geometric, circles, spirals, lozenges, zig-zags and others. The most significant slabs are located around the burial chamber, at specific points in the passage and where light penetrates and illuminates the passage. The same appears to be true of Newgrange, and, no doubt, Dowth (Eogan 1986).

Newgrange is located at the centre of the Boyne complex. It has been restored according to the ideas of its excavator, O'Kelly, and now presents a rather startling white appearance with quartz set into its façade. However, as the more recent excavations at

116   Passage grave at Slibah na Callighe/Lough crew showing the kerb and entrance. Photo C. Malone

Knowth suggest, the surrounding area may have been paved with quartz, rather than having walls faced with the material. The entrance has also been restored to enable public access and is not as it would have been in prehistory. The setting of the site was at the centre of a stone circle that surrounded the mound. The circle was 103m in diameter, and enclosed about a hectare. The mound (78-85m diameter and 13-19.9m high) is defined by a stone kerb of 97 stones, many of which are decorated. The passage ran for 18.9m and was lined by 22 orthostats on the west side and 21 on the east. A curious stone roof box, 1m wide by 90cm high, rests on the passage orthostats and the covering roof slabs. The chamber at the centre of the mound is cruciform, with three side chambers, the largest and most highly decorated being the east chamber, with two granite stone basins set into its base, and single basins in the other two chambers. Burnt and unburnt human remains were scattered around the chambers and amounted to several individuals. Numerous animal bones were also associated, including a dog (O'Kelly 1982) (**110, 113-14**).

Fourknocks forms a small cemetery of tombs, three of which survive, all commanding splendid views from a ridge about 155m above sea level. Fourknocks 1 is a classic passage grave, with the largest known central chamber, 6-7m in diameter and covering an area of 41.92m2. Conversely its passage is a mere 5.67m long. The chamber is a large oval formed by slabs with three small square chambers set in a cruciform pattern, each containing a mass of bone and cremation material. The latter were sealed by stone slabs. Additional piles of cremated bone were placed around the orthostats in the passage, and at lease 65 individuals were buried there (**110**).

Loughcrew (or Liabh na Callighe) lies inland of the Boyne valley, high on the interfluve between the Boyne and the Shannon rivers that drain central Ireland between east and west (see Herity 1974). The core of the cemetery, some 28 tombs, is spread over three prominent ridges at a height of more than 214m, and covers an area of 3.5 x 1-2km, with outliers such as Cairn M on King's Mountain 4km distant. The tombs follow a pattern of kerbed circular stone mounds, each containing a passage and chamber, some stalled, some cruciform in style. The passages were covered by lintel stones, the chambers were corbelled, and the tombs often incorporated decorated stones — at least 120 have been found, engraved with a particular Loughcrew style which include curvilinear, sun and curious daisy-flower patterns. The cemetery is densest on the west, as in the Boyne cemetery. Two tombs (cairns D and L) are

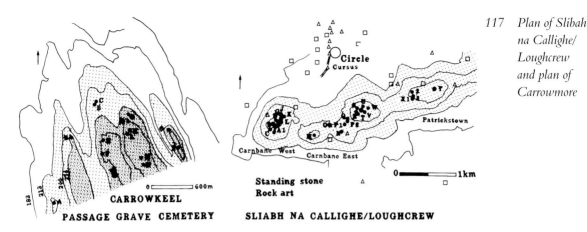

117 *Plan of Slibah na Callighe/ Loughcrew and plan of Carrowmore*

considered to be focal points, intervisible with sites across the hilltops, and associated with a mass of standing stones, a cursus, a circle and rock art, suggesting the whole landscape was cosmologically, symbolically and formally organised (**116-17, 176**).

Carrowmore (Co Sligo) consists of an extensive cemetery of some 50-60 passage graves spread over the plateau and hillside below the prominent peak of Knocknarea. The area has been extensively studied in recent years by Burenhuilt and Berg (see above), providing a detailed survey and dating programme of the sites. Many of the tombs are orientated to the east and are intervisible with other tombs. The typical forms are boulder-built kerbed cairns, with a similar boulder construction forming the interior chamber (**112**).

Carrowkeel is a similarly prominent hilltop, with 14 passage graves spread over its highest peaks and northern slopes with the tombs oriented to the north-north-west. Controversy over the dating of Carrowkeel is centred on the problem of exceptionally early (early fourth millennium BC) dates obtained by Burenhult, which do not tally with the Carrowkeel pottery dates from context such as Ballynagilly that suggest dates in the early third millennium BC (**112b**).

Wedge tombs

Cornwall and the Isles of Scilly

The South-west is typified by small wedge-shaped entrance graves beneath small round cairns. Some 70 sites are known, mostly on the Isles of Scilly (Ashbee 1974), and also in south-east Ireland. The antiquity of the burial tradition is poorly known, and it seems likely that the stone tomb/barrow tradition continued long after the Neolithic, with reuse and even construction in the Bronze Age

The Isles of Scilly specialised in small round cairns (they ranged from 3.5 to 25m diameter) revetted in stone around the perimeter, and containing simple passage graves with chambers constructed of boulders and slabs in various shapes and sizes. Some were constructed around natural rock outcrops, such as Porth Nellick, and others incorporated the wedge-shaped chamber in a kerbed mound, as at North Hill and Samson (**78**).

*118   The cemetery of passage graves of
       Slibah na Callighe/Loughcrew as
       seen from the air, with the more
       recent ridges of cultivation
       surrounding the tombs.*
       Photo CUCAP ANH44

Irish wedge graves *(119)*

The most numerous Irish stone tombs are the wedge tombs, of which 470 are known; the greatest density is the in the west of Ireland from Cork to Clare, with a good number also in Sligo-Mayo and across northern Ireland. They relate broadly to the later Neolithic tradition of larger and more rectangular *allées couverts*, known from Brittany. The favoured locations were prominent, and relatively high (up to 274m), suggesting the tombs reflected the later Neolithic expansion into upland areas. The Irish tombs are normally orientated east-west, with an entrance at the broader west end of the distinctly wedge- or V-shaped structure, and formed around a rectangular stone gallery, which opens from a small antechamber. Large stone slabs and jambs were used to separate the gallery and antechamber and often the side walls were constructed of parallel lines of slabs (such as Labacallee in Co Cork) which were buttressed by smaller stones and the covering cairn (as at Baurnadomeeny in Co Tipperary). The entrance may be marked by a stone façade of standing stones. The burial chamber or gallery was roofed by slabs or lintels placed on the side wall orthostats. Quite often a D-shaped or oval-round cairn was incorporated covering the stone gallery – completely, in the case of the round cairn at Baurnadomeeny, or with a façade of standing stones, in the case of several D-shaped cairns (Boviel, Co Derry). The general pattern seems to be that the round cairns were more southerly in distribution and the D-shaped ones more northerly. Relatively few wedge tombs have been excavated, so dating and details of use or construction are thin. The main funeral rite appears to have been cremation although most excavated sites also include inhumations — up to 12 at Lough Gur. Grave goods included pottery, of which there is material from the first half of the third millennium BC through to Beaker pottery and contemporary barbed and tanged arrowheads. It is unclear whether this was later material inserted or whether the wedge tomb tradition had a very long life into the Bronze Age. This latter is quite likely, given the association of tombs with other later prehistoric monuments and

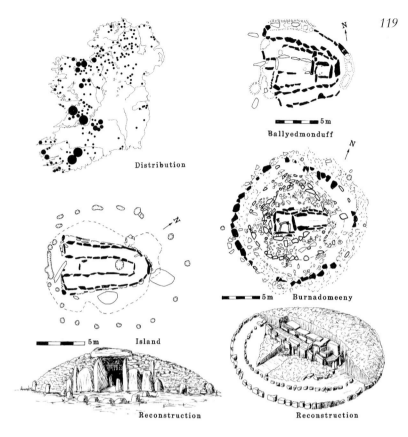

119 Irish wedge tombs were a late development in Neolithic Ireland, and continued in use well into the Bronze Age. They formed long burial chambers encased within round cairns, often encircled with stones and upright posts, as the reconstruction drawings suggest (Ballyedmonduff, Dublin; Island, Co. Cork; Burnadomeeny, Co. Tipperary). After Shee Twohig, Wadell, Eogan and others

Distribution

Ballyedmonduff

Burnadomeeny

Island

Reconstruction

Reconstruction

landscapes in western Ireland, such as Ballintemple and Ballyhoneen in Co Kerry. Although not generally associated with art, several slabs in wedge tombs were occasionally marked with cup marks or incisions (Balleyedmonduff, Co Dublin; Loughash, Co Derry) although these may be later additions to the tombs.

In conclusion, the British Isles and Ireland contain as rich a mix of Neolithic burial rites and tombs as any area of Europe. Over time, the customs changed with the emphasis moving from collective to individual burial rites, and from few grave goods to an impressive array of prestigious artefacts and food offerings. As the discussion has emphasised, the combined variation of landscape topography and geology with different social customs and beliefs promoted the development of the many tomb types that have been recorded. However, even the survival of tombs in many areas is a rarity, so the picture that is presented is wildly regional, and biased towards substantial stone structures. For the bulk of the population, corpses were disposed of without ceremony. Some may have been left on wooden mortuary platforms to rot and be scavenged by birds and beasts, leaving little behind.

Burials and the tombs that house them appear to be such a well known area of Neolithic archaeology, but in truth few sites have been systematically studied, and many types of tomb still await detailed research and examination.

6 Monumental landscapes of mid-later Neolithic Britain

Monument changes of the later Neolithic

The landscapes of the Later Neolithic are usually described as 'ceremonial' or 'ritual' because of the presence of large and apparently non-domestic monuments. Many of these contained inexplicable structures such as lines of posts or stones and huge ditches, in complex arrangements that may have respected both the local landscape and solar/lunar alignments. By 3000 BC the typical causewayed enclosures monuments of the earlier Neolithic and their associated long barrows, cairns and cursuses had been all but abandoned. New types of enclosures were developing, which formed the focal points of more densely settled communities and larger populations in the Later Neolithic. The question of why these changes took place is much debated. Climatic change may be inferred from tree-ring studies (Baillie, pers. comm.) and these suggest episodes of poor climatic conditions around 3200 BC, and again a few centuries later, perhaps triggered by a major volcanic eruption with related deterioration of climate. At the same time, changes in pottery style, burial tradition and more intensive and denser occupation of the landscape seem broadly to tally with these episodes. It is quite possible that environmental changes, population increases and their concomitant social and economic stress were linked, and produced the profound changes archaeology identifies in the later Neolithic.

Firstly, the long barrows and other burial monuments began to go out of use during the final years of the fourth millennium and the early centuries of the third millennium BC, and although some later burials were inserted, they tended to be individual corpses, accompanied by grave goods. New burial monuments included many regional styles and traditions, such as the large round barrows of Yorkshire, cairns and recumbent circles in Scotland, and various cairns, barrows and mortuary houses across much of Britain.

Secondly, the causewayed enclosures were abandoned. Their function was replaced by new, more regular ditched enclosures — the henges, and where these were not part of the local repertoire, especially in the north and west of Britain, circles and enclosures of standing stones or timber posts and pits were adopted as an alternative means of creating defined spaces.

Thirdly, the landscapes around the new monuments were increasingly man-made, and enhanced by ceremonial routes and avenues of stone, earth or posts, which further helped to define the monumental nature of the sites.

Fouthly (but still ill defined), the landscape itself had changed over the early centuries of the Neolithic. Overuse had led to the abandonment of some farmland, the growth of

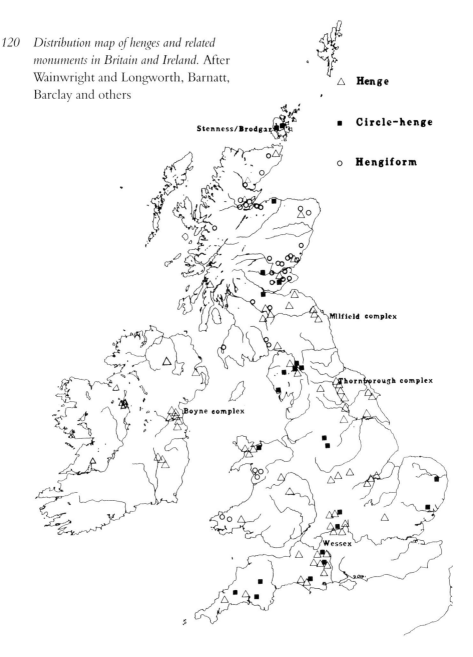

120   *Distribution map of henges and related monuments in Britain and Ireland.* After Wainwright and Longworth, Barnatt, Barclay and others

scrub and heath, and the relocation of settlements. Above all, the once heavily wooded landscape had been progressively cleared of much of the pristine forest that had covered immense areas of Britain, and instead it consisted of relatively open grassland, fields and scrub (**31-33, 37**). Communities could see each other across the landscape, monuments were designed to be visible, one to another, and formerly private and rather secret landscapes had become open and public.

By the end of the second millennium BC, these varied enclosures and structures had reached their peak of development. Monuments such as Stonehenge, Callanish on Lewis, Long Meg and her Daughters in Cumbria, Arminghall timber circle in Norfolk and the Giant's Ring complex of Ballynahatty in Northern Ireland are examples. Many sites suggest an increasing preoccupation with orientation and astronomical concerns, and tombs and circles observed alignments and local topography, further emphasised by alignments of posts, pits and standing stones. Alongside the changes in monument building, houses changed from rectangular to round-oval, pottery and stone developed new styles and forms and elaborate decoration (Grooved ware, Mortlake, Beakers, barbed and tanged arrowheads, flint axes, knives), there were the first tentative uses of metal, and, perhaps most importantly, the use of distinctive art on objects and rocks, marking a distinctively different Late Neolithic world.

Collectively, these varied indicators imply changes in society and its use of the landscape. The numbers of sites suggest an ever more densely settled environment, where structures symbolised territory, ethnic identity, religious beliefs, political and economic power. Change also involved the emerging identities of individuals, with weapons and tombs devoted to them.

Landscapes

The identification and mapping of Neolithic landscapes, often buried and ploughed, relies heavily on relatively new methods of survey and the data are thus very incomplete. Aerial photography has done more than any other method in locating new and unsuspected henge sites and the related monumental constructions around them. Since the 1920s, when Squadron Leader Insall first discovered Woodhenge and other Wessex sites, the number known and investigated has steadily grown, and archaeological understanding has been greatly refined. Some 300-plus henges and enclosures (including timber and pit circles) have been identified.

Henges, timber circles and enclosures

Henges typify the monumental and ceremonial focus of the later Neolithic in many parts of Britain, mostly in the south and east and rarely in the north and west. They have a number of characteristics, which include not only the outer ditched enclosures, but also, setting of posts, pits and stones inside and outside the enclosures. (**120 & 124**)

Henge enclosures
Graham Clark, following his work at Arminghall in Norfolk in 1936, defined a henge as a circular area within which stone or wooden uprights stood, surrounded by a ditch and (normally) an outer bank. Following this definition, Stuart Piggott further refined it with a study of Wessex sites, where he recognised several categories of henge, based on the number of entrances: class I had a single entrance, class II had two or more. Over the years more classification has been applied, so that now Aubrey Burl

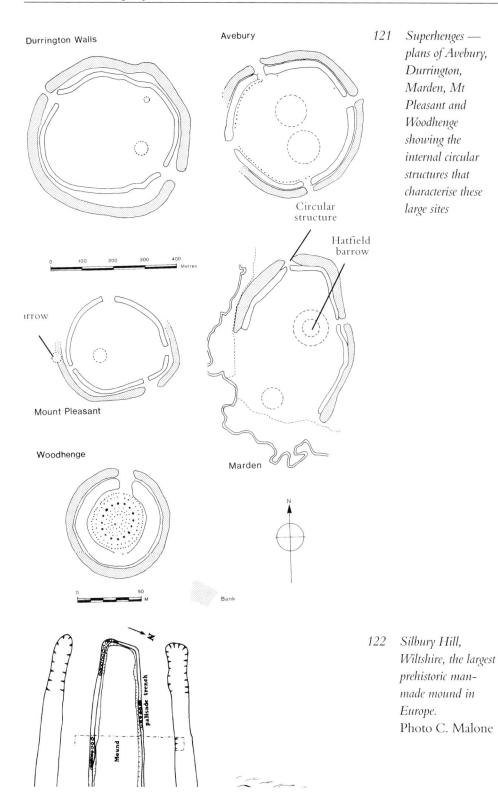

Durrington Walls

Avebury

Circular
structure

Hatfield
barrow

ırrow

Mount Pleasant

Marden

Woodhenge

Bank

N

Mound

palisade trench

*121 Superhenges —
plans of Avebury,
Durrington,
Marden, Mt
Pleasant and
Woodhenge
showing the
internal circular
structures that
characterise these
large sites*

*122 Silbury Hill,
Wiltshire, the largest
prehistoric man-
made mound in
Europe.*
Photo C. Malone

(1991,13) defines henges as shown in the table below, still using class I or II for numbers of entrances:

Table of henge class definitions

Class	Feature	Distribution
I	Single internal ditch, 1 entrance	Widespread in Britain
II	Single internal ditch, 2+ entrances	Widespread in Britain
IA	Two ditches, 1 entrance	Eastern England
IIA	Two ditches, 2+ entrances	Eastern England
IB	Single external ditch, 1 entrance	Very rare
IIB	Single external ditch, 2+ entrances	Very rare
IC	No ditch, 1 entrance	Western Britain, Ireland
IIC	No ditch ,2+ entrances	Western Britain, Ireland

The social landscape of henges

The chronology of henges extends over a long period, from before 3000 cal. BC, to the final Neolithic around 2000 BC. Some sites were periodically refurbished and reinvented, and Stonehenge is probably the best studied and most enduring of these sites, with its elaborations continuing until the middle Bronze Age *c*.1600 BC (see below).

Landscapes with henges usually contained earlier ceremonial sites as well as contemporary monuments that formed the familiar ritual landscapes of the later Neolithic. In several instances (Dorchester, Avebury (Malone 1989), Stonehenge (Richards 1990, 1991), Marden, Dorchester-on-Thames, Yorkshire Wolds. Orkney) there is a clear succession of causewayed enclosure/long barrow/cursus to sites of henge/alignments-avenue /enclosure type. However, other westerly and northerly areas, such as the Mendips of Somerset or Northumbria have henges and circles, but as yet few causewayed enclosures, suggesting that the more thinly populated areas may have felt less pressure to build monuments in the earlier Neolithic. The succession, however, from enclosure to henge or timber circle is not always followed, as shown at North Mains in Perthshire. This site began as a pit containing animal bones, later enclosed by a ring ditch enclosure and then was later covered by a timber circle. Similar pit deposits were found at Balfarg riding school, which later also became formalised as a henge (Ashmore 1996). In the Orkneys, the development of ceremonial sites begins before 3000 BC, and the henge enclosures are amongst the earliest to be constructed, forming a precursor of the ceremonial enclosures of the later Neolithic elsewhere (**152**).

Across the north of Britain, Neolithic enclosures could be buried under riverine silts and peat deposits, or hidden by intensive agriculture or forestry, awaiting discovery through future aerial photography and fieldwork. As the northern examples described above show, the use of wood in many monuments means that their discovery may depend on excavation rather the traditional methods of prospection — fieldwalking, aerial photography and superficial survey.

The topographic location chosen for henges was commonly less spectacular than the earlier enclosures, which were often set in prominent places visible within a forested world from afar. Instead, henges were inserted into an already 'busy' landscape of earlier constructions, settlement and monuments, and located in relatively low lying, inconspicuous places, often associated with streams and water courses (as at Marden,

123 The Priddy Circles (four in all, of which three are visible in the picture) are curious henge structures on the Mendip hills of Somerset. The area was mined for lead during the Roman-Medieval periods creating a chaotic pock-marked surface. Photo CUCAP BFI31

Walaud's Bank, Bedfordshire and Durrington Walls) (Richards 1996). The greatest density of henges lies in the east of Britain, on or near good agricultural land, and frequently in areas where there had already been a long (millennium or more) period of monument building and ceremonial landscaping. Ceremonial complexes with henges occur in eastern Scotland, Orkney, the Milfield basin of Northumbria, north Wales, for example Llandegai (see Houlder 1968), the Thornborough area of North Yorkshire between the rivers Swale and Ure, the Thames basin, the Wessex chalklands, the Mendips, Cumbria (Topping 1992) and the Peak District. Increasingly, new sites are being recognised through fieldwork and aerial photography on the gravel terraces of eastern England. Henges occur in the Boyne valley of eastern Ireland and in Ulster. Henges as defined here do not occur in the rest of western Europe, but along with other monuments (stone circles etc.) they developed from the broader tradition of enclosure to become a phenomenon of the British Isles, a native tradition with sophisticated architecture and calendrical functions.

Most henges have an encircling ditch, and the larger the henge, the less circular and regular it tends to be. Doubtless, there were problems in laying out perfect circles over large areas with simple string and peg techniques, as well as squeezing the sites into the long-occupied local domestic/ritual landscape. The positioning of entrances through the bank and ditch and their relationship to the interior setting of structures (wood, stone or pits) was probably motivated by interest in the cardinal and astronomic points. Several sites have been shown to have orientations towards seasonal solstice points, directed to the rising or setting sun or moon. Stonehenge is of course the most quoted example, and undoubtedly

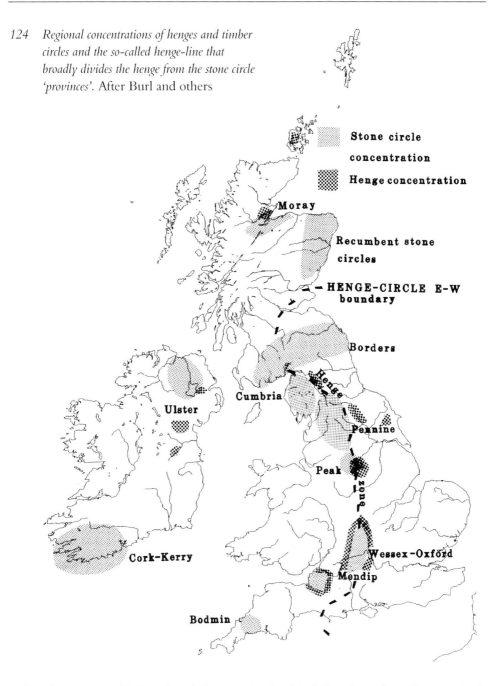

124   *Regional concentrations of henges and timber
      circles and the so-called henge-line that
      broadly divides the henge from the stone circle
      'provinces'. After Burl and others*

it has the most sophisticated and developed calendrical function of any henge. Much research and even more speculation has been directed at sites, especially stone circles, in attempts to discover meaning and pattern in the seemingly random placement of standing stones, posts, pits and their alignments (see below).

Some sites are of enormous size — sometimes called 'superhenges' — and they average more than 300m in diameter (see Wainwright 1989). They include the following:

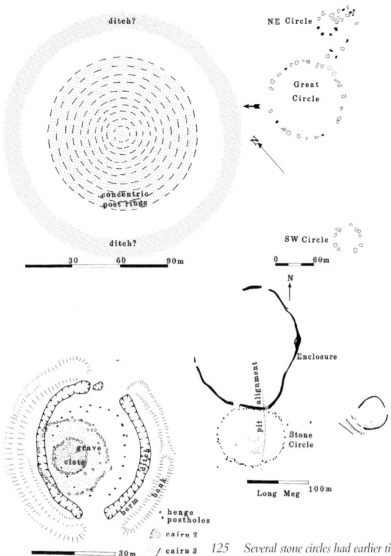

Cairnpapple Hill

125 Several stone circles had earlier timber circles and enclosures. Stanton Drew in Somerset had up to 10 concentric rings of posts prior to its stone circles; Cairnpapple Hill in Scotland was a henge followed by a cist grave, and Long Meg and her daughters in Cumbria included an enclosure and Pit alignment before the stone circle was built [after English Heritage, Grinsell, Historic Scotland & Claire

Site	Class	diameter size	area	ditch depth	width
Marden	IIA	530m	14 ha	9.5m	16-18m
Durrington Walls	IIA	525m	12 ha	6m	16m
Mount Pleasant	IIA	370m	4.6ha	?	17m
Avebury	IIA	347.4m	11.5 ha	7-10m	23.4m

126 *The stone circles of*
     Stanton Drew,
     Somerset, showing
     the three principle
     circles. Photo
     CUCAP AFH48

These immense henges (**121**) dominate their local landscapes, and seem to have been designed as the focal points amongst other impressive sites and landscapes. Their vast ditches and high banks set them apart from more typical henges, and clearly they had special functions. The fact that they are all clustered on the Wessex chalk may be significant — perhaps there were local groups, even chieftains, that promoted a highly competitive local environment, where massive communal sites were part of the local social hierarchy. Certainly, the construction of these henges absorbed immense amounts of time, effort and materials, and outstripped most other enterprises. In competitive tribal societies, and more particularly under chiefs, labour was demanded from members of the clans for collective enterprises and projects (Sahlins 1968), in return for which the worker could access a wide range of social and economic benefits.

Excavations at the superhenges suggest that each enclosure may have contained several structures (wood buildings, alignments, standing stones, pits), and had a multiplicity of functions and activities (see below). The presence of Grooved ware pottery, special flint tools, such as ripple flaked and hollow-based arrowheads, burials, dumps of animals carcasses, antler and other potentially meaningful objects, implies a symbolic importance to the activities and the placement of offerings in ditches and pits. In many cases the offerings were placed at ditch terminals or pits, and emphasised oppositions, such as inside and outside, or male and female, with an intentional patterning of material.

Close to several superhenges are enormous barrows or other constructions, the most impressive being Silbury Hill (**122**) at Avebury. This immense artificial hill had several

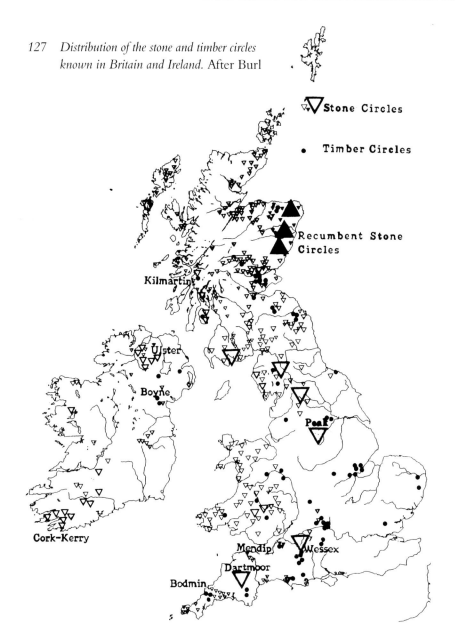

127 Distribution of the stone and timber circles known in Britain and Ireland. After Burl

episodes of construction, from a 5m diameter primary mound at the centre of a 20m diameter area fenced by wood posts. The mound was covered in layers of clay, flint and gravel, turf and soil until it was about 34-36m in diameter and some 5.5m high. The next stage of construction enveloped the original mound in a massive chalk rubble mound covering some 73m diameter, with a deep ditch surrounding the site across a diameter of about 116m and providing the rubble for construction. This mound was then covered again, in a third phase of building, which involved the excavation of a yet larger surrounding ditch. The final stepped mound was some 37m high, over 150m in diameter, and finished off to a regular profile with soil/turf infilling the steps. It is the largest man-made mound in western Europe, and apparently contains no burial or central deposit. The mound at Marden and the barrow at Mount Pleasant may actually contain remains, but the function of Silbury is unclear. The same is true of the so-called Marlborough Mound, some 8km from Silbury. This smaller artificial hill seems to be a similar structure, and prehistoric antler and flint have been found in it. More or less contemporary with the building of Silbury in the first centuries of the third millennium BC, huge tombs were built in several areas of Britain, areas which all have henges close by. The great passage graves of the Boyne valley, Maes Howe on Orkney, Bryn Celli Ddu on Anglesey or great barrows like Duggleby Howe in east Yorkshire within its 10.5ha. incomplete ditched enclosure (Kinnes *et al.* 1983) seem to follow a similar pattern. Other examples of henge-like enclosure, monumental complexes and mortuary mounds in close association are known at Arbor Low (Derbysire) (**142, 143**), Hastings Hill (Sunderland), and the Milfield Basin of Northumbria (Miket 1976, Harding 1981), with its henges, monumental sites and two possible mortuary enclosures. Some Cumbrian enclosures are associated with stone circles, such as the ditched enclosure beside the stone circle of Long Meg and her daughters, or the remaining stone (of a foursome) within Mayburgh henge at Penrith (**125, 139**).

The diameter of henges varies from 200m to under 20m, as at Wormy Hillock in Somerset. Much research over recent years has attempted to further classify henges, and there are numerous articles which argue about whether particular classes of site fit the various definitions (Clare 1986; 1987; Wainwright 1989), but for simplicity, the number of entrances and the interior/exterior ditch and bank are useful criteria.

Site	Class	Diameter
Knowlton north	II	227m
Giant's Ring	?IC/IIC	180m
Dowth Q	IIC	175-165m
Priddy 4	IB	170m incomplete
Priddy 1	IB	158m
Priddy 2	IB	158m
Priddy 3	IB	149-158m
Stanton Drew	?	130-140m
Stonehenge	1B	110m
Brodgar	II	103.7m
Coupland, Milfield	?	95m
Thornborough sites	IIA	92-97m
Mayburgh	IC	90-87m
Stripple Stones	I	69m
Lonstone Rath	IIB	60m
Arthur's Round table	II	44-51m
Stenness	I	44m
Condicote	IA	1.6ha
Gorsey Bigbury	I	40-45m
Wormy Hillock	I	17m

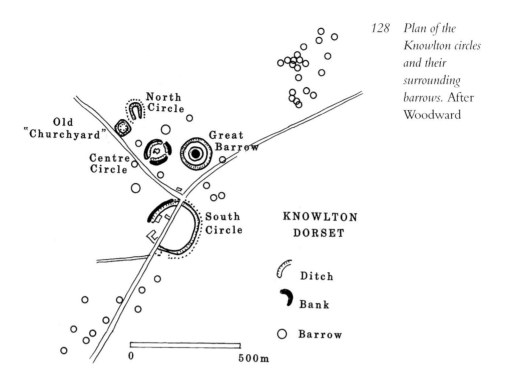

128 Plan of the Knowlton circles and their surrounding barrows. After Woodward

Timber circles and circular houses in henges

Excavation and remote sensing (especially through aerial photography) have identified large circular structures within henge enclosures, and studies began in the 1930s (see Piggott 1940). Often they consist of concentric rings of posts, sometimes with outer ditches, stone settings, pits and entrances. There has been much speculation about how such buildings might have been constructed, whether they were roofed or not, what they represented and how they functioned. It seems clear that these timber circles were not domestic buildings, and the presence of Grooved ware pottery and a lack of domestic waste or hearths further strengthen this view. Domestic houses of the later Neolithic (chapter 3) were usually circular-sub-circular, and at the modest end of a trend of sophisticated construction methods that enabled the building of larger ceremonial houses or timber circles. Several sites have revealed evidence for circular, post-built structures, especially Wessex henges. Recent studies by Alex Gibson (1998) demonstrate that timber circles or circular buildings are numerous across Britain (about 100 known structures, but not all are of Neolithic date). Many were linked to pit alignments and seem to have been part of complex linear arrangements.

Excavation has shown that several of the 900-plus stone circles of the British Isles had a timber phase before later stone construction. Early timber circles have been identified under the later stone circles of Stonehenge, the Sanctuary at Avebury, Stanton Drew (Somerset), Cairnpapple Hill in West Lothian, Croft Moraig in Perthshire and Machrie Moor on Arran. However, since only about 20 per cent of stone circles in Britain have been archaeologically excavated, many more timber settings may have preceded later stone

*129   Three of the
        Knowlton henges
        are visible in this
        photograph taken
        looking west. The
        right-hand
        earthwork contains
        a medieval church;
        a similar sized
        henge is visible as a
        ploughed-out soil
        mark close by, and
        behind these a huge
        henge ditch encloses
        the farm buildings
        and straddles the
        road.* Photo
        CUCAP AGT5

settings. More commonly, timber circles seem to be associated with henge monuments, where they were an important part of the ritual space and the activities conducted in them. Henges were common in eastern-southern Britain (Thames, Wessex, Mendips, Yorkshire), and less commonly in northern England, Northern Ireland and Scotland. Stone circles are more frequent in the north and west, where stone was plentiful, and where the megalithic architectural tradition was already well developed from the earlier Neolithic. The development of the henge enclosure, and its transformation from timber circle to stone circle at Stonehenge, Avebury, Stanton Drew and probably several other sites, is intriguing. Stonehenge, described below, appears to be the culmination of ritual and architectural traditions that mark the final moments of the Neolithic world in Britain. (**131-134, 150**)

The concentric wood circles recently discovered at Stanton Drew resulted from a programme of remote sensing in 1997 by English Heritage. This work identified not only an unsuspected enclosure ditch about 130-140m in diameter, but also a virtual forest of posts set in nine or more concentric rings, the largest about 90m diameter, the smallest 15m, around a central setting. Several stone circles were erected later around Stanton Drew, but systematic excavation of any part is still awaited (**125, 126**).

Woodhenge near Stonehenge was the first wood structure to be recognised in the 1920s by Maud Cunnington, at the same time as Col. Hawley's work at Stonehenge identified the wood structures at the centre of the Sarsen circle. Cunnington then excavated at the Avebury Sanctuary (Cunnington 1931). Since then, systematic work at several sites, including Stonehenge, has revealed a complex succession of several timber buildings at many henges (Cleal *et al.* 1995, 115-65) (**30, 132**).

a

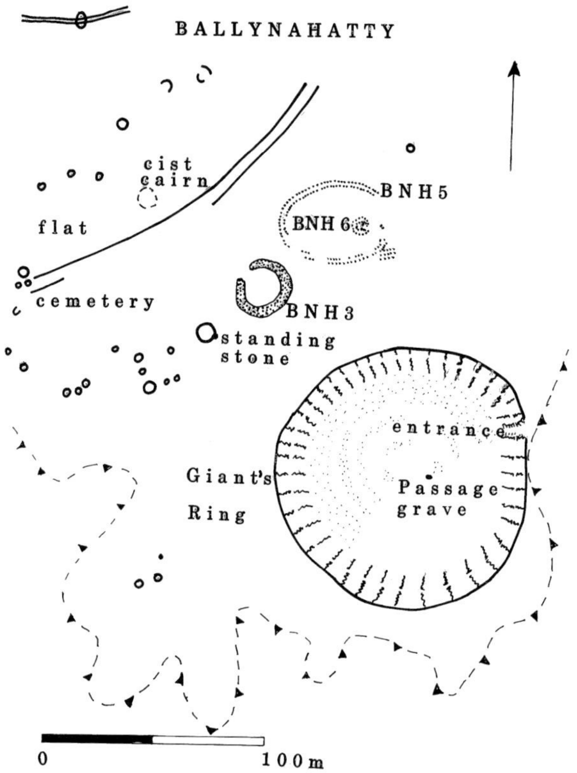

BALLYNAHATTY

130a (right) Plan of the timber circles, the Giant's Ring henge standing stones and barrows/cists at Ballynahatty, Co. Down

130b (below) Detail of Ballynahatty 5 amd 6, the great palisaded timber circles. After Hartwell

cist cairn

flat

BNH 5

BNH 6

cemetery

BNH 3

standing stone

entrance

Giant's Ring

Passage grave

0   100m

b

N

Ballynahatty

BNH 5

BNH 6

Eastern setting

annex

line of sight

Western setting

cist

0   5   10m

o   post

•   post/secondary fill

•   cropmark

x   cremation

p   pit

178

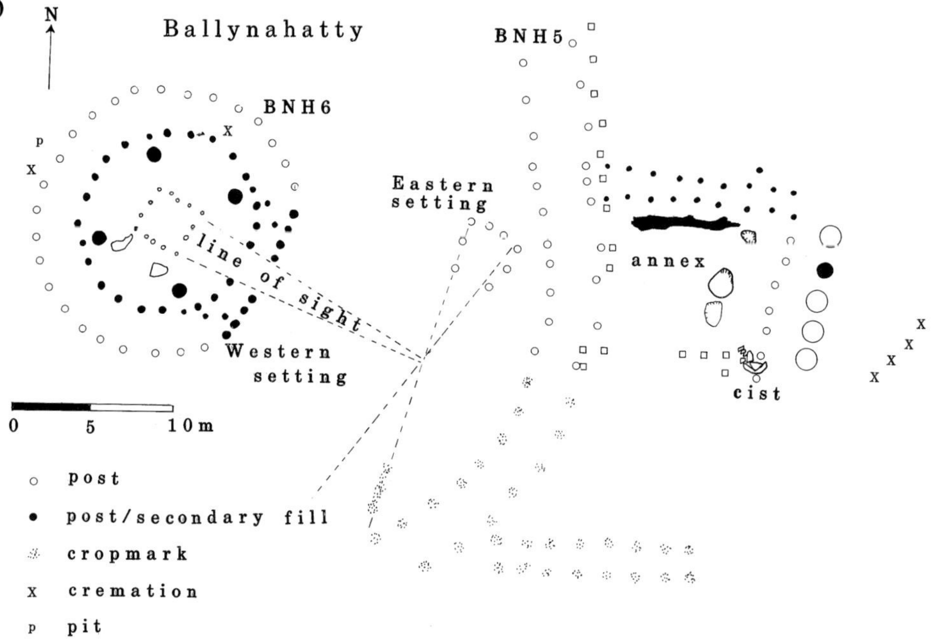

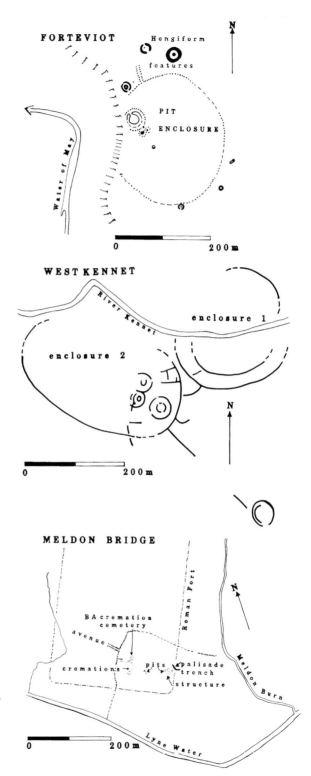

130c Ditched enclosures, avenues and palisades at Forteviot (Scotland), West Kennet (Wiltshire) and Meldon Bridge (Borders), revealed by crop marks, survey and excavation, show how complex these later Neolithic monuments had become

Woodhenge consisted of six concentric ovals marked by holes for timber posts within a ditched enclosure with one entrance. It had a maximum diameter of 43.9m marked by 60 posts. The innermost circle measured 11.7m with only 12 posts. At the centre was a child burial, the site axis was orientated to sun and moon, and its deposits of material appear to be symbolically placed (Pollard 1995). Grooved ware, Beaker pottery and flintwork all suggest high status and symbolic importance. Attempts to design a reconstruction have projected various structures with an apex roof, an open centre, and circles of posts, but its form is still unclear. Carbon 14 dates of 2410-2370 BC place the structure firmly in the later Neolithic (**121**).

Immediately to the north of Woodhenge, the great henge of Durrington was excavated in the 1960s in advance of a new road that cut across the site. Excavations exposed two similar circular buildings both constructed over two phases, which were probably just a part of a complex of other structures within and around the huge henge. The north circle first had a single ring of posts, replaced in its second phase by two rings of post-holes supporting a building only 14m in diameter. Reconstruction has suggested the massive post-holes at the centre supported a 'lantern' above the main roof. The structure dated from the mid-later third millennium BC, and was associated with Grooved ware pottery, antler picks, bone and flint. It was connected to a grand avenue of posts, but was then screened from sight by additional posts in the second phase. This latter phase was dated to 2560-2520 BC. The southern circle was larger, and located just inside the southern entrance to the henge – indeed, it would have dominated and blocked a person's view of the interior as they entered. In its early phase (2850-2800 BC) the circle had four concentric rings of post-holes measuring from 30m to 2.25m diameter. The later phase (from *c*.2580-2200 BC) suggests the building/structure is mid-third millennium (2469-2331 BC). The second phase was larger and replaced the first structure with six concentric rings of posts, measuring a 39m maximum diameter. A large entrance on the south-east side was initially screened, and later enlarged. The building had a central hearth, another hearth outside the entrance and a midden on the north-east side, which suggests that feasting was one of the activities enjoyed within (**30**).

Other henges have revealed similar buildings. Marden had a small circular structure of 21 posts, 10.3m in diameter which, like the Durrington south circle, was located just in front of the (northern) entrance to the henge, dominating the view on entry. Within the huge henge of 14ha there had formerly been a vast barrow — the Hatfield barrow, excavated and destroyed by 1818, and another smaller barrow or enclosure *c*.60m south of it, which has also been flattened (**121, 30**).

Some miles to the north, the Avebury complex includes the potential for several timber buildings, both within the henge underlying the later stone circles (crop marks show prominently in recent aerial photos), and at the Sanctuary on Overton Hill. The Sanctuary was recorded by William Stukeley in the early eighteenth century, as it was destroyed by local builders for its stone. There is now debate over whether it was built in one stage or three (as suggested by Piggott). It consists of six concentric rings of posts. Outermost is a stone ring of 39.6m diameter, then come timber rings of 20.2m, 14.5m, 10.5m, 6.5m and 4.2m diameter; an outer ditch has also recently been identified, which suggests that the site is actually hengiform (Pollard 1992; Pitts 2000). The entrance posts of the north-east of the circle were particularly massive and linked the circle to the West Kennet Avenue and thence to Avebury. The structure was clearly some type of building and similar to Woodhenge and Durrington.

Mount Pleasant contained a timber structure similar to Woodhenge, surrounded by its own ring ditch within the larger henge (Wainwright 1979). Known as Site IV it formed a 38m diameter structure of 52 posts, with four additional smaller concentric rings within, and a square setting of stone and posts at the centre. Recent research suggests that there were aisles set cardinally, marked by blocking stones, and the main aisle led to the entrance at the north side. On the bank of the henge a large round barrow, the Conquer barrow, was 2.7m high and 30m in diameter As at the other main henges with timber structures, Mount Pleasant is associated with Grooved ware and C14 dates range from 2360-2340 BC. The youngest date is associated with the stone setting at the centre (**30**).

Knowlton in Dorset consisted of three henges, one surviving as a substantial earthwork, the others now ploughed flat. Like Marden and Mount Pleasant, the presence of a very large burial mound, the Great Barrow, only 180m from the southern henge, suggests a similar funerary interest in the monument (**128, 129**).

Other circular structures/buildings are known from Wales (Caebetin Hill in Powys, Pont-ar-daf in Breconshire, Sarn-y-bryn-caled in Powys, and the 30-pit 20m diameter circle of Withybushes in Pembrokeshire). In the Walton Basin, Radnorshire (Gibson 1999**)** a timber palisade enclosure, rather similar in style to Meldon Bridge, was nearly 100m in diameter with one boundary formed by the river channel. The enclosure at Hindwell Farm (Radnor Valley) (**61**) was formed by an arc of posts over a diameter of about 400m, with about three posts every 5m. It enclosed an area of 34ha. with what was probably a bank of over 3.3km in length. The Walton basin sites also include standing stones around the complex. Similar circular post-structures are known from Ireland (at Newgrange, Co. Meath, and Ballynahatty, Co. Down) (Hartwell 1998), Scotland and northern England. The site of North Mains in Tayside, Perthshire (Barclay 1983) comprised two timber circles, one within the other, located inside a small henge with two entrances. The larger, with substantial posts, measured 27m with 24 posts, and the smaller measured 22.5m with 18 posts. Early dates of *c*.2930-2460 cal. BC dated the Neolithic activity, and later (early Bronze Age) Food Vessel burials were inserted into the site. Milfield (Northumbria) (Harding 1981) has very similar characteristics with a henge ditch closely surrounding the 36.25m diameter timber structure within. Milfield North formed a single line of timber uprights with some internal pits, and beneath the surrounding henge bank, a ring of additional post settings had once enclosed the site (Speak & Burgess 1999). In southern Scotland one of the most impressive enclosure sites is Meldon Bridge, Peebleshire (**130**). It formed a triangular-shaped enclosure of 8ha defined by a stockade of 3-4m high posts set along two sides, and the river Lyne along the third. The enclosure had a grand entrance avenue of posts 4m wide and 25m long, which may have aligned to the midsummer sunset. The site was constructed *c*.3300 BC and is the type-site for this little-known area. Ceremonial and ritual functions are suggested by the presence of pits containing caches of pottery and charred hazelnuts. The use of wood rather than earth banks and ditches to define the space is significant, and may be one good reason why the location of northern sites has been so elusive. The site is unique, but a close parallel has been found at unexcavated Forteviot in Perthshire (Harding & Lee 1987) where a similar palisaded enclosure and henge avenue of posts have been identified (**130**). Aerial photographs show a circle of pits *c*.40m in diameter located within. Further south, similar

131 Stonehenge from the air — before the era of fences and tourist pathways. The Avenue extends from the henge ditch to the bottom right-hand corner of the picture. Photo CUCAP CS081

structures include Arminghall, (Norfolk) (Clark 1936) where a horseshoe shaped ditch surrounded a curved setting of posts, some 13m in diameter. It had Beaker pottery in the ditch and an earlier C14 date of *c*.3340-2650 BC from its primary phases of use.

The theme of mortuary, excarnation and funerary cults dominates these timber circle sites and perhaps, too, their related henges, enclosures and huge tombs. At Knowth (Co. Meath), excavation of the great passage grave and its surrounds has exposed a timber circle of 21 postholes 8.5m in diameter close to the entrance of the east passage. The circle had a rectangular central setting of posts with a porch and entrance on the east. It had quantities of Grooved ware pottery associated and dates ranging from *c*.2860 to 2520 BC. This structure would appear to be an integral part of the great funerary complex of central passage grave and satellite tombs. Within the complex, several stone rings of small boulders (between *c*.1-2m diameter) of unusual stones (quartz, granite, mudstone) were located immediately against the kerb at the entrance of the eastern passage. They formed a line of six offering areas, many with evidence for burning, and directly in front of the entrance, a circular area 4.2 m diameter ('setting 1') of saucer-like cobbling covered with quartz chips, ringed by larger stones (glacial eratics and ironstone nodules) and centred on a standing stone (Eogan 1984, Eogan *et al.* 1997).

The Ballynahatty complex (Co. Down) (**129**) also implies a mortuary function. Here the timber circle forms part of the Giant's Ring complex (henge, central stone burial chamber), as a double circle of huge post pits — 32 in the outer ring 15m in diameter, and 25 on the inner ring of 10m diameter. A rectangular post setting of 14 posts at the centre may have supported a central mortuary structure or excarnation platform. The entrance

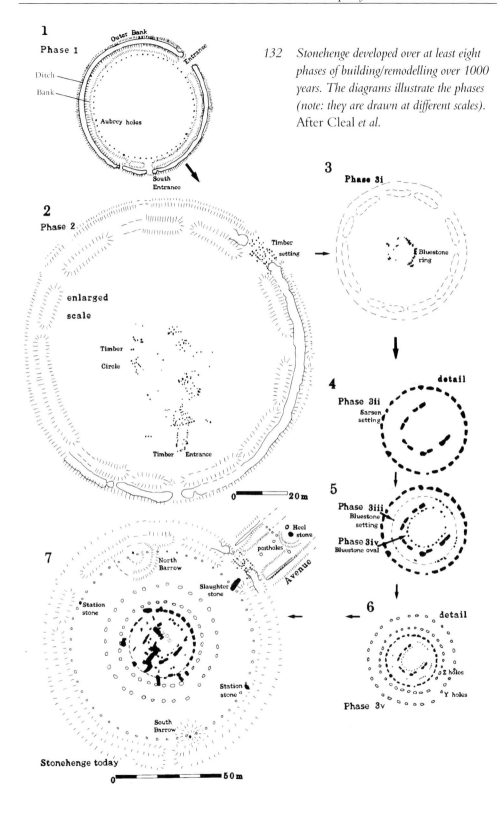

132 Stonehenge developed over at least eight phases of building/remodelling over 1000 years. The diagrams illustrate the phases (note: they are drawn at different scales). After Cleal et al.

133   Avebury Henge in the snow. Photo C. Malone

opened to the south-east, facing the palisade enclosure some *c*.100x80m in diameter. On either side there were smaller open-fronted structures that could only be viewed as a person approached the inner circle and passed their narrow openings. It can only be speculated what they contained — perhaps piles of ancestral bones, cult objects, shamanistic or other necessaries for the rites of passage that these sites seem to imply. Reconstruction of the timber circle suggests that it may well have been a continuous barrier or façade, similar in style to Stonehenge, and perhaps similar to Gibson's reconstruction of the Sarn-y-bryn-caled circle (Gibson 1998 fig. 83) (**61**). Like Knowth, Ballynahatty was associated with Grooved ware pottery. Elsewhere in Ireland, timber circles have been identified at non-henge sites. For example, at Lugg (Co Dublin) three rings of posts (16m, 19m and 21m in diameter) were attached to a post-built avenue, and additional pairs of posts surrounded the circle, suggesting trilithon-like settings. It was later buried beneath a Bronze Age mound. The timber circle tradition continued into the Iron Age in Ireland, at Navan (Armagh) and at Knockaulin (Co Kildare). There, a double ditch/palisade enclosure of 44m diameter surrounded a 25m diameter circle of some 26 posts, and enclosed a small 7m diameter circular setting of posts, with lines of posts radiating from the centre. Many other potential sites of pits and posts set in circles have been identified from aerial photographs, but much more study is needed to fully understand these structures.

Stonehenge

Stonehenge is the most complex of all the henges and stone circles in Britain, and succeeds in combining virtually all the component parts of the monumental constructions of the Neolithic.

The sequence is extremely confusing, but it begins with a banked and ditched enclosure containing a few post and possibly stone settings, and an emphasis on cremated and excarnated human remains placed in the 56 Aubrey Holes dug around the perimeter of the interior. After a period of silting and possible abandonment, the site was remodelled between

134 Aerial view of Avebury stone circle, and the West Kennet Avenue, looking south. Photo CUCAP CKC14

2900-2400 BC in phase 2. This timber phase of Stonehenge bears remarkable similarity to Ballynahatty, even though the plan of the timber structures is very partial due to the succession of later stone structures erected over the site. It consisted of a complex timber circle erected slightly south of the centre of the enclosure. It had of up to six concentric rings of posts, with a central setting (possibly once four posts), and clusters of large holes that may have supported entrance posts. It is now impossible to reconstruct the size or form of the building with any accuracy — some circuits of post-holes suggest a timber circle of over 20m diameter (more likely 30m), and one length of post-holes hints at perhaps as much as 50m diameter. The site is further complicated by posts set within the north-east causewayed entrance to the henge. This consisted of eight to ten lines of posts (**132**) that formed linear screens to the site and may have provided the solar corridor aligned with the rising midsummer sun, along which the sun's rays would have shone, against posts which would have cast shadows. To the south of the timber building an avenue of timber posts extended at least 17m, cut across by a palisade of posts forming a massive screen. As the table above shows, Stonehenge was still at the beginning of its extraordinary development by the time the timber circle was replaced by a succession of stone circles (up to 25m in diameter) built in bluestone and sarsen. It is tempting to interpret the present stone structure as a reinterpretation of the original timber one and, indeed, there is much evidence to support this. The mortice and tenon (peg-hole) technique used to hold the horizontal trilithons in place is surely reminiscent of carpentry methods? The shaping of the blue and sarsen stones is also an unusual feature of Stonehenge, when almost no other megalithic site in Britain can demonstrate more than the crudest reshaping of natural stone blocks. All the Stonehenge blocks are straightened and smoothed through hammering with stone mauls, even though sarsen is a remarkably hard and difficult stone to dress. At Avebury — which is broadly contemporary with Stonehenge and barely 30 km away, no attempt appears to have been made to reshape the stones, and Stonehenge stands out as a unique attempt to build a timber-style monument in stone (**133**).

135   *The henge and stones of the Ring of Brodgar on Orkney form an impressive ceremonial site.* Photo C. Malone

The use of stone may have had profound symbolic meaning, as an essay by Parker-Pearson and Ramilisonina argues (1998) using analogy with ethnography. They suggest that the ancestors were identified with stone, and the living with wood, and that Stonehenge increasingly became a monument to ancestors. Certainly, the presence of scores and perhaps even hundreds of individuals, represented as incoherent cremated fragments placed within the henge, imply a strong mortuary association. Furthermore, the surrounding landscape, littered with some 500 prehistoric burial monuments from the Neolithic to the early Middle Bronze Age, strengthens this idea. However, not all stone circles or henges were necessarily so strongly connected with funerary ritual or ancestors, and other preoccupations may have been more significant at different sites.

The second significant feature of Stonehenge is its calendrical function as an observatory of solar and lunar movements. Many studies have examined the archaeo-astronomical possibilities that the site offers (Burl 1997; 2000; Cunliffe and Renfrew 1997; see also Darvill 1997) and clearly the extreme seasonal movements of sun and moon are well understood. In a Neolithic context, the ability to measure and calculate the seasons, and the birth and death of the year were of great importance. It is not difficult to see that Neolithic communities might have constructed elaborate mythology and beliefs that connected the seasonal celestial movements with the rites of passage of birth and death, and with ancestors. When those ancestors ceased to be important, Stonehenge ceased to be further remodelled or even used, and many sites were abandoned. Barrows were replaced by different types of cemetery and the dead were no longer given such prominence in the landscape. Indeed, by the middle Bronze Age in the mid-second millennium BC, it seems that henges, barrows, astronomically aligned monuments and the very concept of monumental landscapes had ceased to be significant.

Pit alignments, avenues, linear structures and ceremonial enclosures

The earlier Neolithic cursus monuments were replaced by linear constructions in the later Neolithic, very often within the same 'busy' ritual landscapes. The new structures included

136   Aerial view of the Ring of Brodgar, Orkney, set between the lochs of Harray and Stenness, showing its massive rock-cut henge ditch and standing stones. Photo CUCAP

avenues of earth banks such as at Stonehenge, pit or post alignments as at Thornborough in Yorkshire (**146-7**), or stone avenues, as at Avebury. The function of these ceremonial routes may have been similar to the cursus sites — providing arenas within which ritual processions or events took place. However, this superficial similarity does not necessarily extend to the emphasis on funerary ritual at cursus sites (see chapter 4/5) which seem closely to resemble bank barrows and mortuary enclosures. Instead, the new avenues of earth, posts and stone seem to have been designed to link specific monuments (usually henges) or provide a grand ceremonial entrance to them. They were designed within their local landscapes. Their builders intended to provide a dramatic and often unexpected view of the place they enhanced. At Avebury, the stone avenue linked The Sanctuary on Overton Hill almost 2km distant, but maintained a winding route which blocked the view of Avebury until the last moment of the approach. The same is true of the earth avenue at Stonehenge, which takes a similarly tortuous route, with only occasional views of Stonehenge. Drama may have played a part in the planning of these routes, but they may also have been constrained by a much more packed landscape. The Avebury avenue seems to curve around a later Neolithic occupation site, and respected its boundaries. The stone avenues may date from very late in the Neolithic, and certainly they extended well into the second millennium Bronze Age, enhancing stone circles across Britain and Ireland.

Much has been written on standing stones, avenues and menhirs, that range from complex avenues (Burl 1993), to isolated single, paired and dispersed arrangements. Many of these sites may date back to the Neolithic, although dating them can be very difficult, since they often have almost no association or stratified deposits around them. The Heel

137 Callanais Stone circle and central chambered tomb on the island of Lewis, Outer Hebrides is one of the most complex circles, with its avenues still surviving.
Photo C. Malone

stone and the other outliers at Stonehenge, or the remaining central stone at Mayburgh, for example, were erected quite early in the site sequences, and were undoubtedly of Neolithic date. Many megalithic rows and menhirs and the stone circles to which they often attach may well date from the end of the second millennium BC (of Beaker and early Bronze Age date), continuing the earlier traditions of the Neolithic in more durable materials. As Burl shows in his comprehensive study of standing stones, geology naturally plays a vital role in the distribution of sites. Beyond that constraint there are distinct regional traditions of single or multiple lines of stones:

north-east Scotland	long rows of many stones
the rest of Scotland	short rows from pairs to 6 stones
north-central Ireland	long rows and single and tangential stones
Ireland	portal stones, and short rows
Cumbria	portal stones
west Wales	short rows and portals
central Wales	long tangential and rows
south-west England	long rows in various arrangements
Wessex/Cotswolds	avenues
southern/eastern Britain	non-stone avenues and pit alignments

Stone circles

Stone circles offer a tangible glimpse of prehistoric building enterprises, ritual structures and religious activities, but these are often distorted by the perplexing problems which recent over-emphasis and over-interpretation have brought. In the broader context of henges, wood circles, alignments and the multitude of associated structures, circles of stones can be seen in perspective, as part of the increasingly elaborate landscapes of the later Neolithic. Of the 1300 or so that Aubrey Burl has listed over a lifetime of research (Burl 2000), many of the sites visible today are probably not Neolithic in date at all, but are the rebuildings and work of the Copper Age and early Bronze Age. Stonehenge, as

138 *Circle I on Machrie Moor, Isle of Arran with circle XV beyond. The complex is mostly of early Bronze Age date, but some of the structures may have Neolithic origins* . Photo Mick Sharp

discussed above, demonstrates well how a site may begin in the mid-later Neolithic, and be rebuilt and elaborated several times until the early centuries of the second millennium BC. It is surprising how little recent or systematic excavation and conclusive fieldwork has been conducted on stone circles, and information often relies on antiquarian work, surveys of the visible above-ground structures and records of the local topography. When geophysical survey methods are applied — as at Stanton Drew (English Heritage), Avebury (Ucko et al 1991) and the Rollright stones (Lambrick 1988) (**144**) — much unexpected information on dating, buried structures, ditches, stoneholes and the like comes to light. All these investigations have shown that the apparently simple sites are remarkably complex, with long developmental sequences.

Circle numbers and distributions

At least 1300 remnant stone circles still survive in the British Isles and Ireland, with marked concentrations in some areas. Regionally the numbers break down as follows: Scotland has about 40 per cent, England and Ireland about 25 per cent each, Wales only 6 per cent, and the Channel Islands have just six sites (under 0.5 per cent).

The circles divide into smaller and larger sites. Smaller circles with low stone settings are frequent in the Peak District of Derbyshire/Yorkshire, in Cumbria, Wales, northern England and the Scottish Borders, Fife-Angus-Perthshire, Arran and Argyll. Recumbent stone circles are particular to eastern Scotland. Circles with tall stone settings are mainly distributed in Devon and Dorset in two clusters, along the Cumbrian coast and thinly across northern England, Arran, eastern Scotland, Lewis and Orkney. The so-called four-poster circles are known very rarely in Britain, and are mostly from Perthshire, Aberdeenshire and Morayshire. The 'larger circles' include the great Henge-circles and circles of Wessex-Cotswolds, the south-west, Cumbria and Orkney.

139   Mayburgh Henge at Penrith, Cumbria has immense surrounding banks, and contains one standing stone from an original four at its centre. Photo C. Malone

In terms of regional density, some counties have many surviving examples, others have few relics. Cornwall with its relatively well-preserved landscapes of stone-walled fields and pasture, preserves some 29 stone circle complexes, including the Merry Maidens, Leskernick, the Stripple Stones and, on Bodmin Moor, the Hurlers complex of three circles. Devon is especially rich with stone circles, having some 56 complexes (many of which are probably earlier Bronze Age) on Dartmoor, Exmoor and across the pastures of the county. Examples include the Grey Wethers pair of circles and several complex arrangements of stone rows, cairns, field boundaries and circles such as Cosdon on Dartmoor, with its triple stone row and cairn. As one moves eastwards the availability of stone and the density (and probably the survival) of circles declines; Somerset has 13 sites, including Stanton Drew, Wiltshire includes the Avebury complex of some four to six sites, Stonehenge, and a number of other sites across Salisbury Plain and the Marlborough Downs (14 sites). Oxfordshire has three complexes only, Dorset seven, Shropshire seven, and there are some 80 sites across Wales. Once into the stony uplands of the north and west, stone circles become more frequent, with 30 in Yorkshire, 18 in Northumberland, 12 in Lancashire and, according to Burl, 26 in Derbyshire. New research in the Derbyshire Peak District (Barnatt 1990) has re-evaluated the different classes of circle sites which number an astonishing 33-47 sites, depending on how they are categorised. There are only two henge-circles, the Bull Ring and Arbor Low, seven freestanding circles, 19 embanked stone circles, of which the Nine Ladies is a well known example, and 17 Ringcairns (**144, 142 & 143**). Cumbria (Cumberland) is especially rich, with some 27 complexes, including Long Meg and her daughters and the two circles at Castlerigg. Westmorland (now part of Cumbria) includes a further 19, which embraces the Penrith circles of Mayburgh. In Scotland, the western circles are largely ellipses or ovals, and mostly of small size (around 30m diameter) and covering little more than 200m^2. Only the great circles of Orkney, Stennes and Brodgar are large. The large ellipse of The Twelve

140   Castlerigg Stone Circle, Cumbria. Photo J. Cook

Apostles near Dumfries is vast — the seventh largest ring (86 x 79m) in Britain, and not far away, the circles of Broadlees (79m diameter) and Whitcastles (54 x 43m). They may relate to a tradition of circle building that straddled the Solway Firth between England and south-west Scotland. Further north up the coast of Argyll, the valley of Kilmartin includes a dense landscape of cairns, circles, stones and engraved rocks, with signs that much of the visible archaeology may date from the Bronze Age, rather than the Neolithic. In these remoter areas, the traditions of Megalithic building had a Neolithic origin and continued long after they fell out of use elsewhere.

As **127** indicates, the British Isles is divided by a roughly N-S line that defines the henge/stone zones. It relates to geology and to regional traditions. East of the line, almost no stone circles or substantial megalithic monuments dating from the Neolithic are known.

Definitions

As discussed above, circular enclosures formed by earth banks (henges) or wood posts (timber circles) were features of many areas of Britain and Ireland in the later Neolithic, and varied considerably according to local topography and style. The major distribution of these monuments is in the lowland zone, as defined rather deterministically by Cyril Fox in his *Personality of Britain* (1938). He proposed that in areas north and west of the Pennines (the 'henge' line), where stone was plentiful, structures of stone would be common and associated with small communities, whereas the lowland zone had minimal stone and monuments were built instead in earth and timber and served large communities. Henges however, tend to be much larger than timber or stone circles, and cover an average of 3600m^2, whilst the average stone circle covers about 260m^2. The size range of timber circles

141 *The recumbent stone circle of Easter Aquhorthies in Aberdeenshire. The so-called recumbent stone is visible between two tall stones and probably formed the focus for the monument.*
Photo Mick Sharp

is from smaller to larger than the stone versions, especially at sites such as Ballynahatty, but these sites are probably exceptions. Interestingly, the largest stone circles are in the zone immediately outside the henge zone at sites such as Stanton Drew (Somerset), Long Meg and her daughters (Cumbria) and the Devil's Quoits (Oxfordshire) (Barclay *et al.* 1995) (**151, 125 & 126**).

The largest stone circles (after Burl, 2000, Table 4)

Site	Diameter	Area m^2
Stanton Drew Somerset	112.2m	9887
Ring of Brodgar, Orkney	103.6m	8430
Avebury south circle, Wilts	102.4m	8236
Long Meg, Cumbria	109.4 x 93m	7991
New Grange, Co Meath	107.9 x 91.1m	7720
Avebury north circle, Wilts	97.5m	7466
Twelve Apostles, Dumfriesshire	86.6 x 79.3m	5394
Devil's Quoits, Oxfordshire	76m	4537

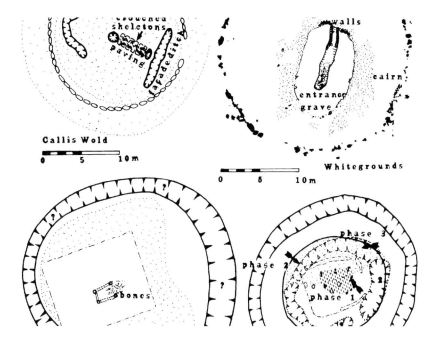

Callis Wold

0   5   10 m

walls

cairn

entrance
grave

Whitegrounds

0   5   10 m

bones

phase 3

phase 2

phase 1

142   *Arbor Low, Derbyshire showing the henge ditch as viewed from the barrow on the bank.*
      Photo Mick Sharp

From Burl's estimates, these huge sites were the exceptions, and 92 per cent of all the stone circles actually average only 13.7m in diameter and have an internal area of $c.150m^2$, very different in scale and perhaps in social function to the massive sites. It is of course impossible to estimate how many people would have fitted into the stone circles to take part in ceremonies. The huge ones could have comfortably accommodated from hundreds to over 1000 active people, the smaller ones, perhaps just a dozen or so participants (see Thorpe 1986 for a discussion on the ritual use of circles).

A superficial survey of stone circles soon shows that most of them are anything but circular in plan, and that a great variety of shapes, sizes and complexities exist. There are regional patterns to these, with islands having relatively few examples. Alexander Thom the astronomer made an extensive and highly mathematical study of the circles of Britain, and attempted to codify his results. He established five main shapes -- the circle, the flattened circle, the ellipse, the egg and the complex. Of these, about 800 are circles, 300 are flattened circles and ellipses and 200 are unclassifiable non-symmetrical shapes. Thom (1967, 1971) claimed that there was precision and geometry in the layout of the circles, and that the 'Megalithic Yard' of 0.829m that he established could be deduced from most of the sites. However, more recent and rigorous survey has suggested that many sites were simply laid out by eye, or, at the most, through simple string and peg survey (Ruggles 1999, Ruggles & Barclay 2000). The more regular circles seem to cluster in the south of England. The elliptical circles may have been much more effective shapes in terms of the visual effect they offered an audience, rather as in the seating plans of ancient (and

143   *Arbor Low henge and circle captured after snow and showing the fallen stones within the henge and the barrow over the bank on the left side.* Photo CUCAP CIS 57

modern) theatres and amphitheatres, which allow much better views of the onstage action. An elliptical shape also allows for a longer axis, and thus a better viewpoint for sighting celestial events against the skyline. There were doubtless many reasons for the shapes of the stone circles which cannot now be deduced, but clearly Thom and others after him (see Mackie 1977) made too much of the astronomical possibilities of what are often almost randomly preserved standing stones.

Other studies (see Burl 2000) have established that there are strongly regional patterns for the different classes of stone circle. Many circles have a central focus around a stone cairn, cists, passage grave, dolmen or cove which implies that there was continuity with earlier funerary sites, and an attempt to incorporate these ancestral and cult places into the later Neolithic ritual landscape. For example the small and damaged passage tomb at the centre of Callanish on Lewis formed a primary focus for the complex of standing stones, circles, ellipses and avenues of the site. The development of the so-called Cove (another term coined by Stukeley) could be a later Neolithic interpretation of megalithic tomb architecture translated into the specially built three-sided stone box construction found at about a dozen stone circles (for example Avebury north circle, Stanton Drew, Arbor Low and Cairnpapple). The development of circles and the translation of the idea of a focal point around an earlier tomb is well shown in north-east Scotland, where the recumbent stone circle form is common. This style of circle may have evolved from the boulder kerbs found around the early passage tombs of Carrowmore in Sligo, the later kerbs around the Boyne passage graves in Ireland and the Scottish Clava cairns and their surrounding circles. Later developments (well extending into the Bronze Age) of this form include the so-called four-posters of Scotland and the five-stone and multiple circles in south-west Ireland. In Cumbria, early stone circles appear to be stone interpretations of henges at sites

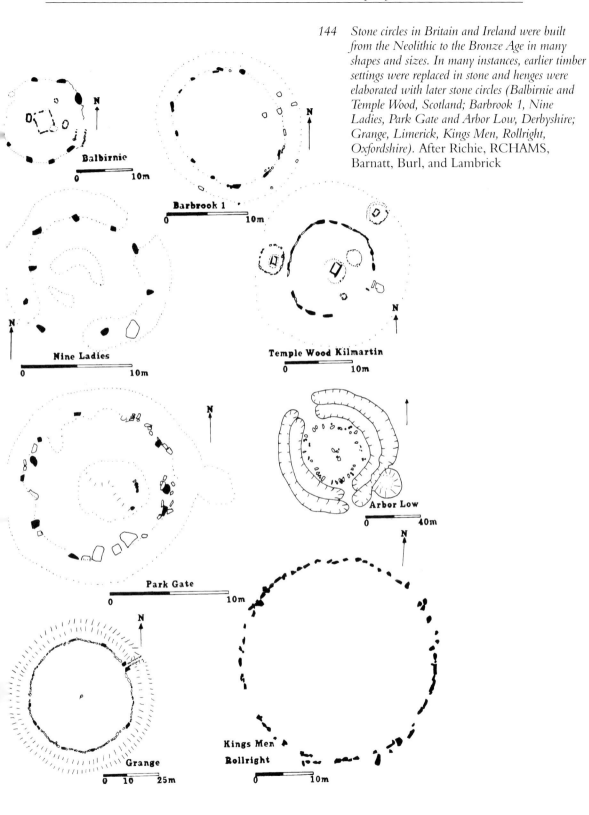

144 *Stone circles in Britain and Ireland were built from the Neolithic to the Bronze Age in many shapes and sizes. In many instances, earlier timber settings were replaced in stone and henges were elaborated with later stone circles (Balbirnie and Temple Wood, Scotland; Barbrook 1, Nine Ladies, Park Gate and Arbor Low, Derbyshire; Grange, Limerick, Kings Men, Rollright, Oxfordshire). After Richie, RCHAMS, Barnatt, Burl, and Lambrick*

145   The Grange Stone Circle at Lough Gur, Co. Limerick, a continuous perimeter of standing stones marked by particularly large stones at the entrance. Photo S. Stoddart

such as Castlerigg E. and are often associated with cairns and cists. In the south and west, the setting of rectangular structures or station stones, as at Stonehenge and King Arthur's Hall in Cornwall, may be inspired from Brittany where parallel constructions exist.

The recumbent stone circles of eastern Scotland (RSC) are a particularly distinctive regional development which span the later Neolithic to earlier Bronze Age. These 80-90 circles have stones graded in height, with the highest stones located between the south-south-east and south-west, and often placed around a ring cairn with a stone kerb, containing cremated bones, and sometimes, pits and burned areas left by the pyres. There may be continuity from earlier mortuary structures like Pitnacree translated into stone as circles and cairns. Similar circles are also known from south-west Ireland: the Carrowmore tombs with their boulder circles and the kerbed cairns and circles of the Boyne are not dissimilar. In the Scottish RSC taller stones are placed close to long low stones, often forming an almost continuous wall. Sometimes the stones themselves seem to have been carefully selected for colour or texture and transported some distance. Occasionally, decoration has been added, such as cup-and-ring marks. It is thought that the stones may have been sighted upon lunar movements. Examples include Easter Aquorthies, Loanhead of Daviot, and Ardlair with its cremation 'pit'.

Some Scottish islands are especially rich in stone circles, where tolerant farmers or sheer numbers have allowed a good number to survive. The Isle of Arran has six circles on Machrie Moor alone, which range from variants of RSC to flattened and eliptical circles, up to some 20m diameter (**138**). The Isle of Lewis lacks the stone tombs of the southern Hebrides, but has a number of stone circles, the most important being the cluster around Callanais. The main elliptical circle is located above a bay opening to the Atlantic, and one of its four radiating stone avenues faces the sea. At the centre, an early chambered tomb forms a funereal focus, and is surrounded by 13 tall stones. The angle and shape of the stones was probably significant, since they provide lines of sight to distant topographical features and celestial (almost certainly lunar) movements (**137**). Several other circles and standing stones are located within a couple of kilometers, and give the impression of a centre of activity in the third to second millennia BC. The Orkneys, so rich in tombs, have just two intact stone circles on the mainland. The largest is the Ring of Brodgar, a vast rock-cut henge of 123m diameter with two entrances. Two very tall stones mark the cardinal south and west points, and some 60 stones mark out the great circle. Within sight a number of other stones and chambered cairns provide potential alignments for celestial observations. The earlier (*c*.2900 BC) and smaller site of the Stones of Stenness is also located within a rock-cut ditch and bank, and is only large enough to accommodate 12 standing stones. The landscape of these circles is extraordinary, since they are sited either side of a small isthmus dividing the Loch of Harray from the Loch of Stenness, and have a decidedly watery character. The isthmus is littered with standing stones and tombs, and clearly was designated a place of ritual in the Neolithic (**152**). Circles are more modest on the Shetland Isles and are often associated with cairns such as Haltadans on the island of Fetlar. Twenty stones enclose a low bank and two central stones. Other sites have up to three banks such as the Rounds of Tivla on Unst, surrounding a stoney area, probably once a cairn.

Mortuary functions of stone circles

The strong association between many stone circles (and indeed timber circles) and burial sites is borne out where excavation has taken place within and around them, and the remains of burials and cremations have frequently been found. Sometimes these are central to the circle (for example Woodhenge) or associated with the individual standing stones (Avebury). However, as Burl puts it:

> Nor is it certain that the cremated human bones interred at the heart of some megalithic ring are those of a person who had participated in the original ceremonies there. As yet the proximity of circle, settlement and cemetery remains inferential. (Burl 2000, 44)

The insertion of burials and cremated remains in and around earlier cult sites was clearly a tradition, and absolute and traditional dating (through comparison of pottery and artefacts buried with the dead) usually demonstrate a time lapse of centuries between structure and later burial. For example, there is a barrow containing an early Bronze Age Food Vessel burial overlying the banks at Arbor Low, and early Bronze Age cists lay within the circle of Machrie Moor on Arran. At Cairnpapple, similar Bronze Age burials overlay and buried the Neolithic levels (**150 & 125**).

146 *The Thornborough
henges, North
Yorkshire, show as
dramatic cropmarks
and survive as low
earthworks.* Photo
CUCAP

Materials and complexity

The construction of stone circles has long been the subject of great fascination and over interpretation (Pitts 1998). Because some researchers have desired a fantastic and extra-terrestial explanation, the raising of the stones of Stonehenge, the exact measurements of circles, perfect alignments and astronomical complexity — to name just a few of the abberations of poor scholarship — have all been claimed at various times as evidence for a lost civilization, men from Mars or similar! However, it should be clear from the discussions above and from the previous chapters that the building of stone enclosures or circles was simply a local interpretation of a broadly similar tradition found across Britain and Ireland and western Europe. It developed quite logically from the technologies of constructing stone cists, cairns, chambered tombs, and timber buildings. The choice of site, the proximity to contemporary Neolithic sites, and the physical geography of an area determined to a great extent the final form of stone circles, along with particular traditions. In most cases, a fairly flat site was chosen, and where flatness was not available, the builders sometimes terraced the area to create a flat zone, as at Kiltierney in Co Fermanagh. The geography and also the social requirements of the site determined its size, which (see above) varied enormously. Sometimes stone was very local, and simply dragged from outcrop or scree to the site, but in rare cases it may have been quarried and transported over considerable distances. The most contentious example of transport is the movement of the bluestones from the Prescelly mountains of Pembrokeshire to Stonehenge (Thorpe *et al.* 1991) which now suggests that, contrary to the belief that the stones were transported by human effort, ice movement brought the rocks as erratics

*147   Plan of the Thornborough south
       henge. After St Joseph*

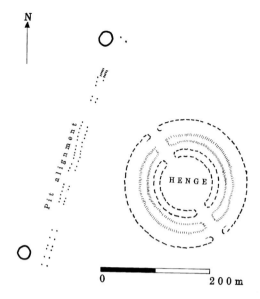

during the Ice Age and dumped them between Wales and Salisbury Plain (eg. Burl 2000, 44). Research and the chemical analysis of Rhyolite across Britain has shown that glacial transportation of the rock, and its use in prehistoric structures, was quite common and that Stonehenge and its use of exotic stone was not unique. For example, fragments of the stone occur in Wiltshire barrows, the Stonehenge cursus, Welsh monuments and standing stones and randomly in modern gateposts and walls. However, other geological studies contest this, and claim that most of the Stonehenge Bluestones are from a specific outcrop in Prescelly (Scourse 1997). Whatever the final outcome of this long debate, some stone was selected and transported for its colour and shape. Circles close to Callanias have standing stones of different colours (pink, white, black) and at Avebury the Sarsens that form the outer circle and the West Kennet Avenue were chosen for their shapes — either triangular or columnar. The Callanais stones were selected and placed for the same reason.

Much experimental transporting and lifting of stone has taken place over the decades, and has resulted in a fairly clear understanding of the methods used. Large stones were probably prised from their outcrops or scree, and levered onto wood rollers, attached to thongs and ropes made of fibres and sinews, and with effort, expertise and experience, dragged to the construction site. Ways of lifting stones into position varied from sinking the butt end of the stone into a dug hole with the assistance of levers, stakes and ropes, to using a complex of wooden supports and earth ramps to gradually heave a large stone into position. The raising of the lintels of the trilithons at Stonehenge, or indeed the capstones of many megalithic tombs, involved elaborate wooden frameworks and a mass of levers. Such methods of construction can still be seen in traditional societies, and it should not be a matter of disbelief that the well-organised and technically sophisticated Neolithic communities of Britain and Ireland were able to achieve such building projects. However, it is this very component of sophistication and organisation that should engage our interest, since this is what underlies the changes and complexities of the late Neolithic world.

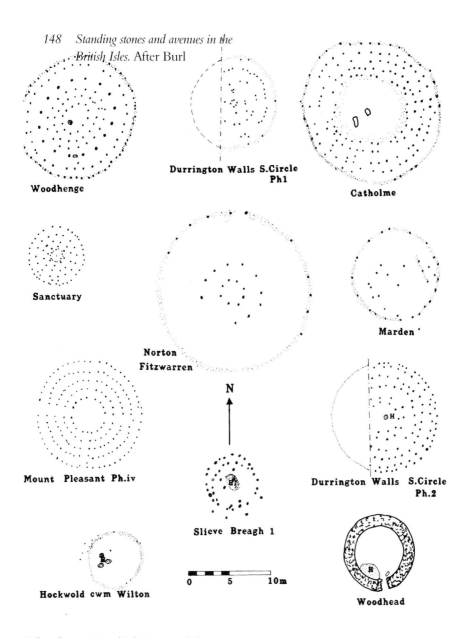

148   Standing stones and avenues in the British Isles. After Burl

The late Neolithic world

People and landscape

Over the 2000 years that spanned the Neolithic in Britain, the world changed irreversibly. From earlier thinly populated landscapes, where trees were the dominant features, the later Neolithic world became a land of large grassy clearings, downland, scrub and arable fields. Of course not all the areas of Britain and Ireland were cleared or intensively used, but much more use was made of the landscape than seems apparent today. Peat and bog had not formed

149   *The Hill o'Many Stanes, Lybster, Caithness forms a remarkable series of low stone alignments now numbering some 200, once 600, stones, and probably dating to the end of the third millennium BC.* Photo C. Malone

in many parts of the north and west during the Neolithic. It was only when the climate became cooler and wetter in the mid-second millennium BC that areas such as Dartmoor, the Ceide Fields of Mayo, and the Pennine uplands were abandoned because of dramatic deterioration in their workability and productivity. By the beginning of the second millennium BC, there were much greater numbers of people living in Britain than before. We know this from archaeological evidence in the form of more and larger sites, environmental data that indicate clearance and cultivation, from the sheer numbers of artefacts in circulation, and from the scale of the monuments. Actual numbers of people of course are impossible to estimate, but the proliferation of round barrows, cemeteries, field systems, boundary markers and settlements in the Beaker-Early Bronze Age period suggest intense use of some areas and high population densities. Over the Neolithic, the way that landscape was marked out, cleared and claimed by communities also changed. We can see these first attempts to make spaces in the causewayed enclosures and their associated cursus sites and barrows, which marked out arenas to celebrate the ancestors. As the Neolithic progressed, these sites were replaced by enclosures and henges, which offered a focus for ritual activities in more dramatic settings. Measurements of the movements of sun and moon together with the emphasis on the dead and the ancestors became more sophisticated and controlled than in the earlier Neolithic. The increasingly high levels of labour invested in the sites of the later Neolithic is a measure perhaps of the growing hierarchies within some communities. The amount of effort channelled into building enterprises may be another

150 Aerial view of Cairnpapple Hill under excavation in 1949, showing the various circles, henge and cairn. Photo CUCAP DH49

measure of the levels of social cohesion or, perhaps more realistically, social control. For example it has been estimated that an average long barrow in the earlier-middle Neolithic probably required about 10,000 man-hours to build. A causewayed enclosure like Windmill Hill required some 62,000 man-hours to complete. By the later Neolithic a modest 110m diameter henge-stone circle like the Devil's Quoits required some 26,000 man-hours and the ditches alone of a superhenge like Durrington Wall needed perhaps 900,000 man-hours to excavate 50,000 cubic metres of earth and build the bank. An Avebury superhenge of 347m diameter and up to 200 great megalithic stones required massive labour investment (between 650,000 and 1,500,000 man-hours) and a vast artifical mound like Silbury something between 2 and 3 million man-hours to build. Stonehenge is on a similar level of investment, with its transportation and shaping of stones representing a vast time-labour investment.

What do these figures really tell us about the changing Neolithic? Certainly they imply that more people and labour were harnessed in the later period in the creation of vast ceremonial monuments. How people were organised or ruled is another problem, however, and we are left with ethnographic analogy and speculative theories to explain Neolithic society. At a very simple level of explanation, societies are seen to evolve from mobile family bands (in the Mesolithic) to loose tribal groups of household-based family lineages. These were supported by domestic scales of subsistence and hamlets; villages and regional confederacies made up 'tribes' in the Neolithic (see Sahlins 1968). Such societies have no central political organisation, but instead a segmentary hierarchy of groups that collectively have a tribal identity linked by kinship, language, customs and ancestors. As population levels increase, tribal structures become more formalised, and may develop increasingly towards chiefdom organisation. These societies still have family-based units, villages and lineage identities, but chiefdoms impose an additional level of political centralisation over these groups. At the simplest level, control might be organised by a petty chieftan or headman who is appointed by the community to organise particular matters. Sometimes, other leaders emerge as self-appointed Big Men able to harness resources, provide feasts, exert their personality and for a time at least, control the community for their own ends. Tribes are rarely totally self-sufficient, and ethnography shows that their

151 Long Meg and her daughters stone circle, Cumbria, from the air. Photo CUCAP — BE90

character and scale vary according to local resources and economic success. Exchange and trade between different groups ensure that restricted resources are obtained, often reinforced by marriage payments and gift exchange.

Chiefdoms are far more formal political entities than tribes, and have administrative hierarchies overriding local communities and their identities. Societies organised into chiefdoms identify a common ancestor, and make up extensive common descent groups. Hierarchy within the social order dominates chiefdoms, where lineages are ranked in the power structure according to their genealogical distance from the ancestor and from the chief. Status becomes very apparent, with individuals (often male and first born) and clan groups distinguished by wealth, political and economic influence. Other specialist groups may also become separated from the rest through their role in crafts, warfare, administration and religion. Some groups (especially political and religious classes) may live apart in demarcated settlements or enclosures to distance themselves further from the rest of the clan. In some societies, such as the Maories of New Zealand, ethnographers noted that everyone claimed to be of high status, even though clearly some individuals had far more power. The importance of chiefdom organisation is that it relies of the production of surplus, and lower ranking members are obliged to give their labour, agricultural products and loyalty to the chief when called upon, in return for protection, inclusion, and the redistribution of food and materials when needed. Chiefdoms give otherwise disparate clans and groups a larger identity, and can often harness enormous levels of labour and resource. Large building enterprises, such as mounds in Polynesia, or indeed henges in prehistoric Britain, are made possible through such political unity, which under small-scale lineages could not be achieved.

Analogy with ethnographic examples is helpful in trying to understand the changes that we see archaeologically in the Neolithic Age of Britain, although no exact comparisons can be drawn between entirely different times and places. What is apparent is that some areas had exceptional levels of organisation at certain times; Wessex is the most obvious example, and others are the Boyne in Ireland, Orkney and the many areas of dense monument building discussed in earlier chapters. Social change rarely follows a linear or irreversable evolution, and at times with climatic deterioration, soil exhaustion, marginality and

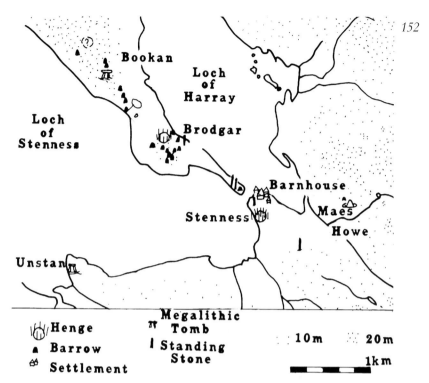

152 *Map of the
monumental
landscape
between lochs
Harray and
Stenness on
Orkney.*
After Ritchie

isolation, chiefdoms would have reverted to simpler tribal systems. In some instances, the apparent flowering of a monument-building episode may actually have been a last-ditch attempt to salvage an already precarious social system. The very coincidence of apparently declining agricultural productivity in the middle-later Neolithic around 2900-2400 BC marks the beginning of massive social enterprises such as Silbury Hill, Stonehenge, and the superhenges. At the same time, new experiments with more extensive forms of agriculture, such as upland grazing and secondary animal products like cheese, wool and animal traction, may be responses to a difficult economic environment. Population levels may also have grown to the point where tribal lineage systems were ineffective over formerly extensive and thinly populated tribal areas. The emergence of chiefdoms and their building projects at such a time could be seen as a social response, to refocus and reorganise disparate and warring communities under a more peaceful common identity.

By the end of the Neolithic (*c*.2300-2000 BC) chiefdom organisation seems to be less obvious in the archaeological record. The great building enterprises ceased, and instead new social identities, Beaker pottery, individual high-status burials, metalwork, long-distance trade and internationalism dominate the picture. Gradually, new settlement systems and economic strategies had begun to have an impact in Britain, and whilst individual status was increasingly celebrated at death, monuments became less impressive. Characteristic constructions are stone rows and circles, small enclosures, barrow cemeteries, demarcated landscapes of fields and grazing land and small but distinct villages of a more permanent character than found in the Neolithic. Can these too be inferred as the product of chiefdom politics, or a different level of control?

Finally, archaeology has no means to observe prehistoric social structures beyond those represented by material remains. It can only extract and interpret evidence that might, or might not, imply a scale of society and organisation, and through analogy and parallels, suggest what could have been.

Phase	Phase 1 Middle Neolithic 2950-2900 BC	Phase 2 Later Neolithic 2900-2400 BC	Phase 3 – Final Neolithic – Beaker – Early Bronze Age 2550-1600 BC
Landscape	Wooded – cleared for grazing land and crops	More open	Grassland, Fields, short-lived settlements
Linear monuments	Greater and Lesser Cursus constructed	Timber avenues. Palisade ditch to N dividing landscapes E-W, with entrance near Stonehenge	Earth Avenue links Stonehenge to River Avon to E.
Burials – Mortuary	Long Barrows going out of use	Cremations and excarnated remains in monuments	Single burials in round barrows in cemeteries in distinct areas around site
Enclosure	Causewayed enclosures at Stonehenge and Robin Hood's Ball	Henges at Durrington, Coneybury, Woodhenge, Stonehenge	Enhancement of Superhenges
Structures	Segmented Ditch. Bank inside and externally, 3? entrances, Aubrey Holes. Circular setting of posts around inner edge of bank.	Complex timber structures include timber circle, screens, avenue, entrances.	Axis modified. Sarsen and Bluestone settings erected and re-erected 5-6 times i) Bluestone in Q and R hole – dismantled
			ii) Sarsen Circle set up with Bluestone
			iii) Trilithons and Bluestones dismantled
			iv) Bluestone circle and oval with Sarsn Circle and Trilithons. Bluestone arc removed to form:
			v) Bluestone Horseshoe with Bluestone Circle
			vi) Y and Z holes dug for stone but never filled or completed
Settlement	Small clusters – King Barrow Ridge, Wilsford Down	Within 1km, associated with pits, pottery and flint working	Scattered settlement shortlived and mobile
Phasing	Dark soil suggests periodic abandonment	Ditch part backfilled or silted,	Beaker Pottery in deposits contemporary with stones
Deposits	Cremation deposits, artefact deposits. Ox remains placed at terminals of ditch segments.	Deliberate deposits in ditch of pot and bone, human remains. Cremations in bank?	

Table of the stages of development at Stonehenge

Phase	Early Neolithic c4000-3200 BC	Middle Neolithic C3200 – 2800 BC	Later Neolithic C2800-2000 BC
Land-scape	Wooded landscapes	Semi-cleared landscapes Some regeneration	Open landscapes, extensive pastures
Population	Low levels of population	Growing population	Regionally dense populations
Pottery	Round-based pottery – little decoration – Windmill wares etc	Peterborough and decorated pottery – round and flat based	Grooved wares, Beakers, flat based decorated and plain pottery
Projectiles	Leaf arrowheads	Oblique arrowheads	Barbed and tanged arrowheads
Hosues	Rectangular houses Balbridie, Knap of Howar	Oval – round houses, Skara Brae	Oval-round houses – sometimes replaced by barrows
Enclosures	Causewayed enclosures	Enclosures-henges, timber circles	Elaborated henges and stone circles
Linear Monuments	Cursus monuments and mortuary enclosures	Avenues and alignments	Stone rows, avenues, pit alignments
Burial Monuments	Long Barrows, bank barrows, long cairns, stalled cairns, portal and court tombs	Oval barrows, great passage graves, court tombs, recumbent stone circles, stalled cairns	Pit graves, late passage graves, wedge tombs, cairns Round barrows
Burial Rites	Collective burial rites – excarnation	Increasingly individual burial	Individual burials
Flint Mines	Sussex flint mines	Grimes Graves flint mines	Grimes Graves Flint Mines
Axe production	Developing axe trade	Height of axe trade and quarry exploitation	First experiments with copper
Astronomy	Tombs face east or to the cardinal points	Growing com-plexity of align-ments to cardinal points and sun-moon	Monumental landscapes aligned to lunar-solar movements. Obser-vation markers
Economy	Subsistence Cattle farming & cereals, woodland management	Emphasis on pig rearing for feasts + cattle and arable – possible surplus	Pastoralism cattle and pig, arable. Wool, milk and traction from stock
Society	Small household units within loose tribal networks	Increasingly un-stable and hierarchial tribal groups. Emerging big-men and chiefs	Chiefly organisation and growing social hierarchies, boundaries and warfare

Table of the broad characteristics of the Early to Later Neolithic

7 Artefacts, technology and craftsmen

Evidence of past societies is preserved in very limited forms, as sites, material culture, anthropogenically created rubbish, or as indirect human interference on the environment, such as pollen from plants. Artefacts remain as one of the most potent links we have with the prehistoric past. Through them we can reconstruct much about everyday life, and imagine more vividly how Neolithic people managed their world.

Pottery and stone tools are the most durable remnants of Neolithic cultures in Britain. Together with the less common or hard-wearing objects, they are essential evidence in recognising and categorising these cultures in their varied regional and chronological manifestations. As the previous chapters have shown, Neolithic sites and landscapes abound across the British Isles, but they are recognised, dated and interpreted by their associations with specific artefact types of pottery, flint, stone and bone. The different assemblages are often diagnostic of a particular period of the Neolithic and indicate the broad dates of use and burial; thus Windmill Hill style pottery is associated with the earlier Neolithic before 3000 BC, but Peterborough and Grooved ware pottery after 3000 BC represent the later Neolithic. However, objects can tell us far more than just their approximate date. They may be interpreted as part of an economic model; for example, a proliferation of axes could suggest tree clearance and agricultural expansion; or an emphasis on flint saws, burins and points might imply leather and wood working. Objects did not have just functional use, and there are symbolic dimensions to be explored, such as notions of aesthetics, craftsmanship, value and cultural identity, which can be extracted from the study of material culture and its archaeological associations (Coles 1973, Hodder 1990). These studies rely on good archaeological records, statistical studies, experimental materials and technological research and ethnographic analogy. The body of evidence for Neolithic, as opposed to later prehistory, in Britain has always been difficult to assess, since most sites produce relatively few examples of pottery or bonework, and the greatest quantity of material is usually flint. Not surprisingly few corpora of Neolithic artefacts have been attempted, and it is not yet possible to lift a volume from the shelf entirely devoted to British or Irish Neolithic pottery, flints (except arrowheads) or bonework to compare material, unlike the metalwork or pottery of the Bronze Age. Much Neolithic artefact research still remains to be done! This chapter aims to introduce the main categories of Neolithic artefact from Britain and Ireland and explain and present the broad characteristics of typology and style.

Exchange and production

Throughout prehistory people sought high quality materials for tool making and special objects such as jewellery, and often travelled great distances to obtain them. The best

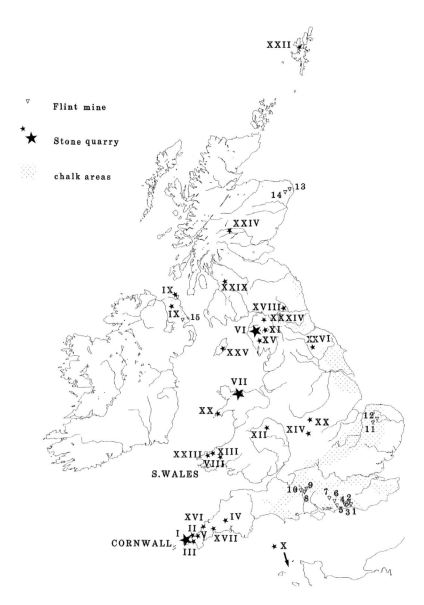

153   *Map of rock and flint sources in Britain and Ireland exploited in the Neolithic (sources —
various). The hard rock sources have been assigned to specific geological 'groups' as follows:
I=UralitizedGabbro; I-III=Epidorite or Greenstone; IV=Altered Picrite/Sheared Greenstone;
VI=Tuff; VII=Augite Granophyre; VIII=Silicified Tuff; IX=Porcellanite; X=Dolerite;
XI=Tuff; XII=Picrite; XIII=Spotted Dolerite/preselite; XIV=Camptonite; XV=Micaceous
sub-greywacke; XVI and XVII=Epidorite/greenstone; XVIII=Quartz dolerite;
XIX=Greywacke; XX=Epidotized and ashy grit; XXI=Baked shale; XXII=Riebeckite felsite;
XXIII=Graphic pyrocene granodorite/quartz dolerite; XXIV Calc-silicate hornfels;
XXV=Altered quartz diorite/tonalite; XXVI=Carbonate mudstone; XXVII/
XXVII=Greywackes; XXVIII=Quartz dolerite; XXIX=Essexite; XXX=Horneblende
lamprophyre; XXXI=Basic andesite; XXXII=Epidiorite or altered diorite; XXXIII=Biotite-
Silliminite-quartz-schist; XXXIV=Leucogabbro. After Clough*

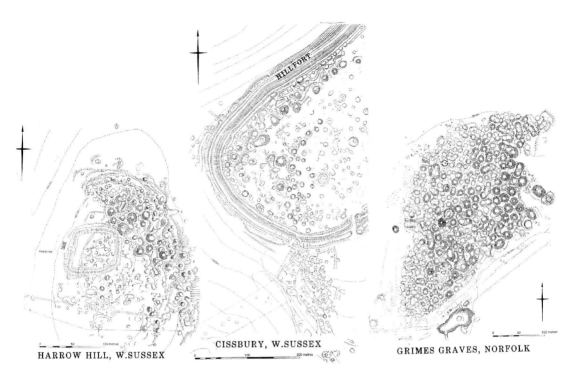

HARROW HILL, W.SUSSEX

CISSBURY, W.SUSSEX

GRIMES GRAVES, NORFOLK

*154   Plans of Neolithic flint mines at Harrow Hill and Cissbury in West Sussex (earlier
Neolithic) and Grimes Graves, Norfolk (later Neolithic) showing the many pit shafts and
their surrounding dumps of spoil that still cover the landscape.* After Barber *et al.*

materials may be sparsely scattered across the landscape, and in the case of specific
minerals, such as greenstone, copper, tin, amber, jet, or even fine flint, they may have been
concentrated in distant, alien lands, across the sea or at least in other political entities. The
Neolithic represents a period when the search for ever more attractive and suitable
materials became intense and, as can be seen from the axe trade, enormous organizational
effort was invested in obtaining, making and trading axes and maces of many different
materials. It may be possible to interpret the distribution patterns of the different axe
materials in relation to each other, and to other materials against an increasingly precise
chronology and reconstruct, at a broad level, the political and economic alliances that may
have existed over the Neolithic period.

Anthropological work has examined exchange and gift giving in traditional societies,
and this offers some important examples of how polished axes and other 'primitive'
valuables were prized in such societies. The Kula — a system of gift-exchange-partners
across the small islands of the western Pacific in the Trobriand islands — is an interesting
and useful ethnographic comparison. It offers a means to explain some of the distribution
patterns of prehistory. The work of Marcel Mauss especially (1954), following on from
fieldwork of Malinowski, examined what gift giving symbolized and entailed. He showed

that the Kula gift was organized between distant partners, who were obliged to pass on a symbolic prestige object — a shell arm-ring or necklace, an axe or suchlike. The object often had a venerable history, reputation and name, and the very ownership of it conferred importance and status on the owner during their possession. However, under the traditions of the Kula, they were obliged to pass the gift on to another exchange partner. Thus the object kept moving over space, to new 'keepers', and could end up far from its point of origin, and sometimes eventually return in the cycle of giving. The process of Kula exchange had many purposes. Most importantly, it enabled ordinary market exchange to take place peacefully between the communities of the gift partners. The isolated Pacific islands had limited natural resources, and gift partnerships ensured both good relations between island communities, and offered access to vital but rare commodities. The Kula also provided a means to exchange brides between different communities, and to forge political links. In an unstable tribal world where intertribal warfare was usually endemic, and alliances with other groups, gift giving and marriage alliances reinforced links. Kula exchange ranged from subsistence products to prestigious symbolic gifts, and distinctive venues were used for the different exchanges. Usually, flamboyant feasts and celebration accompanied the gift giving, whilst other goods were literally unloaded from canoes on the beach for exchange. The Kula and other gift-giving traditions are important to archaeologists because they indicate how prestige goods were obtained over great distances, and help to explain the extensive distribution patterns of rocks, amber, jet, obsidian and, later on, metal.

Raw materials and their extraction

Quarries and mines, clay and other materials
The geology of the British Isles is amongst the most varied and complex in the world, and contains a wealth of useful raw materials. Many stone resources were exploited in prehistory and the Neolithic represents a period when prospection for new materials was particularly active. Mesolithic communities certainly understood and exploited some resources, such as chert and flint, but they did not excavate flint mines or quarry for rock and clay. Neolithic enterprises were on a quite different scale, and the reconstruction of their industrial operations paints a vivid picture of new levels of organisation and technological development.

The metamorphic, igneous and sedimentary rocks in the north and west of Britain provided much of the raw material for axes and stone tools. Mining and quarrying operations represented a considerable investment of time and expertise in prospection, in setting up temporary work camps (often far from permanent settlement), and in the extraction and reduction of workable nodules. Some rock is found as river boulders and pebbles, but by far the more important sources were from the parent rock outcrops in the upland and mountainous regions (**153**). In some places, such as the Cumbrian Lake District, extensive quarrying and chipping areas have been located, and these offer an insight into a major industrial activity from the middle of the fourth millennium BC. Flint was of great importance for the everyday tasks of Neolithic life, and it was obtained mostly

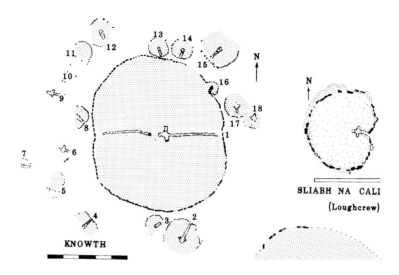

SLIABH NA CALI
(Loughcrew)

KNOWTH

155   Grimes Graves flint mine (Norfolk) from the air, showing the scores of extraction pits and dumps that pock the surface. Photo CUCAP

from the lowlands and downland of southern Britain. Although flint occurs widely scattered in glacial deposits, gravels and shingle, the best high quality flint was mined. Several mines have been identified in the chalklands, from East Anglia to Dorset, and some mine shafts have been excavated to reveal a complex and dangerous activity.

The axe trade

The scientific study of stone axes began in earnest in the 1930s following the excavations at Windmill Hill, where Alexander Keiller and others took thin sections of axes for petrological study. This initiative was embraced by the 'South Western Museums Committee on the Petrological Identification of Stone Axes'. Several reports then followed synthesising the data. Petrological research concentrated on England and Wales;. Irish axes have been studied comprehensively and the sheer numbers have confounded the researchers, who expected about 10,000 axes to exist but found in excess of 20,000. Numbers in England and Wales (about 4000 in 1972) are more modest, and reassessment is now needed. However, the samples nevertheless show important patterning and have firmly established the bulk of geological sources for most axes in Britain, and their broad distribution patterns.

At least 34 distinct geological sources (**153**) have been established for British axes. These vary from small and rarely exploited sources (for example XXIX in Ayrshire, or XXX in northern Scotland) to the well-known and hugely exploited outcrops of Gabbro (Penzance — Group 1) and Augite granophyre of north Wales (Group VII). Many more sources remain to be confirmed in Britain and Ireland (Clough & Cummins 1979, 1988).

Distribution patterns from the various sources differ greatly over space and probably over time. For example, the Cornish Group 1 Greenstone axes tend to be clustered either close to Cornwall and the West country, or else at 500km distance around the Thames

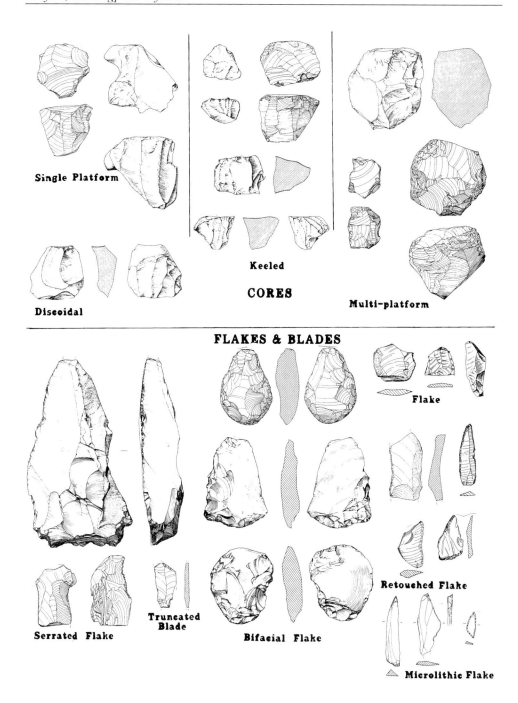

Single Platform

Discoidal

Keeled

CORES

Multi-platform

FLAKES & BLADES

Flake

Retouched Flake

Serrated Flake

Truncated Blade

Bifacial Flake

Microlithic Flake

156 *Flint cores, flakes and blades, showing some of the basic categories (material from Walton Basin, Maiden Castle, Annaghane, Tormore, Brackley, Grimes Graves: various scales).* After Sharples, Gibson, Eogan, Henshall and Mercer

Estuary area and the Fenland. The low density of axes in the regions between allows us to speculate that perhaps whole boatloads of axes were transported directly from their source to Essex or the Wash, where patterns of local redistribution then took place. Distributions of Group VI axes from Great Langdale in Cumbria show a similar pattern of concentration on the opposite side of the country, but this time almost certainly carried overland. The greatest concentrations of these Tuff axes are found 200km to the east in East Yorkshire and Humberside — areas that naturally had no local hard stone, but an intensive agriculture and dense populations. A striking example of a trade monopoly is suggested by the very large numbers of group VI Great Langdale axes in the East Riding of Yorkshire and Lincolnshire during the earlier-middle Neolithic. Over 50 per cent of Group VI axes have been found within 120km of the River Humber, and nationally Group VI axes may represent 40 per cent of the total of all hard stone axes in circulation in Neolithic Britain. Although Group VI axes were in active competition with local axe sources, they were highly prized, which accounts for the large numbers found in central Britain and in 'prestige' contexts such as enclosures.

The major source of axes from north Wales — the Group VII Graig Lwyd — Augite granophyre, was in competition with axe Groups I and IV, but shows a different fall-off in distribution, with concentrations gradually declining with distance from the source. Group VII axes are found in low densities in central England, Wales and in the south east where they were surprisingly abundant. Almost none have been found in East Anglia outside the Fenland, showing that other axe sources (Group IV and Grimes Graves Flint) had the local monopoly. The importance of the distribution studies is that they provide a measure of the movement of material, the frequency of particular sources in an area, and may describe the mechanisms of distribution from one community to another.(**163**) (for example see Darvill 1989, Cummins 1980) (**165, 166 & 157**).

Changing distribution and exchange patterns in the later Neolithic, suggested by the different distribution and frequency patterns of axes, show that the Group VI Cumbrian Axes became progressively rare in the south, but remained popular in East Anglia and Yorkshire where they are found in late Neolithic contexts. Meanwhile, axes from Cornwall (Group 1) became common in the south, especially the Thames area, and similar patterns of replacement are suggested by axes from other sources in Britain. Axe distributions are distorted by the amount of fieldwork done, the accuracy of records and the often unrecorded quantities of flint axes which locally may have been frequent and significant

Quarries

Recently interest has been revived in the study of stone quarries, and especially in the Great Langdale area, where Richard Bradley has led investigations with Mark Edmonds (Bradley & Edmonds 1993). The remote location of some rock sources, and the lengths to which the prospectors went in obtaining the raw material is often astonishing. This work showed that some of the finest axes, which sometimes come from symbolic contexts like tombs, were quarried from the most remote and inaccessible outcrops. The nearer the summit the better, it seems, to obtain rock for axes that perhaps embodied mythological

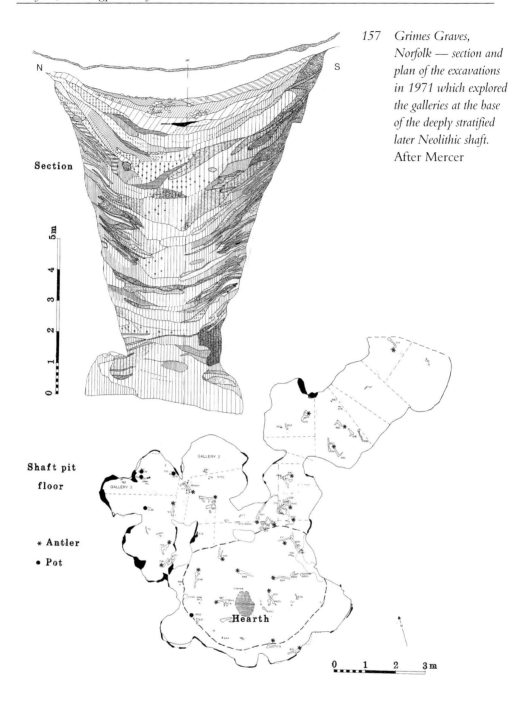

157 *Grimes Graves,*
Norfolk — section and
plan of the excavations
in 1971 which explored
the galleries at the base
of the deeply stratified
later Neolithic shaft.
After Mercer

Section

5m
4
3
2
1
0

Shaft pit floor

GALLERY 2

GALLERY 3

Hearth

* **Antler**

● **Pot**

0   1   2   3 m

identities and were objects to be treasured. It has also been possible to identify areas of quarrying around the outcrops, and map the vast areas of scree covered in waste flakes and abandoned roughouts left since the Neolithic. The actual exploitation of rock seems to have begun in the Mesolithic in the Great Langdale area, north Wales and Ireland, near sources of fine-grained rock. As time progressed, it appears that quarrying became more and more organised, and zones were demarcated to divide up the extraction. Bradley believes that unlike the increasingly haphazard production of flint tools in the south of England, the Tuff axes were being produced under ever more strict and organised conditions, supplying an increasingly demanding market in the east. Work is progressing on Scotland's axe industry, where many potential rock sources were used (Sheridan 1992).

The Irish Stone Axe Project has recently attempted to study the findspots and forms of over 20,000 Irish stone axes (Cooney et al. 1998). The results present some unexpected data. For example, nearly half the axes appear to come from rivers, lakes, bogs and dredging operations, suggesting deposition may, like bronze weapons and tools in the Bronze Age, have been closely associated with water cults or with watery activities. Another interesting finding has been that Cumbrian Group VI axes were imported into Ireland in some number and, likewise, the porcellanite axes (Group IX) from Tievebulliagh and Rathlin Island in northern Ireland travelled across the sea to Britain, together with Irish flint.

Jade and greenstone axes

An example of even longer distance trade is represented by the magnificent jadeite axes that were imported to Britain and Ireland from the Jura and Alps 1200km distant. These distinctive, often pointed, green axes were clearly prestigious objects, and their findspots have often suggested they carried status and cult significance. Of the 100 or so known, one, dating from early in the Neolithic, was found within the Sweet Track of the Somerset Levels, another was found in Canterbury, some in the tomb of Cairnholy I in Scotland and some in clusters in Wessex and East Anglia (Cambell Smith 1963). Similar artefacts from France appear to come from the same Alpine sources. This huge pattern of distribution shows that from early in the Neolithic continental scale exchange networks were active, with jadeite traded as far as Malta, central Europe, northern Scotland and Ireland.

Flint mines

The most important cutting material in Neolithic Britain was flint, a fine silica-rich glassy material that had reliable flaking properties, and was widely available. Flint (or its coarser relative, chert) is found in two main locations — as re-deposited material in rivers, gravels, clays or beaches, or as tabular 'wet' flint formed within sedimentary chalk deposits. The former was the most widely available and provided reasonable material for knapping. However, temperature and humidity changes, movement and impact all damage the structure of flint, creating cracks and weaknesses, which limit the production of large and regular flakes. Tabular flint is far superior, but only available from specific locations, and often at quite deep levels that require mining and an industrial level of extraction and production. In Britain, there are several early mines, and a long history of excavation and research that allows insight into flint mine development (see Barber et al. 1999, Holgate 1991). The mysterious deep nature of some of the flint mines may, like the remote axe quarries, have endowed the extracted material with special character. The remains of offerings in mine shafts suggest ritual significance alongside the economic extraction.

Early flint mines have been located in Sussex at Blackpatch, Cissbury, Church Hill, Long Down, and Harrow Hill. These seem to have been active from about 4000 BC and throughout the fourthmillennium BC. Mines in Sussex appear to have supplied a large amount of flint throughout southern England. They competed successfully with other source areas, even where local supplies were good, as in East Anglia. Later Neolithic flint extraction took place on an industrial scale at Grimes Graves, Norfolk and Easton Down in Wiltshire from the third millennium BC. At Grimes Graves, on the edge of the Breckland of Norfolk, some 360 shaft depressions have been recorded over an area of 37ha., making it the largest prehistoric flint mine in Britain (**154, 155 & 157**). The shafts, sometimes 4-6m in diameter, were sunk from the surface to the seams of black flint that lay in layers, sometimes 12m deep. Seams of flint were followed along passages, which occasionally met up with neighbouring shafts. A complex system of ladders, ropes and baskets must have been employed to excavate the shafts, and remove the spoil and flint to the surface. This was dumped back into worked-out shafts leaving a strange pockmarked surface to the landscape. An average-sized shaft probably produced about eight tonnes of flint, but 1000 tonnes of chalk had to be excavated to reach it. Shafts of similar mines have been found on the Sussex Downs, in Hampshire and in Wiltshire. Other chalkland areas like Dorset, Kent, Surrey, Buckinghamshire, Berkshire, Hertfordshire, Cambridgeshire, Lincolnshire and Yorkshire have the potential geology to have had flint mines, but as yet evidence has not been firmly established that flint was extracted this way. Instead, dense surface spreads of clay-with-flints in addition to traded flint may have provided sufficient material for local consumption. Flint cobbles were extracted in quantity (some 300 shafts) from Den of Boddam, near Peterhead (Scotland) around 3000 BC. Shafts were sunk through glacial till to the layers of flint cobbles beneath. In Ireland, flint is rare, and seems to have been quarried mainly from Antrim, in the north east and especially from Rathlin Island where knapping areas have been identified. An opencast mine was identified at Ballygalley Hill, in association with earlier Neolithic settlement and flintworking areas. The flint was so fine that it was exported to south-west Scotland, and a recent hoard of several finished axes and tools from Campbeltown indicates the importance and local rarity of flint in the region.

Sometimes the flint miners left curious offerings of antlers, pottery, bird and animal remains, chalk carvings or finished axes at the base of the shaft. At Grimes Graves one particular carving was of a strange female figure, and another was a phallus. Similar phalli have been found at the causewayed enclosure of Windmill Hill.

Although flint was the dominant material used in flaked stone tools in Britain, other materials were also exploited, including the lower grade Chert, which is like flint but has a higher sand content and more granular texture. Chert was routinely exploited in south Dorset where Portland chert was available and used for distinctive petit tranchet arrowheads. Other areas exploited similar local sources. A finer but volcanic glassy material rather like obsidian is Arran pitchstone, found only on Arran in western Scotland. This was exploited from Mesolithic times and throughout the Neolithic, as a fine local substitute for flint, and distributed in south-west Scotland and north-west England.

Flint tools

This section includes the common types of flint tool that are found in the Neolithic, with descriptions of form, manufacture and typological names. It cannot be comprehensive, because typologies are changing, incomplete, and widely debated between different specialists, but is offered here as a simple means to recognise and categorise flint material.

The illustrations attempt to show the broad range of tool types, but as yet, no single scheme is published. Instead, different lithic specialists use various names and criteria to describe the very varied industries of Neolithic Britain (see Edmonds 1995 for a general introduction).

Cores are the primary nodules of stone or flint from which blades or flakes were removed. When found on sites, cores are often worked down to a small size through the removal of flakes, and sometimes converted into tools. Neolithic cores may have one platform from which the flakes have been removed, two platforms, usually end to end, or two or even three striking platforms at oblique angles from which flakes have been taken. 'Keeled' cores had flakes taken off at angles. The study of cores is important because they reveal the precise technology used in the stone industry at a site. The size, complexity and the level of reduction of cores suggests the availability of raw materials and the need to extract the maximum from each core. The pattern of development seems to be from single platformed cores which were common in the Mesolithic, to more complex and, in particular, keeled cores in the later Neolithic, which were effective in the production of oblique and chisel arrowheads.(**156**)

Blade technology
Scholars measure the width and length of flakes or blades in order to determine their ratio, and thus assess the type of technology and style of knapping of a flint industry. Mesolithic blades were long and narrow (ratio 1:5-2:5) in comparison to Neolithic blades, which became much wider in relation to length (normal ratio 3:5-5:5) as time progressed. In turn, early Neolithic blades were narrow in comparison to later Neolithic examples, as their cores similarly indicate. The changing technology from Mesolithic to Neolithic related to the specific types of tools to be made. Mesolithic flakes were suitable for simple, snapped and geometrically knapped blades forming geometric arrowheads and composite tools. The wider Neolithic blades, on the other hand, were designed as complete tools, retouched and shaped into scrapers, arrowheads, laurel leaf points and the many other tools employed.

Many flakes were left unretouched and show slight scars from utilisation, whilst others have restricted areas of retouch resulting in slight shaping, blunting or sharpening. Such flakes are difficult to recognise as tools, and have to be categorised by their length-width ratios and from the type of retouch (for details of technologies and further reading see Andrevsky 1998, Lord 1993). Other flakes were tools in their own right. Sharp, unretouched edges were used for cutting, shaping and trimming all manner of materials. Some were intentionally worked with serrated edges to cut wood or bone. Far more easily categorised are the worked tools of the Neolithic. Scholars continue to categorise material, but the following are commonly accepted types:

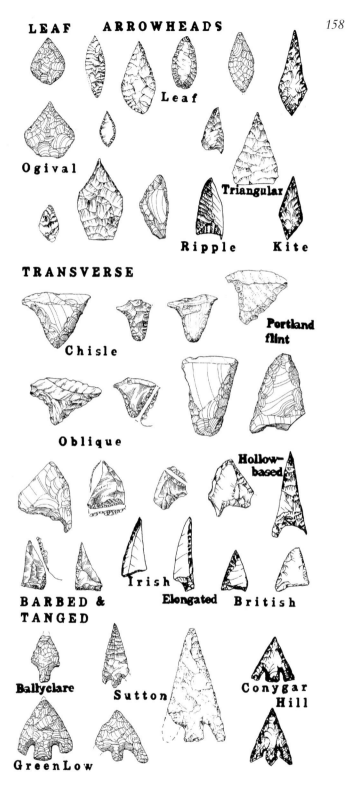

LEAF ARROWHEADS

Leaf

Ogival

Triangular

Ripple   Kite

TRANSVERSE

Chisle

Portland flint

Oblique

Hollow-based

BARBED & TANGED

Irish   Elongated   British

Ballyclare   Sutton   Conygar Hill

GreenLow

158   Flint arrowhead types (from Maiden Castle, Durrington Walls, Cranborne Chase, Duggleby Howe, Etton, Walton Basin). After Sharples, Barrett and Bradley, Wainwright and Longworth, Kinnes, Gibson, Green and Pryor

Stone projectiles were weapons fixed to a shaft or arrow by gum, tar, fibres or sinews, and thrown or shot at a target. Projectiles were very important before the Neolithic when hunting was a fundamental subsistence activity. Not all arrows or spears necessarily had stone tips: many may have been simply made of sharpened and fire-hardened wood. Arrowheads and larger projectiles were important throughout the Neolithic for hunting and warfare. The latter became an increasingly important activity as the Neolithic period progressed, with evidence for attack at sites and on people. Curiously, perhaps, as metal became increasingly used, flintwork became cruder and larger and Bronze Age flint arrowheads are often large and cumbersome in comparison to Neolithic examples.

Arrowheads are formed from single flint flakes and usually retouched on both sides (bifacial) with considerable skill into a number of different forms. The development of different shapes and forms reflects the chronology of the Neolithic and Beaker periods, and have been confirmed through C14 dating of contexts and by association with pottery. Arrowhead forms changed from predominantly leaf and ogival-shapes, associated with earlier-middle Neolithic Windmill Hill and Peterborough-type pottery, to oblique, chisel and transverse shapes in the middle Neolithic (Peterborough pottery) to barbed and tanged forms in the later Neolithic (Grooved ware and Beaker periods). Large laurel leaf points (often 9-10cm long) are rather crude versions of the leaf arrowhead and were in use at early sites like Hurst Fen (Suffolk) and Windmill Hill. Arrowheads were dependent on wood shafts and on wood bows to project them effectively at the target. Several wood bows have been found, and show how elaborate and decorated they were in the Neolithic (Clarke 1963) (**175**).

Where steady research of a landscape has found concentrations of arrowheads, the numbers are often fairly evenly spread between the earlier leaf forms and the later barbed and tanged forms, suggesting that this is a chronological distinction. Stephen Green (1980) has made a detailed study of British arrowheads and provided a definitive typlogy based on length, retouch, shape, and symmetry. He found that the largest numbers known came from the sandy Brecklands of E. Anglia, the Yorkshire Wolds, and the north Cotswolds, where Neolithic settlement may have always been especially dense. However, arrowheads seem to be present across all types of land, reflecting perhaps, the intensive way in which the small space of the British Isles was exploited in prehistory. Raw materials were found to be important in determining the size and form of arrowheads, and in the north and west, where good flint and chert are rare, arrowheads remained small and simple – i.e. they are often leaf forms. Some areas favoured certain materials, for example Portland chert in the south, where people persisted in making the petit tranchet and chisel types that were suited to it.

Leaf arrowheads range from slender to squat in width, and from small to very large in length, and form 12 'types' according to Green's typology (**158**). Subdivisions include the *ogival* forms which have concave upper sides, *attenuated* which are squat shapes with sharp points and *kite-shaped* which tend to be symmetrical in the lower and upper halves. A rare addition is the polished form, which comes from Ireland. Generally, leaf arrowheads in the west of Britain are smaller, reflecting the poorer quality of the raw materials. Research suggests that leaf arrowheads from domestic and communal sites like causewayed enclosures were less fine and elaborate than those deposited in tombs or other 'special' places. Examples of fine large arrowheads mainly come from long barrows, particularly those associated with Towthorpe pottery, and similarly, the kite-shaped examples seem particularly associated with burials of the 'Duggleby' phase (Yorkshire). Some leaf arrowheads are very late, and the form was still in use in the Bronze Age.

Transverse arrowheads are sometimes known as *petit tranchet* and incorporate a range of asymmetrical shapes on simple flakes, where the unretouched edge is part of the weapon. They are generally considered as middle-later Neolithic, and many have been found at henge monuments in association with Grooved ware pottery. The industrial flint production at Grimes Graves in Norfolk has shown transverse arrowheads to be stratified with Grooved ware pottery.

The *chisel arrowhead* form used the unretouched edge as the impact point, and retouch on the rear of the flake enabled it to be fixed to the arrow haft. It is thought that these arrowheads were especially effective in shooting birds and would have stunned the prey, even if not entering the body. They are found in some chambered (passage grave) tombs and most especially associated with the Woodland Grooved ware. They were common in the Brecklands and Yorkshire Wolds. Chronologically chisel types may precede the oblique types, which occur in later contexts.

Petit tranchet arrowheads are rare in Britain, especially in the highlands and Ireland, but present in the south and Yorkshire Wolds. They are rather similar to chisel types, but formed from snapped blades, with a longer, sharp unretouched edge, and steep retouch on the narrowing sides. They would also have been effective on birds and small creatures.

According to Green's study, *oblique arrowheads* have a different length/width ratio. In general they form a triangular shape, with retouch on the base and one side, and employ the sharp unretouched edge of the flake on the other. 'Ripple' flaked transverse arrowheads were common only in the Yorkshire Wolds, and had fine retouch on one side, worked into a barb at the base. It has been suggested that the finest ones may have been made in just one workshop near Bridlington. Like chisel types, obliques were also common on the Brecklands and in association with later Neolithic material, from Grooved ware to Beaker. The so-called Irish oblique arrowheads range from asymmetrical triangles with regular retouch on one side and the base, and little or no barb, to elongated forms, with pronounced retouch on one side which extends into the barb.

The *'British' type of transverse arrowhead* has a more isometric triangle shape, with shallow retouch pressure flaking on at least two edges, and some examples have a pronounced barb worked at the base. They are the only arrowheads associated with 'pure' Grooved ware sites. A variant is the *hollow-based arrowhead*, which is rare in Britain, except in Ireland, Wales and Cumbria, and is more common in continental Europe. Unlike the oblique types with barbs, these have two barbs of equal length and regular retouch.

Later Neolithic arrowheads, and those associated with Beakers and the early Bronze Age, are typically *barbed and tanged* in shape. In graves, these are frequently associated with male burials. The finest examples tend to come from East Anglia, where flint was being mined and worked, but good examples occur everywhere, suggesting they may have been exchanged. There are many regional varieties defined from the form of the tang, and the shape and type of barb. Green divides these into non-fancy (Ballyclare, Sutton) and fancy types (large, small, Conygar Hill, Green Low, Kilmarnock).

There is clear chronology associated with barbed and tanged arrowheads, and only this variety is found in Beaker burials (**183**). In Beaker settlements, they are always twice as

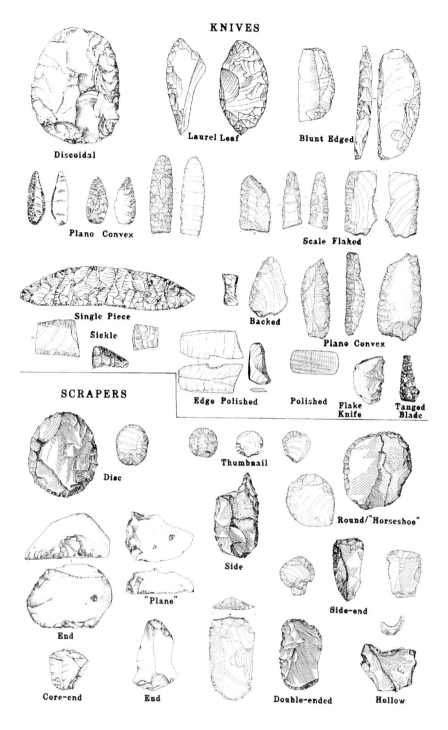

159 *Flint knives, sickles and scrapers (from Grimes Graves, Hurst Fen, Barnes Lower, Handley
Common, East Knoyle, Unstan, Duggleby Howe, Etton and Durrington Walls).* After Mercer,
Clark, Barrett and Bradley, Henshall, Pryor, Wainwright and Longworth, and Gibson

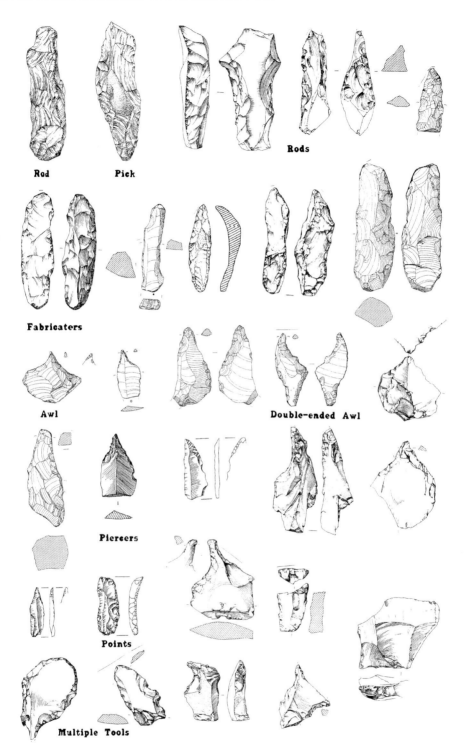

160   *Flint tools: rods , fabricators, awls, piercers, points (from Cranborne Chase, Grimes Graves, Walton Basin, Hurst Fen, and Etton). After Barrett and Bradley, Mercer, Gibson, Clark and Pryor*

common as other arrowhead forms, although oblique types sometimes occur on late Beaker settlements in southern England.

The *Ballyclare* type is small, weighing less than eight grams, and is a long narrow form, ranging from simple angled 'shoulders' without barbs to oblique barbed points as long as the tang. The *Sutton* type has round-square or pointed barbs, which are rarely as long as the central tang

The *Conygar* Hill type has square tangs and barbs, which can form a convex base to an almost equilateral triangle shape. They are not found associated with Beaker graves but are frequent in Food Vessel cremation graves, showing they belong to the Early Bronze Age. *Green Low* types, which are wholly English-Welsh in distribution, form a convex shape with the barbs and tangs cut oblique or square, and with the barbs always longer than the central tang, forming a convex outline at the base. They are particularly found associated with southern Beaker inhumation graves, but never with collared urns, indicating a chronological cut-off by the early Bronze Age.

The *Kilmarnock* type is mainly Scottish in distribution, and is a long and solid shaped arrowhead, with a wide long tang and shorter barbs, with minimal removal of material between them. The barbs may be triangular, pointed, oblique or square. Their chronology is late, tallying with Beaker to middle Bronze Age, and they are found associated with inurned cremations.

Cutting tools (knives, sickles, razors, polished discoidal knives)

Many flint tools were designed as cutting tools for meat, leather, wood and fibres including straw and plants. Knives were made from large, wide blades, with retouch to shape them. The simplest types are straight-edged knives where retouch along one edge forms a blunted side, and the unworked side forms the cutting edge. Some knives show signs of sheen or sickle gloss from the silica derived from plant fibers, and microwear analysis has shown that knives and other cutting tools were often used on specific materials, which left their characteristic microscopic marks. Small finely-worked knives were a feature of later Neolithic and Beaker industries.

Technically complex and dating from the mid-later Neolithic to the early Bronze Age are the bifacial *plano-convex or discoidal knives*, which were often worked into smooth and regular forms varying from leaf-shaped to almost circular. They occur across the country, including the Orkneys in Rinyo contexts and have often been found in association with burials, which suggests the knives were prized objects. Some knives of this type were also ground and polished along one or more edge to a smooth finish. Whether this polishing (and indeed blunting) really improved the cutting quality is debatable, but perhaps there was an aesthetic component involved, since polished knives have been found in chambered tombs and barrows.

Laurel leaf points are similar and so too are the large single piece sickles of the later Neolithic. These tools employed the fine pressure flaking techniques used on arrowheads, but at a larger scale, to produce single piece tools. The sickles are generally slightly curved with retouch and flaking on both sides and both edges. The worked piece was then set into a wood handle, and would have been effective in cutting grass and straw crops. The function of laurel leaf points is not clear; perhaps they were spearheads, perhaps they were used as knives, perhaps they were status symbols. The early Neolithic

161   The Neolithic polissoir stone in-situ at Fyfield (Wiltshire) showing the deep grinding scars from hours of axe polishing and sharpening.
Photo Mick Sharp

site of Hurst Fen was especially rich in these 'tools' and Clark (Clark & Longworth 1960) speculated that the lack of a sharp point seemed to suggest that they were not used as projectiles (**159**).

Points (burins/piercers, gravers, serrated blades, rods)

Palaeolithic flint tools were characterised by a great number of pointed tools used for opening shells, drilling holes in bone and skin and in decorating stone, bone and wood. By the Neolithic, the forms had changed to simpler, sturdier examples, employed in similar tasks working and turning raw materials into useful objects. Burins, awls or piercers were flakes worked into sharp narrow points. In some cases these are symmetrically placed at the end of a flake, in others they were asymmetrical and worked on one side, along with shaping retouch that blunted the sides of the flake. Some piercers were worked on thick triangular flakes, and were hefty enough to make holes in wood and may have been used in carpentry as drills. The range and weight of this class of tool are very great but relatively little study has been made of them. However, it can be assumed that tools for making holes, slits and grooves had great utility in a culture that required the construction of many new timber items, such as simple furniture, domestic fitments, house timbers and carvings, leather clothes, bone and antler work and much more. Some large examples are called spurred tools, but they seem to have functioned in the same way. Together with particularly long points, they were in use in the later Neolithic. By then, flintwork was frequently heavy duty and robust, and many forms of tool seem to have became cruder and stronger.

Saw-like blades were developed as serrated blades and even recognisable flint saws, which were clearly intended for working wood. Large examples had regular notches removed from the cutting edge to make a toothed saw and others had smaller notches nibbled from the edge. It can be presumed that such flakes may have been set into a wood or bone/antler handle, and perhaps several were employed in one effective saw.

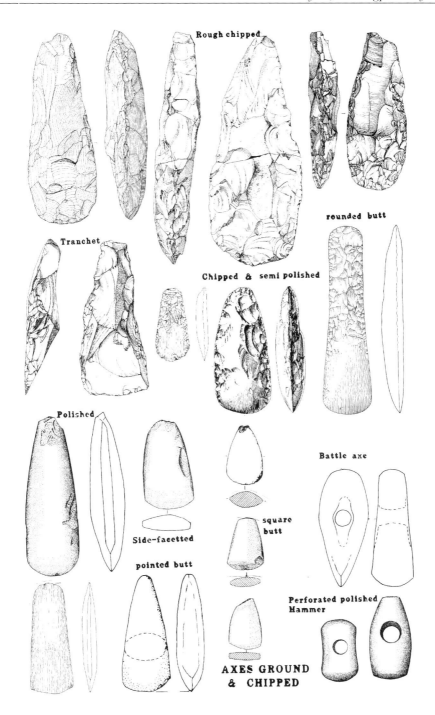

162   *Chipped and polished stone and flint axes, hammers and maces , showing how the tools range from crude chipped objects to finely polished tools (from Knowe of Lairo, Durrington Walls, Grimes Graves, Fyfield, Bavant, Ormiegill, Isbister, Creevykeel, Mullaghcrew, Duggleby Howe, Claigharg, Walton Basin). After Henshall, Mercer, Gibson, Barrett and Bradley, Eogan, Kinnes*

Forming tools

Denticulates, notched blades

Some flint tools were worked with concave retouch on one side of the flake, forming distinct notches or denticulates. These may have been used to trim, form and straighten arrows, to make bone points and needles, and in the manufacture of smooth and regularly shaped material. Some flakes demonstrate a number of distinct types of working and retouch, with points, scrapers and notches on them — the 'Swiss Army knives' of prehistory, able to undertake a number of tasks in one multi-use tool.

Scrapers

Scrapers are probably the commonest tools found on Neolithic sites, after utilised and worked flakes. A great variety of scrapers from very small thumb scrapers to large pieces the size of a clenched fist represent a utilitarian tool employed in many tasks. The most obvious use was the scraping of animal hide clean of hair and meat, and the preparation of leather. However, the sheer range and number of scraper-type tools means it is likely that they had many other tasks. Scrapers would have had a use in whittling wood, working bone and forming wooden vessels in basketry and suchlike. In essence, a scraper is a thick flake with steep regular retouch around one or more of the edges, removed from one side of the flake only. At their simplest, side scrapers had retouch on just one edge and end scrapers on the narrow end, usually opposed to the striking platform scars. The latter were especially characteristic of the earlier Neolithic with its narrower blade technology; particularly narrow worked ends are known as nosed scrapers. Sometimes double-ended scrapers were formed, perhaps with slightly different working at each end so the tool had multiple functions, a multiplicity of uses which is further enhanced in double-sided or double-sided end scrapers. Horseshoe scrapers are large rounded flakes with retouch around the curved edges, leaving just the striking platform unworked. Round scrapers are worked all the way around, like large examples of thumbnail scrapers. Some flakes were worked aound a concave edge, making them hollow scrapers to function like denticulates. Worked out cores were also formed into scrapers and are recognisable from the scars left on thick facetted pieces of flint. Core scraper tools were formed into steep planes for fashioning wood and, like all scrapers, seem to have been hand held, rather than set into a handle or haft.

Scrapers changed over the duration of the Neolithic, and small thumb scrapers were common in the later Neolithic and Beaker periods, many having been found in burials as part of the essential kit of a Beaker burial (**159**).

More heavyweight equipment is seen in objects called fabricators and rods. Fabricators are thick flakes, triangular or squarish in section, with steep secondary retouch around the edges, forming a rough knife shape. Rods and picks are generally much thicker in section, with very steep rough retouch along the sides, and are pointed at one end. They might have functioned in drilling holes in wood, or in cultivation if set into a haft (**160**).

Axes

The most characteristic of all Neolithic stone tools, in flint or hard stone, were the chipped or ground axes and adzes. These were essential tools for clearance, tree-felling, cultivation and forming timber for construction purposes. Mesolithic toolmakers had already developed chipped axes (using the tranchet technique of forming a sharp cutting edge by removing a flake across the base of the axe). These tools were probably used for clearing and cutting wood, but never in the intensive fashion required by Neolithic farmers. Whether made from flint or stone, the manufacturing process was similar. First nodules or boulders of suitable, unfractured stone had to be broken into suitable thick flakes. Selected flakes and natural stone cobbles were then flaked from both sides into a triangular to oblong shape. Finer pressure (or invasive) flaking smoothed the surface and profile into the final or near final shape. In some flint axes, the cutting edge was sharpened and used in its fairly rough state, in others the lower section was semi-ground creating a good cutting edge, and the upper part which was inserted into the haft was left rough. The most effective axes for tree felling were polished all over. This investment in finishing the surface meant that the axe had no rough areas to catch on the wood and cause friction, which would probably lead to the axe either sticking in the tree trunk or breaking. Axes were also used for cleaning felled timber, forming wood and in carpentry, where deep cuts were not needed, and so only the immediate cutting edge had to be polished. Many axe-like tools were probably used as adzes and hafted at a steep angle so that they were effective in trimming felled timber, forming dugout canoes and suchlike. Sometimes this use is revealed through the angle and wear of the ground edge. Celt is the term given to heavy duty tools of the axe and adze type from antiquarian times. Here it refers to axe-like tools used for cultivation as hoes. The fact that many semi-polished/ground axe-like tools are found at random in the countryside rather suggests that cultivation may have been just as important as tree-felling, which is the usual explanation given to these tools.

Typology and chronology of axes

Neolithic axes range from triangular to oblong in shape, but no one form or style defines early as opposed to later axe shapes. One distinctive early feature was side facets formed in the grinding process, especially found in porcellanite axes from Tievebulliagh/Rathlin, tuff axes from Great Langdale and some flint axes from the Yorkshire Wolds. Cumbrian axes sometimes also have a pronounced butt (non-cutting) end facet, conforming to the rather angular shapes preferred in the earlier Neolithic. Plain chipped and pecked axes are less likely to have the side facets (a particular feature of Scandinavian forms). Some Scandinavin axes may have been imported into Britain and have influenced the style of axe production in northern Britain. Fine imported jadeite axes, perhaps from France, often had a pointed butt end and a triangular shape. Late Neolithic axes seem to become more oblong in shape, longer in relation to their width, and the pointed butt of early axes was replaced by rounder or squarer shapes. Some later Neolithic burials and hoards in north-east England include waisted shaped axes with expanded cutting edges, and ground edge axes, very different in form to the early Neolithic.

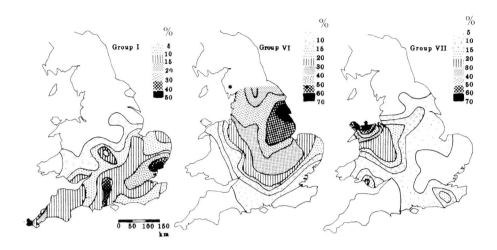

163   *Distribution patterns of axes from Graig Llwyd and Great Langdale (after Clough &*
      Cummins); and Cornwall

Axe hammers, maces and perforated 'battle' axes became a feature of the later Neolithic.
These required more skilled manufacture to form the perforated drilled or ground hole for
the wood haft. A bow-drill and sand were probably used to drill the hole from either side,
which was a lengthy business and often resulted in the breakage of the tool. However, once
achieved, the axe or mace could be firmly set on the haft or handle and used. Maces were a
feature of the later Neolithic, and seem to have been status symbols, perhaps to be wielded
by emerging chiefs in battle or political activities. Some are elaborately polished or carved in
stone such as the fine examples from the Orkneys and Knowth (Co Meath), or carved in
antler, as from the tomb at Duggleby Howe (see Roe 1979). Alongside these objects were
curious stone balls, carved into elaborate shapes and from attractive stone. Many come from
Scotland, and may have a symbolic importance similar to the maces.

Axes, whether polished or chipped, were always set into hafts, so that they could be
effectively manipulated in cutting operations. Wood hafts have occasionally survived in
rare wet conditions. The different woods selected are as follows:

Site with haft	Region	Wood
Sulishader	Isle of Lewis	Hawthorn/apple
Coll	Isle of Lewis	Hawthorn/apple
Maquire's Bridge	Fermanagh	Hawthorn/apple
Solway Moss	Cumbria	Hawthorn/apple
Etton	Cambridgeshire	Alder
Edercloon	Co Longford	Alder
Ehrenside Tarn I and II	Cumbria	Beech/oak
Port Talbot	Glamorgan	Birch
?	Co Monaghan	Pine

These hafts are rarely well preserved, but show sufficient detail of size and form. The Etton example was 56cm long and made from a split alder log. In some cases, antler was used as a primary sleeve to protect the axe from the greatest shocks, and this sleeve was then set into the wood shaft. The axe was normally set through the haft, and then secured with leather and fibre thongs. Some axes were left intentionally rough and unpolished just where the axe fitted through the haft, ensuring that they were less slippery and easier to secure firmly.

Axes clearly suffered from the work they did, and most axes show signs of breakage, chipping, resharpening and repolishing. Sometimes axes of particularly fine, colourful stone were reground several times, until the final object was almost too small to use. Axes placed in special deposits — perhaps as cult offerings — were sometimes pristine, of exotic source and thus rare and valuable. As discussed above, in many traditional cultures, fine axes were used as symbolic gifts, passed between communities (**164 & cover photo**).

Stone — polishers, rubbers, saddle querns

Less glamorous classes of stone object are the many querns and polishing stones that were essential for food processing and tool making. Domestic sites and causewayed enclosures normally produce evidence for these, but their deposition in tombs or ritual sites is rare, since they had little status. Hard, fine sandstone was especially favoured for saddle querns and rubbing stones. The slabs were pecked into shape — a concave base and a flattish-convex shaped rubber. Smaller stones were used for polishing, and sometimes have distinct grooves where pins may have been shaved and straightened, or concave areas where beads or small objects were fashioned and polished. Axes were ground on large, sandstone boulders or outcrops and stones showing the dished, concave grinding areas have been indentified across the country. Sometimes there are narrow grooves alongside, where the cutting edge was ground and sharpened. Three good examples lie close to Avebury, one near the Ridgeway path, another one of the sarsen standing stones of the West Kennet Avenue and another is set within the main passage of the West Kennet long barrow. The distinctive grinding hollows have been inadvertently exposed in the stone's reuse in the tomb passage. Very small polishing stones have been found in tool kits, from caches or graves, sometimes along with axes, adzes and sickles (**161**).

Pottery

Pottery is often considered to be a classic Neolithic invention that developed in response to the innovations of cereal food cooking and storage, and to sedentary life. Certainly, in Britain, pottery was present as soon as domesticated plants and animals were introduced and it is an important indicator of Neolithic occupation. Fired clay was a new medium in Neolithic communities, used for pottery and for daub on house walls. It was widely exploited, since good clays occur across the country. Some clays are highly distinctive because of the parent rock, as in the case of south-west Britain where Gabbroic rock and clay are easily identified. Whatever its source, clay was dug, seasoned and cleaned, mixed with various fillers, such as crushed burnt flint, shell or straw, and fashioned into vessels at a local level of production. All Neolithic pottery was hand-made, and built from simple coils or slabs into the great variety of forms and styles that characterise Neolithic ceramics. Regional and chronological identifications rest upon the overall shape of the pottery, round or flat based for example, on the shape of the rim, on the style of decoration, such as impressed bands, all-over patterns, top of rim patterns and so on. The addition of lugs, knobs, handles and cordons (applied bands to strengthen the pot) also makes the styles distinctive. The names given to pottery and their associated assemblages are usually type sites, although some groups are named after the pottery style itself, such as Grooved ware or Beaker. Pottery was fired at relatively low temperatures in bonfires and simple pit-kilns (often to less than *c*.850-1000°C), using a simple and uncontrollable technology that remained in use for several millennia. The low firing temperature and the large inclusions in the fabric combine to ensure that much Neolithic pottery barely survives once frost, water and plant roots penetrate the structure and reduce the pottery to little more than crumbs and putty-like mud. However, sufficient remains and Neolithic pottery has been much studied (see Gibson 1986; Gibson and Woods 1997 for a good introduction), and scholarship has produced a confusing variety of styles, forms, phases and distinct distributions. These are represented here in the illustrations, which aim to show the changing forms and decorative styles.

There is more to pottery than simply typology, chronology and distribution, however, and whilst it is important to retain the notion that pottery had practical functions for particular types of food preparation and presentation, notions of cultural identity expressed through distinctive form and decoration show vessels had many levels of symbolic meaning. These more elusive attributes become apparent when pottery is analysed in relation to its archaeological context and its associations. Clearly some material was given meaning through its burial, for example in tombs and ritual sites, where it may have been used as containers for gifts of food. In later prehistory, specific types of vessel were made to house the remains of the dead (burial urns), or as special offerings with them. The idea of structured deposition, where the fills of pits and ditches appear to contain intentional arrangements of pottery, rubbish, bones and suchlike, has become important over recent years. For example, the vast numbers of pig bones, and their emphasis on the right side of the skeleton from the West Kennet enclosures, appear to be highly structured and full of meaning. The same may well be true of much Neolithic pottery, as suggested by the associations of pot, bone, flint and skulls at Staines. Pottery also had exchange value, and in both Britain and Europe there are examples where fine pottery (such as the Cornish Gabbroic wares) was distributed over great areas, far from the original source. The great variety of different styles present at some causewayed enclosures such as Windmill Hill suggest that pots were traded or presented alongside products like axes, fine flint and doubtless other organic goods.

The earliest widespread pottery is the *Grimston-Lyles Hill* style (*c*.3750-2500 BC), which relates to parallel west European Earlier Neolithic styles like Michelsburg, Wijchen and Hazensonk. Pottery-making reached Britain *c*.4000 BC with the first elements of farming and settled society. Aspects of the Grimston-Lyles Hill style persisted for perhaps 1000

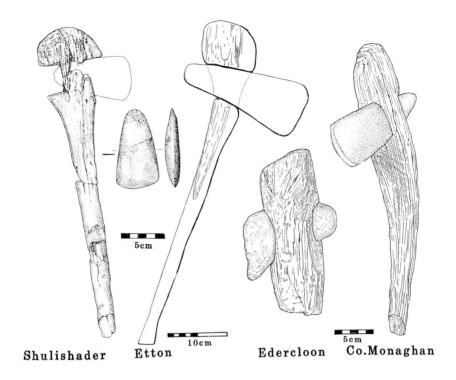

164 Hafted axes sometimes survive with handle and axe intact (from Etton, Cambridgeshire, Edercloon, Co. Longford, Co. Monaghan, Shulishader (Lewis) and Etton. After Pryor, Sheridan et al.

years across the eastern side of Britain, as indigenous developments began to dominate the repertoire. From *c*.3750 BC, the early undecorated carinated bowls that represent the earliest pottery were replaced by regional styles. In the south of Britain the *Windmill* culture (which includes *Abingdon)*, the Devon-Cornwall *Hembury* style and the *Whitehawk Hill* style of Sussex are associated with the long barrows and causewayed enclosure sites of the period *c*.3750-3000 BC. *Mildenhall* and *Broome Heath* are the contemporary styles in East Anglia. In the north-east midlands and north, *Grimston*, *Heslerton* and *Towthorpe* pottery styles, together with Windmill Hill-type monuments, are found in Lincolnshire and Yorkshire. Elements of Grimston pottery extend into Scotland and as Lyles Hill in Ireland.

Typically, Grimston-Lyles Hill pottery is found as plain, fairly shallow bowls, with simple everted, rolled rims and rounded bases. Sometimes a carination below the rim forms a shoulder, and small lugs were applied as decoration to a lightly burnished surface, which is a characteristic of the north-west European carinated bowl style, seen in France and across Britain and Ireland. Like many early ceramics, Grimston pottery was made of clay mixed with vegetable temper, and has an open cork-like fabric. The regional variations conform this pattern. The Heslerton style (only found at the typesite) has an S-shaped profile, and the Towthorpe variety has distinctive out-turned rims. The dark,

231

*165   The dramatic lakeland landscape of Great Langdale (Cumbria) was the scene of massive
        quarrying and axe making, and the Pike o'Stickle valley side — visible at the top right of the
        photograph (arrow), was where the finest tuff for Group VI axes was extracted.*
Photo CUCAP 17AG 268

burnished, Scottish Boghead Bowls (*c*.3000-2900 BC) are similar to the Lyles Hill style. These typically have fluted or ripple-burnished decoration on the inner and outer rim and neck area, above a slight carination. (**169**)

The East Anglian Mildenhall style is far more decorated although the overall shape is similar to Grimston-Lyles Hill. The decoration is impressed as lines and dots around the rim and shoulder of the pottery, with emphasis on the marked carinations. Forms include the typical open, round-based bowls of the earlier Neolithic as well as more closed jar forms.

The Windmill Hill styles form the pottery of the middle early Neolithic in the south-west of England (*c*.3700-2900 BC). First recognised at the type-site in north Wiltshire, the

166   *The axe quarry at Graig Clwyd in north Wales was so productive that the profile of the mountain is scarred with a deep notch.* Photo Mick Sharp

term was used generically but is now considered as a regional variant. Shallow, round-based, baggy pots and jars typify the style. Rims are simple or thickened, and sometimes decorated with incised lines and dots/stabs frequently repeated on the neck of carinated forms, and around the upper section of the vessel. Small oval lugs placed on the shoulder or upper part of the pot were sometimes perforated for suspension. The south-eastern variant is the Whitehawk Hill ware, which employs the familiar S-shaped profile vases, open bowls, and closed jar forms. The pottery is decorated with simple stabs, lines and whipped cord impressions around the neck and rim. Abingdon pottery (*c*.3500-3000 BC) of central southern England includes round-based shallow open bowls with and without carinations at the rim and deeper, rather shapeless pots. Rims are simple, rolled, everted and T-shaped and sometimes curved into carinated shoulders, which may be decorated with perforated lugs and the surface polished and burnished. The style typically has some decoration in the form of stabs, lines and impressed twisted cord marks around the rim, neck and shoulder. Abingdon ware is associated with limestone areas and the clay often includes shell and burnt flint. In the far south west, Hembury ware forms a distinctive, early simple round-based pottery. The 'classic' material was made from dark Gabbroic clay

167   *Schematic map showing the earlier Neolithic regional pottery styles of the so-called Western Neolithic, and distinctive northern and southern traditions in Britain and Ireland*

from the Lizard peninsula, although the style was widely imitated in local clays elsewhere. The forms are generally open bowls, and lugs and distinctive trumpet-shaped handles (**170**). The Irish pottery of the early Neolithic (from *c.*4000 BC) is the western Neolithic *Carinated Bowl* tradition, which seems to be ancestral to Grimston-Lyles. The pottery is round-based, mostly open bowls, usually dark red in colour and burnished, with a

168   Schematic map showing the later Neolithic regional ceramic styles within the Peterborough and Grooved Ware traditions

distinctive carinated shoulder, concave neck profiles, and rounded or slightly pointed everted rims. Decoration is simple and is little more than fluting or rippling burnished lines on the surface (similar to the *Boghead* bowls of Scotland) (**171**).

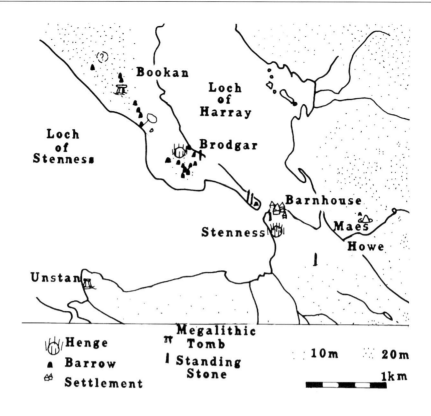

169   *Earlier Neolithic pottery of the Grimston Lyles-Hill tradition in Northern Britain*
      (Towthorpe, Heslerton, Grimston, Beacharra, Boghead and Unstan). Examples from
      Carnaby Top=CBT; Heslerton=Hes; North Canby=NC; Kilham=Kil; Thirlings=Th;
      Hanging Grimston=HG; Dyffryn Ardudwy=DA; Clegyr Boia=CB; Cairnholy,
      Beacharra=B; Boghead=BH; Clettravel=Cl; Kenny's Cairn=KC; Pitcapple=Pit;
      Pitnacree=Pitn; Archnacree=Ach; Rudh an Dunain=RD; Northton=N; Unstan=U;
      Midhow=M; Nether Largie=NL; Camster Long=CaL; Unival=Unv).
      Sources and scales — various

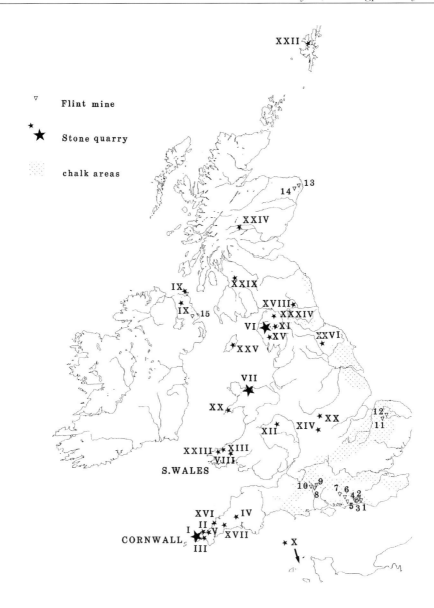

170   *Earlier Neolithic pottery traditions of southern Britain (Windmill Hill, Hembury, Mildenhall, Whitehawk, Hembury, Abingdon and Broome Heath). Etton=E; Hurst Fen=HF; Windmill Hill=WH; Abingdon=A; Whitehawk Hill=WhH; Hembury Hill=Hembury; Haylands House=HH; Coombe Hill=CH; Maiden Castle=MC; Carn Brea=CB; Chelms Coomb=CC; Norton Bavant=NB).* Sources and scales — various

There were several regional developments after around 3500 BC, including the *Limerick* and the classic *Lyles Hill* styles. These vases become thicker, more vertical and deeper, have a longer 'neck' between a markedly angular or T-shaped rim, and the noticeable angular carination that forms the curve for the base. Limerick pottery also has decorated rims and incised-ripple burnished patterns on the lower base section and lugs on the carination. Some vessels have suspension holes. Middle Neolithic derivatives of Lyles Hill pottery (from *c.*3500-2900BC) are more decorated and have cord impressed patterns arranged in triangles, rectangles and bands. These styles (if indeed they really are separate styles) include the so-called *Goodland bowls* (from Antrim) with simple inturned rim forms; the *Sandhills* pottery, *Dundrum* bowls, the broad-rimmed forms, *Murlough* bowls and *Carrowkeel* pottery. These all employ more exuberant use of stab-drag, cord and finger impressed decoration, lugs, larger and heavier rims or collars and, in the case of Carrowkeel, highly decorated bases. Bipartite forms develop in the Middle Neolithic from the carinated bowl tradition (see below).

Later Neolithic styles

Pottery of the middle to later Neolithic from around 3200 BC, in southern and eastern Britain, is dominated by the so-called Peterborough styles. This is the now generic term for several regional and chronological developments. This material typically has flat bases and decorated, prominent rims

The flattened or slightly rounded bases of this well-developed pottery and its transition to flat base tells us more, perhaps, about changing attitudes to food and furniture than simply a typological change. Flat bases may imply that pottery was used at a table and was required to stand steady on a flat surface, whereas the round-based vessels were ideal for placing on the hearth, on an earthen floor or on mat rings of straw or similar material. Pottery forms thus imply that table manners and food preparation had evolved considerably between the earlier and later Neolithic.

Peterbrorough styles

Ebbsfleet pottery distribution is focused around Kent and the Thames basin although, together with *Mortlake* pottery, it is found as far away as Wales and the Midlands. They have rounded bases, long S-profile rims and wide necks with decoration, and further decoration on the sharp carination and shoulders formed by impressed whipped cord impressions. Although simple, the decoration includes criss-cross and herringbone patterns covering a large surface area. Mortlake pottery probably develops from Ebbsfleet and is distinguished by a heavier, more rounded or angular rim below which is a thinner neck. There is much variety in the decoration covering the upper part of the vessel, which involves designs of herringbone and circles using cord and other impressed and stamped patterns from bone, tools and fingers. *Fengate* pottery differs from the two previous styles in having a tapered and very small flat base and a heavy rim-collar, but it seems to follow a logical evolution from Mortlake to Fengate. Although all three styles occur together at some sites, as at West Kennet long barrow before 2500 BC, Ebbsfleet is present before 3000 BC, and forms of Fengate persist until as late as 2000 BC, suggesting a very long duration of Peterborough styles. The Fengate style anticipates several elements of the early

Bronze Age collared urns, with its heavy collared rim and decorative motifs. The northern Peterborough tradition has strong Mortlake elements, and includes *Rudston* in Yorkshire, *Meldon Bridge* in the Scottish Borders and the Northumbrian *Ford* styles. Rudston has some Mortlake elements, flat bases were favoured, and the rim forms a T-section profile, much in the tradition of the earlier local *Towthorpe bowls*. Decoration is over the rim and body of the pot in bands of lines and herringbone motifs. *Meldon Bridge* pottery is round-based and similar to Mortlake, but the rims are more angular and finished with a bevelled angle and heavy rim-collar, which anticipates later Food Vessel forms. The pottery is decorated with cord and bird bone impressions arranged in herringbone motifs. *Ford* pottery links the Meldon Bridge and Rudston styles across space, and is distinguished by a large rounded rim above a concave neck, below which the body was lavishly decorated with cord and linear patterns.

Later Neolithic styles in Scotland also reflect the Mortlake tradition of impressed decoration and round-based forms, especially at *Glenluce* on the west and *Brackmont Mill* on the east. By the later third millennium BC a rich variety of styles had developed, including the baggy forms of the *Rothesay*, and the earlier carinated forms of the *Beacharra* styles of the Clyde area (formerly known as the Clyde-Carlingford culture). The decorated panels around the carination have close parallels to the Orkadian *Unstan* style and *Hebridean bowl* pottery, which predominated in the earlier third millennium BC. Round-based, with heavy, vertical collar-like rims, these styles have parallels with Irish bipartite vessels. Decoration is limited to the collar as triangles and lines made by stab and drag techniques. (**169 & 172**)

Grooved wares

Once named the Rinyo-Clacton style, Grooved ware pottery has increasingly become synonymous with later Neolithic ritual sites in southern Britain, and with settlements in the north (Cleal & MacSween 1999). The style developed in Scotland in the early third millennium BC but later, perhaps around 2500-2300 BC, became frequent in the south. It is distinct from the Peterborough styles, with its chunky flat-based bucket forms, heavy grooved patterns and rusticated ribs and cordons. Four distinct sub-styles are currently recognised. The *Clacton* has a simple rounded rim, with an exterior of grooved or plastic decoration of triangles, lozenges and rectangles with stabbed infill, and incised and filled chevrons. The Clacton type-site was a settlement on the Essex coast. The *Durrington* (or *Woodhenge)* style is associated with the Wessex henges and has six distinct characteristic elements. These are an internally bevelled rim which can be decorated on the inside, grooved spirals and circles and the exterior divided into panels by vertical grooved cordons, which may be filled with triangles and incised lines. The decoration is made by impressed cords and incisions. A parallel style, the *Woodlands* grooved ware, has been found on settlement sites, and differs from the henge material. The vessels are smaller and decorated cordons are applied across the body of the pot, forming a ladder-like pattern. Small knobs mark the crossings of the cordons and are also placed around the rim. The cordons have small slash line decorations as well as fingernail impressions. The *Rinyo* of Scotland and the north is mostly known from domestic sites like Skara Brae. It has rims bevelled on the interior and sometimes scalloped on the outside. The grooved decoration is arranged on cordons and in parallel grooves (MacSween 1995).

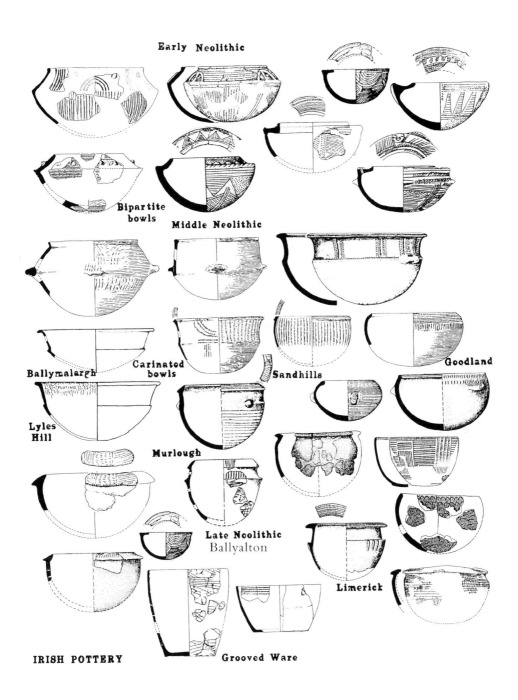

171   *Irish Neolithic Pottery: carinated bowls — Boghead, Limerick, Dundrum, Carrowkeel,
Murlough, Sandhills. Broad-rimmed pottery — later Neolithic Irish carinated bowls,
Ballyalton bowls*

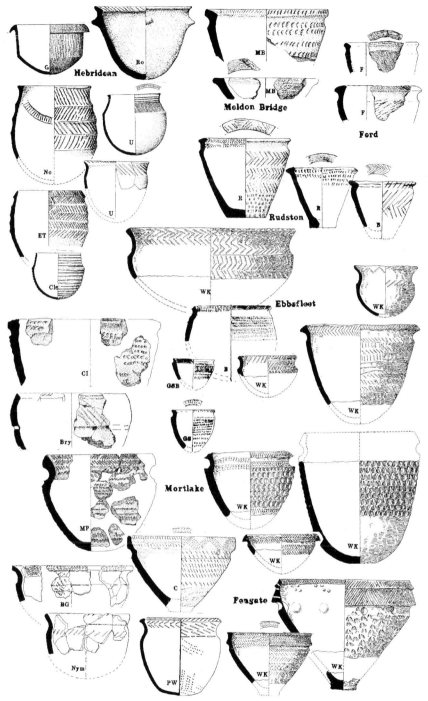

172 *Middle-later Neolithic Peterborough style Pottery had many local interpretations of the impressed decoration and elaborate rim-forms (B = Boynton; GS = Garton Slack; GSB = Garton Slack Barrow; MP = Mount Pleasant, Wales; WK = West Kennet long barrow; CI = Caldey Island; Bry = Brynderiwen; C = Cam; BG = Burnt Ground; Nym = Nympsfield; PW = Pole's Wood; R = Rudston; F = Ford; MB = Meldon Bridge; G = Glenvoidean; Ro = Rothsay; No = Northton; U = Unival; Cle = Cletraval; ET = Eilean an Tighe).* After Henshall, Manby, Burgess, Piggott, Darvill, Gibson and others

Irish later Neolithic pottery

Developing from the Irish Carinated bowl tradition, closed and bipartite forms and more elaborate pottery typify the later Neolithic styles from before 3000 to the Beakers of the early second millennium BC, as a stylistic development towards Grooved Ware. *Ballyalton* bowls have sharply angled shoulders and an inturned rim forming a narrow-mouthed jar. Cord decoration and parallel grooved line decoration are typical and there are strong parallels to styles in Scotland. Grooved Ware appears in the early third millennium BC in Ireland as the distinctive flat-bottomed flowerpot shaped pottery. Typically this material has parallel grooves for decoration and has particularly been found at Knowth and Newgrange in the east (see Sheridan 1995).

Pottery of the final Neolithic and Copper Age

The emergence of metal technology in the final centuries of the third millennium BC brought indigenous ceramic styles and cultural isolation in Britain to an end. There were increasing trade links to Europe, and new ideas in artefact production and materials began to have a profound impact on the British Isles. The Beakers especially are seen as one of the major European trends that were adopted. Beakers are more than pots, since they seem to be associated with many new social, technological and economic changes. They were often placed in burials, along with barbed and tanged arrowheads, copper daggers, distinctive V-perforated buttons, pins, jewellery made of amber, jet, bone and stone, archer's stone wrist guards and flint scrapers and tools. The most obvious change was that the graves were invariably the burials of one (or a very few) individual(s), instead of the great collective graves of the Neolithic. The style of grave varied across Europe, from Poland to Ireland, from Scandinavia to North Africa, and so did the artefacts, societies and pottery. But nevertheless, the Beaker culture seemed to link this immense area, through similarities of artefacts and burial rites, and perhaps a growing interest in communal drinking and perhaps alcohol production. In some areas Beakers are found on settlements, but the best evidence for the new fashion is invariably offered by the graves of well-equipped archers and budding warriors. This culture honoured a new breed of male warriors using the latest in metal weapons, and indicates the beginning of a much more stratified and belicose society than was evident in the Neolithic (Clarke et al 1985).

British Beakers have been much studied, and here is not the place for more discussion. Briefly, the pottery begins to appear from *c*.2500 BC, still well within the late Neolithic period. The early Beaker style was probably closely related to Beakers in the Netherlands, and made from fine, often reddish clay, with a gentle S-shaped profile forming a low belly to the pot, with everted rims. There was decoration all over the body of the pot, incised with carefully executed cord and comb patterns in horizontal bands.

The middle period of Beakers in Britain saw them become more decorative, with wider bands, employing larger diamonds, triangles and filled/open patterns often executed with fingernails, cords and shaped tools. The neck area of the pot became shorter, wider and often more curved to the belly area of the vessel.

By the later Beaker period, between *c*.2000-1700 BC, the shape changed considerably, anticipating the early Bronze Age pottery that followed. The neck of the pot became clearly distinguished from the previous sinuous profile, and is marked by a straight almost vertical neck above a comparatively short bulbous body. In some instances, Beakers have handles and look almost like beer mugs with patterned bases. The patterns are divided into two main zones, the neck and the belly, and different patterns, such as cord impressions or zones of filled geometric motifs and zig-zags; some Beakers have rough, rusticated surfaces and are very large (**183**).

Alongside the Beaker developments, an indigenous style emerged from the northern Peterborough and Meldon Bridge traditions. This was the *Food Vessel and Urn* style, centered on the north and west of Britain. The pottery is mostly quite small, rarely more than 20cm in height, with a flat base, and a bipartite form with a heavy rim below which is a marked concave 'cavetto' neck and a wide belly. The shoulder groove varies, and may be emphasised by a handle or knobs and cordons with incised decoration, especially in the Yorkshire type. In the south, more angular forms predominate and these have less elaborate decoration in bands of impressed or incised lines and motifs. Some examples have applied cordons in vertical patterns, the so-called *Ridged vases*. The simplest forms of *Food Vessel* are the bucket shaped types, including *Globular British bowls*, which are squatter and shallower than the typical Food vessels. Scottish and Irish examples — the *Hiberno-Scottish bowls* — are the most elaborately decorated of these forms, employing combed patterns and applied relief zones. The bowls range from simple forms to waisted styles with horizontal cordons defining a marked concave waist. The waisted form develops into Tripartite bowls which have several horizontal ridges and troughs, decorated with bands of incised/impressed patterns. Deep grooved decoration, which seems to develop from Grooved ware traditions, is employed across the belly of some pots, especially in the north Although the name Food Vessel implies a domestic use, the pottery was also used in burial contexts across the north of Britain. It seems to have gone gradually out of use in the first third of the second millennium BC, to be replaced by *Encrusted urns* and other styles typical of the Bronze Age. Concurrent with the Food Vessels at the beginning of the second millennium BC were *collared urns*. They were widely distributed across Britain and Ireland, but were rare in northern Scotland. The heavy collared rim seems to have evolved from the Fengate style of the later Neolithic Peterborough wares, and also contains elements of Beaker decoration, comb impressions in particular. The form, like the Food Vessels, employs a thick rim set vertically to diagonally above a curved concave neck. Decoration is reserved to the collar and the neck/shoulder area of the vessel. These vessels seem to have been made particularly for cremation burials.

In Ireland, Beakers follow the same stylistic evolution as in Britain, from the early All-Over Corded style, to the later more elaborate comb decorated forms. The final Irish Beakers tend to be insular in style, with tall, wide everted rims and employing a broad range of decorative motifs and techniques. Although most of the known sites lie in the northern half of Ireland, this reflects the levels of research and fieldwork, for where research has been intensive, as at Lough Gur, considerable numbers of Beaker settlements and tombs have been found. The development of *Food Vessels* and *Food Bowls* follows a similar course to mainland Britain, but Food Bowls are far more frequent in Ireland, where hundreds of findspots are associated with cist and pit graves, and occasional megalithic sites. Some pottery has been found on settlements, but the main association is with burial sites. The bowls range from simple and bipartite forms and bowls with necks to more complex tripartite and rib-decorated examples, which sometimes, especially in the north, have lugs.

Rinyo style

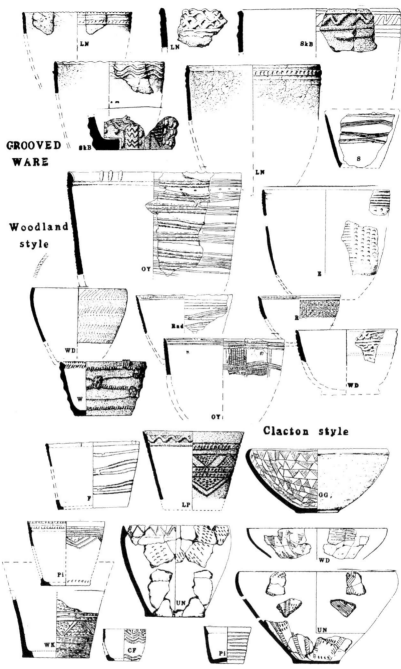

173 Grooved Ware pottery styles of the Rinyo, Clacton and the Woodlands sub-styles. Upper Ninepence=UP; Corp Farm=CF; West Kennet Long Barrow=WK; Wyke Down=WD; Grimes Grave=GG; Etton=E; Old Yeavering=OY; Woodland=W; Flamborough=F; Lion Point=LP; Roughground Farm=R; Radkey=Rad; Stenness=S; Skara Brae=SkB; Links of Noltland=LN

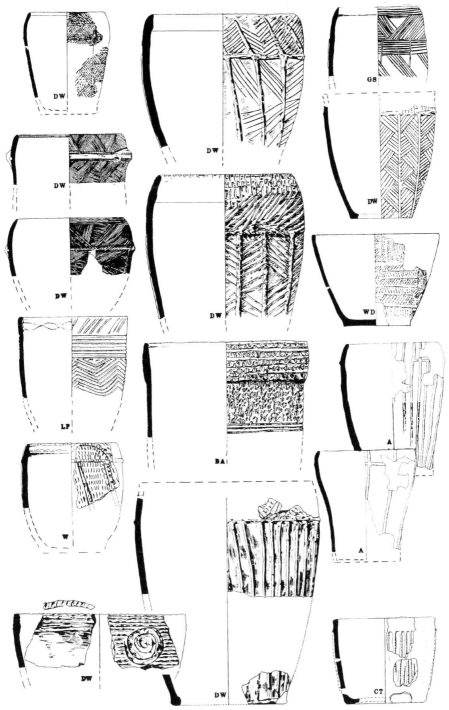

174   *Grooved Ware pottery of the Durrington style.*
Burton Agnes=BA; Willingdon=W; Lion Poin=LP; Garton Slack=GS; Durrington
Walls=DW; Carnaby Temple=CB; Abingdon Common=A; Wyke Down=WD).
Sources and scales — various

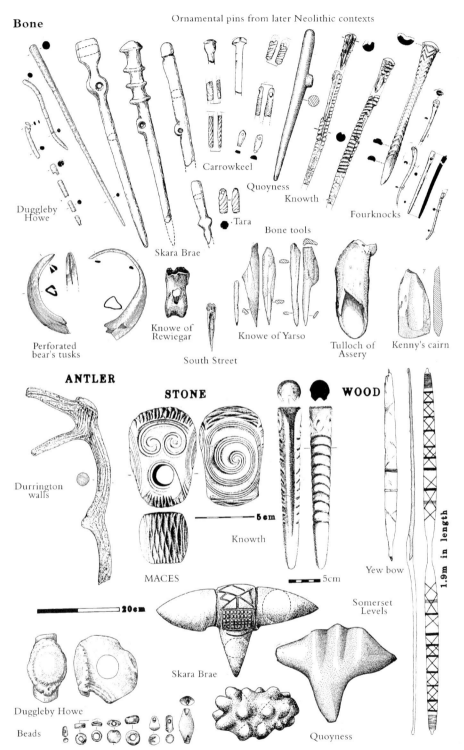

Bone

Ornamental pins from later Neolithic contexts

Carrowkeel

Quoyness

Knowth

Fourknocks

Duggleby Howe

Tara

Skara Brae

Bone tools

Perforated bear's tusks

Knowe of Rewiegar

South Street

Knowe of Yarso

Tulloch of Assery

Kenny's cairn

ANTLER

Durrington walls

STONE

WOOD

Knowth

MACES

5cm

Yew bow

Somerset Levels

1.9m in length

20cm

Skara Brae

Duggleby Howe

Beads

Quoyness

5cm

175 *Decorative bone and stone from late Neolithic burials, antler, beads and utilitarian points. Yew bow from Somerset levels. After Henshall, Eogan, Kinnes, Ashbee, Clark, Coles*

Other materials

Local materials predominated in the domestic needs of Neolithic communities and wood, bone, stone, antler, horn, twine and vegetable fibres and leather were generally sourced close by (**175**). Most of these materials do not survive the ravages of time, soil and later disturbance, so a biased picture of stone and pots emerges that dominates our idea of life in the Neolithic. Unless burnt and preserved as carbonised remains, organic materials (wood, bone, fibre and so on) only survive in exceptional conditions — either very dry or very wet (only the latter applies to Britain!). Wetlands such as the Cambridgeshire fens, Irish bogs and Somerset Levels preserve Neolithic wood, baskets and fibres, but bone and untanned leather are usually destroyed. The settlements of the Swiss lakes provide a vivid picture of the organic materials that were used in typical Neolithic sites, and analogous materials doubtless were in use in Britain. Prehistoric trackways from the peatlands of Somerset and Ireland are impressive examples of organic preservation, showing the complex technology employed in shaping timber, hurdles and wooden objects like canoe paddles, bows and wooden bowls. This evidence not only demonstrates the technical aspects but the different qualities of the woods selected for particular types of tool and object.

Crafts — weaving, woodworking, house building, dress and ornament

Many crafts in the Neolithic were less distinctive of the period than pottery or stonework, and some varied little in style or technology from the Mesolithic to the medieval. Animal bone, preferably hard and fine-grained like sheep carpels or bird bone, was routinely worked. Split into sharp pointed pieces, it could be worked into points, needles, pins, decorating tools, combs, buttons, toggles, spoons and spatulae. Most domestic sites in non-acidic conditions have revealed examples of worked bone, horn and antler, and the qualities of the materials meant they could be used for many items that were later made of metals or plastics, horn for spatulae and drinking vessels, and antler for hafts, combs, picks and maces.

Basketry is a very under-represented craft in material surviving from the British Neolithic, but rare examples and impressions on pottery show a complex range of plaiting and twisting techniques. Contemporary Swiss lake villages have preserved examples, and in modern traditional societies basketry is still a major method of making storage containers, room dividers, furniture and suchlike. Similarly, weaving, rope-making and textiles of all types are rarely preserved, although impressions on pottery again provide some clues. The full weaving of wool or linen, knitting, crochet, knotting and suchlike were late developments, and are attested by the presence of loom weights, needles, combs and spindle whorls, associated with the later Neolithic and Beaker periods. Early Neolithic textiles may have been simple weaves and mats of fibres, but the dominant form of material seems to have been leather, suede and animal skins, which were perhaps stitched simply together through holes punched by flint piercers and bone points. As was shown recently in research of the alpine Ice Man's clothes, early leather was not tanned using conventional tannins, and thus was not preserved unless frozen. It is unlikely these very specific conditions will be found in the British Isles.

Grooved wares

Dates Cal BC	South East	South West/S Wales	Midlands	North	Scotland	Ireland
4000	Grimston Whitehawk	Hembury Windmill Hill Abingdon	Grimston Mildenhall	Grimston Heslerton Towthorpe	Grimston	Carinated & Lyles Hill Limerick Decorated Bowls Goodland/Sandhill
3500	Fengate Peterboro Mortlake Ebbsfleet	Fengate/Ebbsfleet/ Mortlak Peterboro	Fengate Peterboro Mortlake Ebbsfleet	Ronaldways Peterboro Meldon Bridge Rudston	Meldon Bridge/ Hebridean/Rinyo Ford/Unstan/ Rothesay Beachara	Bipartite Bowls/Ballyalton Grooved Ware
3000		Grooved Ware		Ford Peterboro Fengate Food Vessles		Knockadoon
2500	Grooved Ware Beakers/ Food vessels	Beakers/ Food Vessels	Grooved Ware Beakers Food vessels		Grooved Ware Beakers food vessels	
2000						

Wood was undoubtedly a major craft material, used for construction projects of many types. Without metal saws, the working of wood was arduous, but techniques were developed to speed the process. Axes were used to fell timber and clean branches. Logs could be split by the gradual insertion of wooden wedges, hammered longitudinally along the felled trunk. Once split, planks were formed, and from these, smaller pieces of wood were fashioned into tools, building materials, or whatever was required, using flint and stone tools. Canoes were hollowed out of large tree trunks, using adzes. Experimental archaeology has shown that technique and practise are far more effective in working natural materials than particularly sophisticated tools.

8 The Neolithic achievement

Conclusions

The aim of this book has been to try and summarise what we do, and what we can, know about the Neolithic in Britain, and also to suggest where new research is needed to explore different areas of evidence. Many of the most famous sites have been deliberately played down, since entire libraries exist to ponder on them, and instead lesser-known sites are discussed, in the hope that new generations of scholars and field workers will look more broadly across the vast canvas of the Neolithic. What should have become apparent to the reader, from the innumerable examples presented here, is the great amount of information that has come to light about this remote period, the range and diversity of artefacts, sites and landscapes across the British Isles and Ireland, and the many questions that archaeologists are beginning to ask of them. But there are nevertheless gaping holes in the narrative, and it is not clear whether evidence survives to fill them.

The lack of settlements, and thus understanding of their nature, size, longevity, economy or location, over most of the region means that some first principles cannot be addressed. We cannot know the scale of Neolithic societies at the household level, village level or local level without settlement and population evidence, and building models for reconstructing social organisation is also fraught with uncertainties. Without settlement evidence it is extremely difficult to assess the economic basis of daily life. Instead, curious ritual sites that were probably on the margins of everyday life must suffice in painting a picture of Neolithic subsistence.

The people themselves are only partially represented, although one or two notable sites like Hazelton North and Isbister give graphic indications of whole tomb populations. For the most part, excavation has explored only damaged sites (like Callis Wold) or parts of larger burial complexes (such as West Kennet Barrow). Far too many of the precious burial sites were looted and wrecked by antiquarian diggers. The remaining tombs are mostly preserved as Scheduled Ancient Monuments and are technically protected from archaeological or other disturbance, although they are still subject to damage from erosion, ploughing and time itself. Whilst preserving sites for the future is ethically sound, the result is rare samples of bones but not whole tomb populations, and we can guess numbers of burials (like the supposed population of Quanterness) but no more. Equally, modern excavation techniques are far more likely to extract information from burial sites than old digs were, but such opportunities are rare indeed. Beyond the burial evidence of skeletons, the personality, tastes and identities of Neolithic people are almost impossible to envisage. Little evidence that might relate to identifiable individuals exists, and inevitably people of the Neolithic remain very hazy and uncertain. We can not even know

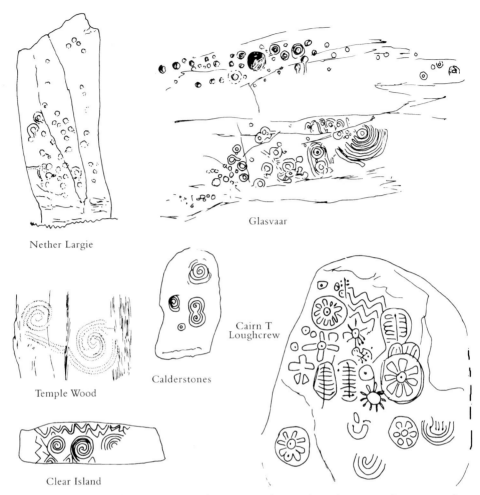

176   Examples of Neolithic/Bronze Age rock art: cup marks, spirals, and more complex patterns of tombs, standing stones and natural rock (Nether Largie and Temple Wood — Scotland; Clear Island and Loughcrew — Ireland; Claderstones — Liverpool). After RCHAMS and Herity

how they dressed, other than assume that simple skin, fur, roughly woven linen and fibres formed clothing secured by bone toggles and crude stitching.

Neolithic landscape studies are a fruitful area of research at the present time, with a variety of approaches and new methodologies attempting to examine the broad trends of settlement, monuments and change (Topping 1997). Extensive gravel quarries provide unprecedented opportunities for far-reaching landscape research, with notable examples in the Thames valley in Oxfordshire (Hey 1997), the Trent valley in Derbyshire/Nottinghamshire and in the river systems of Cambridgeshire, Bedfordshire and Northamptonshire. These interventions allow entire buried landscape to be examined minutely, and often unseen features are found relating to more obvious monuments, such as the ring ditches associated with cursus sites, as seen at Brampton in the Ouse valley of Bedfordshire-Cambridgeshire (**60**) (Dawson. 2000)

Knowth Rectilinear art in eastern tomb

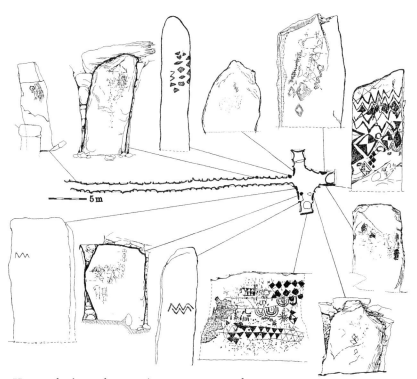

Knowth Angular art in eastern tomb

177   Passage grave art styles and their locations in Knowth, Co. Meath. After Eogan

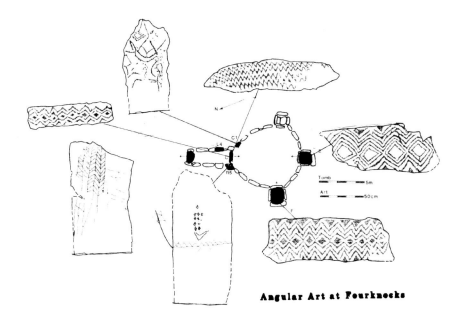

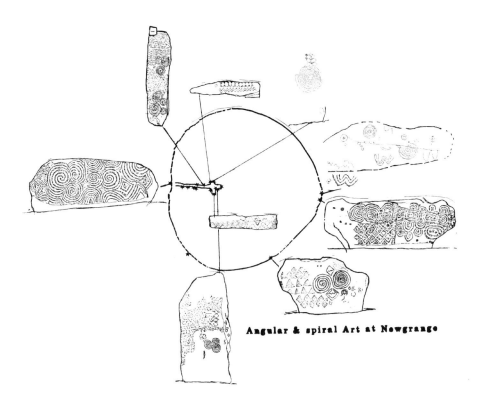

178   *Plan of decorated stones in Newgrange and Fourknocks (Co. Meath) show that particular areas of passage and chamber were given special significance.* After Eogan

179   Decorated kerb stone at Newgrange, Co. Meath. Photo C. Malone

Artefacts have traditionally been a rich research province, and until two decades ago many research projects were focused on the classes of lithic, pottery or bone. Fashions changed, perhaps temporarily, while other forms of data and investigation became relevant, such as landscape phenomenology. The artefacts remain in many museum stores as one of the richest sources of data on the Neolithic, however, and await new researchers and questions.

Recent research includes the scientific analysis of materials such as pottery, their fabrics and investigations of their organic contents (such as milk or vegetables). In time, this may show that particular types of pottery were used for specific tasks or foods, and perhaps had specialised functions and identities. Such studies have become routine for later periods, but Neolithic pottery is still a rare and relatively little studied class of artefact. The same is true of bone-work, which is known from pins, awls, toggles and spatulae, but has received little comprehensive treatment. Microwear analysis of lithics has also been an area of intense study, showing that some tools were used for specific types of material and activity, for example harvesting reeds for thatch, cutting leather, or paring wood. Yet the technique relies on material from pristine contexts and these are often rare in Neolithic sites.

A particularly rich area of study that has recently become important is Neolithic rock art, especially the engraved patterns on passage graves and in the wider landscape (Bradley 1993; 1997; Eogan 1986; Shee Twohig 1981; Beckensall 1986, 1999). 'Art' sites are often difficult to date, but the presence of the rich designs in the passage graves from the beginning of the third millennium BC implies many of the rocks in the landscape were decorated at much the same time. Rock art studies in many continents has become very fashionable of late, and it is tempting to over-interpret it and assume that in the twenty-first century we can 'read' the meaning of patterns and symbols. However, Bradley points out that mobile people such as those who might have grazed stock in the remoter rocky

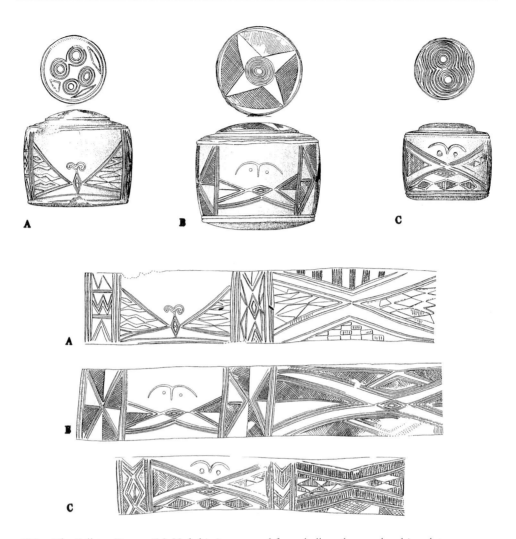

180 *The Folkton Drums (N. Yorkshire) are carved from chalk and were placed in a later*
Neolithic grave. Their complex patterns are some of the most enigmatic known from Neolithic
Britain. After Longworth

uplands of Britain, and taken paths to quarries or sacred places, would have identified their
routes by the paths and sites marked along them. Distinct from territorial monuments
which marked the land, paths through places and the views from them become all
significant. Marking the rocks with designs and symbols was a way of identifying them,
investing meaning and place in them, and communicating through symbols and
signatures of ownership. The rock art consists of zig-zags, concentric rings and cup marks,
linear and geometric patterns of triangles. It is never naturalistic in Britain (unlike
Scandinavia or the Alps), except in rare examples from the early Bronze Age when daggers
and similar objects were depicted. Instead, the patterns are mysterious, with forms that
might be likened to the shapes of henges, houses and passage tombs, to torcs and rings, to

181   Map of rock art in the British Isles

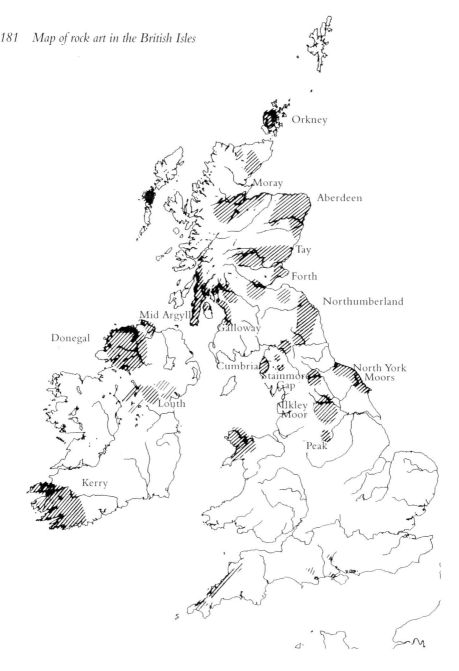

the sun, moon and stars and early metalwork spirals. They occur in the Peak district, Ilkley Moor, the North York Moors, the Stainmore Gap, Northumberland, Cumbria, Galloway, Argyll and Strath Tay, and in Ireland in Louth, Donegal and Kerry. Exceptional sites also occur associated with tombs on Orkney, Clava, and the Boyne area.

Bradley's work suggests that many British rock art sites were inter-visible with each other or with ceremonial sites in the landscape. Apart from the sheer interest of these sites,

*182   The Folkton Chalk Drums (N. Yorkshire) from a later Neolithic burial are some of the finest
examples of later Neolithic art. There are strong similarities between the motifs on the drums
and Grooved ware pottery patterns and some rock art.* Photo British Museum

the presence of rock art in the remotest places of Britain shows that *all* the landscape was
known and visited. No part of it was excluded, and Neolithic people exploited, identified,
marked and knew their land very well.

Art in tombs and other 'material culture'

The increasing use of 'art' on rock faces and on objects is a particular feature of later
Neolithic, with close parallels to the spiral and geometric repertoire repeated across
Europe, from Scandinavia to Malta. One particularly intriguing example is seen in the
chalk Folkton Drums from a later Neolithic burial in Yorkshire. The patterns on all faces
of these inexplicable objects are almost anthropomorphic, which may indeed have been
the intention of the prehistoric carver who made them (**180, 182**).

Passage grave art, engraved on the megalithic blocks of passages, chambers and kerbs,
represents a remarkable source of 'art' in late Neolithic Britan and Ireland. Eogan has
shown how particular groups of pattern apppear to be intentionally located and
symbolically used, as at Knowth and Newgrange. The repertoire of patterns and designs
is broad, and there are many combinations. Interestingly, similar motifs (triangles, zigzags,
dots, lines, filled and unfilled shapes and so on) are repeated on much of the more
decorated pottery styles (see chapter 7). The repertoires of design might be linked in a
general way, as evidence for Neolithic tastes in decoration, and perhaps, more subtley, in
meaning and ethnic identity (**176-178**).

Decoration of other craft objects seems to conform broadly; an example of a highly-
decorated object is the Somerset level Yew Bow. Less fine (and possibly even faked) chalk
carvings are known from the mine shafts at Grimes Graves and include a possible figure
and odd phallic objects. A more convincing example of art in chalk was unearthed during

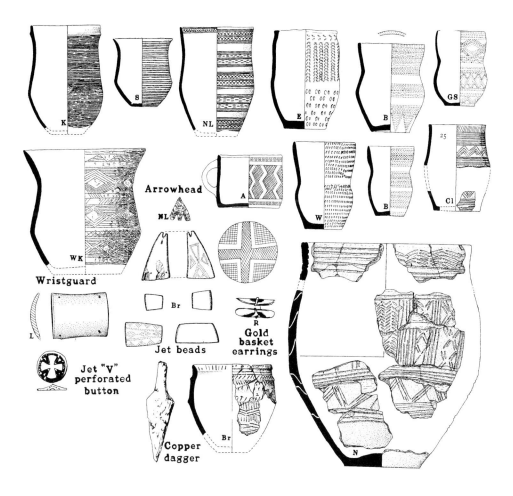

183   *Pottery-Beaker traditions and the later Neolithic — Early Copper Age Beaker assemblage.*
K = Kicoys; S= Sandywell; NL = Nether Largie; E = Eynsham; B = Broomend;
GS = Garton Slack; WK = West Kennet long barrow; A = Aldro; W = Wilsford;
Cl = Cletraval; L= Liveras; Br = Brackley; Rud = Rudston; R = Radley;
N = Northton. After Henshall, Case, Piggott, Gibson, and others

the Dorchester bypass construction work, when a series of incised lines/patterns were identified on the side of a cut chalk ditch. Rather similar linear 'patterns' have been recorded at Skara Brae.

Unlike southern and eastern/central Europe, Britian and north-west Europe seem to have no tradition of making plastic clay figures or convincing attempts at human or animal forms. Indeed, realistic or even schematic artistic representation appears to be missing from Neolithic or Bronze Age cultures in the region.

Prehistoric (and Neolithic) art should naturally be a theme of great interest. Rock art has rather dominated study, when in fact there are many areas of craft and decoration that can quite justifiably be called 'art'. The most obvious is the detailed decoration (mentioned in chapter 5) of megaliths in passage graves.

Changing visions of the Bronze Age

What sort of world greeted the societies of Britain at the end of the third millennium BC? A number of adventurous imaginative novels have been penned on this subject, mostly using Stonehenge as the central pivot of the stories. Their authors are to be applauded for trying to paint vivid pictures of the status-conscious, male-orientated and, frankly, pugnacious world that seems to characterise the Beaker and Early Bronze Age in Britain. However, there is no beginning or end that conveniently marks the change from Neolithic to metal-using societies; indeed, it is probably retrograde, 'Three-Age-System' narrowness that still allows us to call the Neolithic and the Bronze Age these names at all! But what else is better? Dating and the fashion for naming episodes after millennia can come unstuck too, as new calibrations and refinements show that a millennium can be a very long time, even in prehistory. Culture names are a little more appealing, although they focus the mind on type sites, technologies and pots, which are useful aide-memoires but not representative of the whole. The Beaker people undoubtedly have had the misfortune to be called after their drinking pots at the expense of anything else. But it is with the Beakers that this book must finish.

In Europe, the betwixt and between episode of the Copper Age (or Eneolithic or Chalcolithic) occupies a much clearer space in archaeology than it does in Britain. Metal technology came late and came fast in Britain, compared with other parts of Europe where a millennium or more was spent experimenting with copper, silver and gold, before methods of alloying tin with copper introduced bronze (Brodie 1994). The earliest copper objects in Britain predate the appearance of Beakers, but it is with Beaker that the new technology was most prominently displayed, on the person, in battle, and in burials. The typical Beaker male burial, from *c*.2400 to 2000 BC, most likely includes a fine decorated Beaker pot, barbed and tanged flint arrowheads, a copper tanged dagger, a stone wristguard, possibly a stone axe or slate polisher, personal ornaments made of amber, gold, copper or bone. It is probably in a single grave (perhaps under a low mound), and perhaps with other family members inserted close by. Female Beaker burials do not contain weapons, but often include a beaker pot, shale and jet beads, a copper or bronze awl, bone and antler tools and flint knives. Status and hierarchy were prominent in many Beaker burials, as in the Barnack (Cambridgeshire) example. A ring ditch 11.5m in diameter contained a central grave (of an adult male with beaker, bronze dagger, bone pendant and wristguard) surrounded by 15 further graves, of which only three had any gravegoods at all. The whole group was then buried under a mound. Unlike the collective burial rites of the earlier Neolithic, the Copper Age Beaker people appear to have celebrated the status of just one (invariably male) individual, and to have accepted their lowly status in relation to him. By the early Bronze Age, in the first centuries of the second millennium BC, this trend for high status and richly endowed individuals had reached its zenith in the so-called 'Wessex Culture' in southern Britain, and in comparable expressions of wealth elsewhere.

Under impressive tumulus mounds arranged in cemeteries in prominent places, the chiefly rulers of the region developed even further the traditions of status and wealth that their Neolithic and Beaker predecessors had begun. Fabulous goods made of gold, jet, amber, bronze, stone, flint and bone/antler represent some of the finest products of the prehistoric craftsmen of ancient Britain. In some ways, though, only the bronze technology, in the form of daggers, pins and rings, was new. The other technologies — fashions in ornament, ritual treatment of the dead — were the final products of the Neolithic that had emerged over the previous two millennia, changing gradually and finally into the Bronze Age.

What next for the Neolithic?

The body of archaeological evidence that now constitutes our knowledge of Neolithic Britain and Ireland has been documented over many decades of fieldwork and scholarship. At last perhaps, some regions and some themes are becoming well enough known for scholars to begin to pose searching questions about the period and its communities. The reader may have gained the impression that the sheer range of sites and types and forms discussed here constitutes sufficient, but we are really only just starting to understand that remote place — the Neolithic! Recognition is a beginning, but even expert surveyors lack the terminology to categorize the vast range of Neolithic monuments — for example, a cursus is a cursus in all the lists and studies, but there is massive variety in just this 'class' of monument. The same is true of most of the field monuments, and even more obvious in artefact definitions. There have been studies of some categories — arrowheads and Grooved ware pottery for example, but the rest still need study. And this study needs to go beyond the simple 'stamp-collecting' excercise of lists and distribution, and needs to examine the minutiae of context and association and seek understanding of the role of each artefact. The same demands are being sounded from other periods of archaeology, and there is much to be done across the many specialist fields of archaeology from survey and new excavation, to new scientific analysis and interpretation.

Sites to visit and museum collections

Over 600 Neolithic sites are listed here, which remain visible and sufficiently coherent and interesting to justify visiting. A star indicates public access (English Heritage, National Trust, Local Authority, Parks etc.). Many other sites are close to public footpaths or roads, but visitors should check access with landowners before entering private land. Six-figure (and some four-figure) Ordnance Survey grid references are given for each site to aid location. Readers are advised to use 1:50,000 or 1:25,000 scale maps. Many regional guidebooks and manuals (English Heritage, Historic Scotland etc.) provide detail of individual sites. Some chambered tombs allow access to the chambers, and viewing benefits from a torch.

The internet now has excellent data on British and Irish sites and their monument archives. Consult RCHAMS (Royal Commission for Historical and Ancient Monuments in Scotland — CANMORE database), English Heritage's National Monument Record (NMR), the Welsh Royal Commission for Historical Monuments (Wales) and CADW, and the Irish Heritage Service (DUCHAS), which have increasingly sohisticated access to information, maps, photographs and archives.

England
Reading
T. Darvill 1987 *Prehistoric Britain*. Batsford. London
James Dyer 1973 *Southern England: an Archaeological Guide*. Faber
James Dyer 1973 *Ancient Britain*. Faber
V. Megaw & D.D.A. Simpson 1979 *Introduction to British Prehistory*. Leicestershire University Press
Shire Archaeological Guides
English Heritage regional and site guides
National Trust site guides
Historic Scotland Regional guides. RCAHMS guides.

Bedfordshire
Galley Hill, Streatley; Barrows; TL092270
Maiden Bower, Houghton Regis; Enclosure; SP996224
*Waulud's Bank, Luton; Henge; TL062247

Berkshire
*Inkpen long barrow, Coombe Gibbet; Long barrow ; SU365623
Lambourn long barrow; Long barrow; SU323834

Buckinghamshire
Whiteleaf Barrows; Oval Barrow; SP822040;

Cambridgeshire
Thornhaugh; Henge; TF066008

Cornwall
Brane; Entrance grave; SW402282
*Carn Brea, Redruth; Enclosure; SW685407
Carn Gluze; Barrow??; SW355313
Castilly Luxulyan; Henge; SX032627
Castelwich; Henge; SX371685
Chun Quoit; Burial chamber; SW402339
Giant's Quoit, Caerwynnen; Burial chamber; SW650373
Giant's Quoit, St Breoc Down, Pawton; Burial chamber; SW966696
Helman Tor, Lanlivery; Tor enclosure; SX168607
Lanivet Quoit, Lanhydrock; Chamber tomb; SX072628

*Lanyon Quoit, Madron; Long cairn (rebuilt); SW430337

Men-an-tol, Madron; Burial chamber; SW427349

Mulfra Quoit, Madron; Burial chamber; SW452532

Nine Maidens, St Colomb Major; BA stone circle; SW937676

Notter Torm Caradon; Tor enclosure; SX271737

Pennance; Entrance grave; SW447376

Pawton; Long barrow??; SW966697

Roughtor, St Breward; Tor enclosure; SX147808

Stripple Stones; Henge I/circle; SX144752

Stowe's Pound, Caradon; Tor enclosure; SX257724

Tregiffianm St Buryan; Entrance grave; SW430244

Trencom Castle, Ludgvan; Tor enclosure; SW518362

*Trevethy Quoit, St Cleer ; Portal dolmen; SX259688

Zennor Quoit, Zennor; Portal dolmen; SX469380

Isles of Scilly

*Bants Cairn, St Mary's; Entrance grave; SV911123

Cruther's Hill, St Martin's; Burial chamber; SV929152

Innisidgen, St Mary's; Entrance grave; SV921127

*Porth Hellick Down, St Mary's; Entrance grave; SV928108

Samson Hill, Bryher; Burial chamber; SV879142

Cheshire

Bridestones; Barrow; SJ906622

Cumbria

Carrock Fell, Allerdale; ?Enclosure, cairns; NY342336

Casterton Circle; BA?Stone circle; SD640799

*Castlerigg, Keswick; Stone circle; NY292236

Gamelands, Orton; ?BA Stone circle; NY640079

Green How, Allerdale; ?Enclosure; NY237374

Greycroft, Seascale; Stone circle; NY034024

Howe Robin, Asby; ?Enclosure; NY624104

*King Arthur's Round Table; Henge II; NY523284

Lacra, Millom; 5 Circle, avenues; SD150814

Langdale Pikes; Axe factory/quarries; NY280070

Leacet, Brougham; BA? Stone circle/cairn; NY563263

Lowther; Barrow??; NY537243

*Long Meg and her daughters; Stone circle; NY571373

*Mayburgh, Yanath Penrith,; Henge IC/stone; NY510285

King Arthur's Round Table; Henge; NY523284

Rayseat Pike, Crosby Garrett; Long cairn; NY872132

Shap Circles; Stone circle, avenue; NY567133 and Thunder & Goggleby Stone etc.; NY552157, 555152, 550184

Skemore Heads, Urswick; ?Enclosure; SD274751

Swinside, Millom; Stone circle; SD172883

Derbyshire

*Arbor Low; Henge circle+; SK160636

Bull Ring; Henge/barrow+; SK078783

Five Wells; Chambered cairn; Sk124710

Gardom's Edge, Baslow; Enclosure; SK272729

Gib Hill; Long barrow; SK158633

Gospel Hillocks; Long barrows; SK086714

Green Low; Chambered cairn; SK232580

Barborough Rocks; Chambered cairn; SK238549

Harrod Low; Long barrow; SK098805

Long Low; Chambered cairn+; SK121539

Longstone Moor; Long barrow; SK197747

Minninglow; Chambered cairn+; SK209573

Pea Low; Chambered cairn+; SK130564

Perryfoot; Long barrow; SK109811

Ringham Low; Chambered cairn; SK169664

Rockhurst; Long barrow; SK214573

Smerill Moor; Chambered cairn; SK186608

Stanton Moor, Nine Ladies; Circle, tombs; SK249636

Stoney Low; Chambered cairn+; SK217578

The Tong; Long barrow; SK116781

Wind Low; Chambered cairn; SK114751

Devon

Butterdon Hill; Long barrow; SX660586

Cookoo Ball; Long barrow; SX660582

Corringdon Ball, South Brent; Long barrow; SX670614

Hembury; Enclosure; ST113031

Spinsters' Rock, Drewsteignton; Stone tomb remains; SX700908

The Dewarstone, Meavy; ?Enclosure; SX539640

Whittor, Peter Tavy; ?Enclosure; SX542786

Dorset

Came Wood, Whitcombe-Broadmayne; Long/round Barrows; SY699855

Dorset Cursus, Bokerley-Thickthorn; Cursus; ST970123, ST040191

Grey Mare and her Colts, Long Bredy; Chamber, Long barrow SY584871

Hambledon Hill; Enclosure, barrow; ST849122

Hell Stone, Portesham; Long barrow; SY606867

*Knowlton; Five henges/barrow; SU025100

Long Bredy; Bank barrow; SY572911

*Maumbury Rings; Henge I; SY690899

*Maiden Castle, Winterborne Monkton; Enclosure; SY669884

Martin's Down. Long Bredy; Bank barrow; SY571911

Nine Barrows, Corfe Castle; Long barrow; SY995816

Nine Stones, Winterborne Abbas; Circle ?BA; SY610904

Pimperne Long barrow; Long barrow; ST917105

Thickthorne, Gussage St Michael; Long barrow; ST971123

Wor Barrow, Handley; Mortuary enclosure/barrow; SU012173

East Sussex

Cliffe Hill, South Malling; Long barrow; TQ432110

Coombe Hill, Jevington; Enclosure; TQ574021

Firle Beacon, West Firle; Long barrow; TQ486058

Hunter's Burgh, Wilmington; Long barrow; TQ550036

Litlington; Long barrow; TQ535006

Long Burgh, Alfriston; Long barrow; TQ510034

Money Burgh Barrow, Piddinghoe; Long barrow; TQ425037

Whitehawk Hill; Enclosure; TQ330048;

East Yorkshire/Humberside

Willie Howe; Round mound; TA063724

Gloucestershire

Avening; Burial cairn; ST879984

*Belas Knap, Charlton Abbots; Chambered cairn; SP021254

Birdlip Camp, Cowley; Enclosure; SO924150

Cow Common, Swell; Chambered tombs; SP135262

*Crickley Hill, Coberly; Enclosure, fort; SO928161

Druid Stoke, Bristol; Burial chamber; ST561762

Gatcombe Lodge; Chambered cairn; ST884997

*Hetty Pegler's Tump, Uley; Chambered cairn; SO789000

Lamborough Banks, Bibury; Chambered cairn; SP107094

Leighterton, Boxwell; Long cairn; ST819913

Lodge Park, Farmington; Long barrow; SP142125

Lower Swell; Long cairn; SP170258

*Notgrove; Long cairn; SP095212

Nympsfield, Frocester; Long cairn; SO794013

Pole's Wood East, Swell; Long cairn; SP172265

Pole's Wood South, Swell; Long cairn; SP167264

*Randwick; Long cairn; SO825069;

Soldier's Grave, Nympsfield; Round cairn; SO794015

Tingle Stone Long cairn, Avening; Long cairn; ST882990

West Tump. Brimpsfield; Long cairn; SO912133

Windmill Tump, Rodmarton; Chambered cairn; ST932978

Hampshire

*Danebury Long barrows, Nether Wallop; Three long barrows; SU320383

Duck's Nest Barrow, Rockbourne; Long barrow; Su104204

Giant's Grave, Whitsbury; Long barrow; SU139200

Grans Barrow, Rockbourne; Long barrow; SU090198

Houghton Down, Broughton; Long barrow; SU330357

Knap Barrow, Martin; Long barrow; SU089199

Lamborough Long Barrow, Bramdean; Long barrow; SU593284

Moody's Down, Barton Stacey/Chilbolton; Long barrows; SU426387

Isle of Wight

Afton Down, Freshwater; Barrow cemetery; SZ352857

The Longstone, Mottistone; ?Long barrow; SZ408843

Herefordshire.

Arthur's Stone, Dorston; Chambered tomb; SO3184431

King Arthur's Cave, Whitchurch; Cave; SO545155

Hertfordshire

Therfield Heath cemetery, Royston; long and round barrow cemetery; TL342402

Kent

Addington Park, Addington; Chambered barrow; TQ653591

Chestnuts Tomb, Addington; Chambered tomb; TQ652592

Coffin Stone, Aylesford; ?Burial chamber; TQ739605

Coldrum Tomb, Trottiscliffe; Chambered tomb; TQ654607

Juliberrie's Grave, Chilham; Long barrow; TR077532

*Kit's Coty House, Aylesford; Burial chamber; TQ745608

Lower Kit's Coty House, Countless Stones; ?Burial chamber; TQ744604

Upper White Horse Stone, Aylesford; ?Remains of tomb; TQ753603

Lancashire

Bleasdale; BA Stone circle; SD577460

Cheetham Close; Stone circle; SD717158

Druid Temple, Birkrigg Common; Circle, cairns; SD292739, SD285744

Holme Stone Circle; BA? Circle; SD879302

Pikestones, Anglezarke; Trapezoidal cairn; SD627172

Skelmore Heads, Urswick; Burial chamber; SD262744

Lincolnshire

Deadmen's graves, Claxby; Two long barrows; TF745608

Giant's Hill, Skendleby; Long barrow; TF428711

Norfolk

Arminghall, Bixley; Henge; TG240060

Broome Heath, Ditchingham; Long barrow; TM344913

*Grime's Graves, Weeting; Flint Mines; TL817898

Salthouse Heath, Cley and Salthouse; Barrow Cemetery; TG069421, TG077423

West Rudham; Two long barrows ; TF810253

Northumberland

Debdon; ?BA cairnfield, cupmark stone; NU055029/056029

Doddington Moor; ?BA cairns, cupmark stones; NU008318/013324

Cartington; Stone circle, cairns; NU111028

Duddo; four stones, druids' circle, stone circle, cairns; NU049053

Ilderton; Stone circle; NT971205

Milfield; Henges, barrows etc.; NT934352

Keilder; Devil's lapful, long cairn and cairns; NY641928

Dod Law; north, sheepfold, quarry, cup-ring rocks; NU001323, NU007319, NU014333

Roughting Linn; Cup-ring rocks; NT983367

Windy Gyle; Russell's Cairn, cupmark stones; NU098225

North Yorkshire

Duggleby Howe, Kirby Grindalythe; Enclosure/round mound ; SE880668

East Heslerton; Long barrow; SE939753

Eskdaleside; High Bride Stones; BA barrow, stone row; NZ8000

Thornborough; Henge IIA; SE285795

Hutton Moor; Henge; SE2879

Rudston; Monolith, standing stone, cursus; TA0668

Kepwick Moor; Long barrow; SE492904

Kilham; Long barrow; TA0567

Scamridge; Long barrow; SE892861

Westow; Long barrow; SE759652

Willerby Wold; Long barrow; TA029761

Oxfordshire

Devil's Quoits; Henge circle; SP411048

Hoar Stone, Enstone; Burial chamber; SP378236

Hoar Stone, Steeple Barton; Long barrow; SP458241

Lyneham Long Cairn; Long cairn; SP297211

*Rollright Stones, Rollright; King's Men Circle; SP296308
 King's Stone; Remnant stone
The Whispering Knights; Portal dolmen; SP299308

Slatepits Copse, Wychwood; Long cairn; SP329165

*Wayland's Smithy; Chambered barrow; SU281854

Somerset

Devil's Bed and Bolster, Beckington; Long barrow; ST815533

Gorsey Bigbury

Ham Hill. Stoke-sub-Hamdon; Possible enclosure; ST483164

Hautville Quoit, Stanton Drew; Cove; ST602638

Pen Hill; Long barrow; ST562486

Priddy Circles, E.Harptree; Four henges; ST540530

Stanton Drew; Three stone circles; ST601634

South Cadbury; Possible enclosure; ST628251

*Stoney Littleton, Wellow; Long cairn; ST735572

Wick Barrow, Stogursey; Long barrow; ST209456

Tyne and Wear

Hastings Hill; Enclosure/settlement; NZ355540

West Sussex

Barkhale; Enclosure; SU976126

Bevis's Thumb, North Marden; Long barrow; SU789155

Blackpatch, Patching; Flint mines; TQ094088

Church Hill. Findon; Flint mines; TQ114083

Cissbury, Worthing; Flint mines; TQ136079

Court Hill, Singleton; Enclosure; SU897137

Halnaker Hill, Boxgrove; Enclosure; SU920096

Harrow Hill, Angmering; Flint mines; TQ081100

Stoke Down, Funting; Flint mines; SU832096

Stoughton Down; Two long barrows; SU823121

The Trundle; Enclosure; SU877110

West Yorkshire

Baildon Moor; Cup-mark stones; SE137400; Stone circle; SE138399

Bradley Both; Long cairn; SE009476

Bradup, Keighley; ?BA Stone circle; SE090440

Devil's Arrows, Boroughbridge; Three monoliths; SE391666

Ilkley Moor (Rombald's Moor); Decorated stones; SE104470; BA Cairns, Circle; SE144442; SE132458, 125540,084471

Twelve Apostles, Burley Moor; ?Stone circle; SE126451

Green Howe-North Deighton; Barrow SE3851

Wiltshire

Adam's Grave, Alton Priors; Long barrow; SU112634

★Avebury; Henge II; SU103699; and Avenue, SU107692; Long Stones, Beckhampton, SU089694

Devil's Den, Fyfield; Burial chamber; SU152696

Durrington Walls; Henge; SU15043

East Kennet long barrow; Long barrow; SU116669

Fyfield Down; Fields; SU142710; Sarsen stone; SU143688

Giant's Cave, Luckington; Long cairn; ST820829

Giant's Grave, Milton Lilbourne; Long barrow; SU189583

Kitchen Barrow; SU066648

Knap Hill; Enclosure; SU121636

Lanhill, Chippenham Without; Long cairn; ST877747

Lugbury Long Barrow, Nettleton; Long barrow; ST831786

Manton Long Barrow, Preshute; Long barrow; SU152714

Marden; Henge; SU091584

Normanton Down, Wilsford; Barrow cemetery; SU118413

Robin Hood's Ball; Enclosure; SU103460

Ryebury; Enclosure; SU083640

★Silbury Hill; Mound; SU100685

★Stonehenge; Henge-circle; SU123422

Stonehenge Cursus; Two cursuses; SU124430

Tidcombe; Long barrow; SU292576

Tilshead Old Ditch; Long barrow; SU023468

★Tilshead White Barrow; Long barrow ; SU033468

★The Sanctuary, Overton Hill; Timber circle; SU149763

★West Kennet long barrow; Long barrow; SU104677

★ Windmill Hill; Enclosure; SU087714

Whitesheet Hill; Enclosure; ST802352

Whitesheet Barrow; Long barrow; ST942242

Winterborne Stoke ; Long barrow/cemetery SU101417;

Windmill Hill, Avebury; Enclosure; SU087714

Woodhenge ; Henge timber circle; SU150434

Isle of Man

Ballafayle; Long cairn; SC476901

Cashtel yn Ard; Clyde tomb/façade; SC463893

King Orry's Grave; Chambered tomb; SC440844

Wales
Reading

Christopher Holder1974 *Wales: an Archaeological Guide*, Faber.

Anglesey

★Barclodiad y Gawres; Passage grave; SH383693

★Bodowyr; Passage grave; SH463682

★Bryn Celli Ddu; Passage grave; SH508702

Bryn yr Hen Bobl; Chamber tomb/façade; SH519690

★Din Dryfol; Chamber tomb; SH395724

★Lligwy ; Chamber tomb; SH501861

★Presaddfed; Chamber tomb; SH347089

Pant-y-saer; Chamber tomb; SH509824

Plas Newydd; Chamber tomb; SH519697

★Trefignath; Chamber tomb; SH258805

★Ty Newydd; Passage grave; SH328708

Caernarvon

Bachwen Burial chamber; Chamber tomb/cup-ring marks; SH407495

Mynudd Cefnamwlch; Cromlech, chamber tomb; SH230345

Mynydd Rhiw ; Axe quarry; SH234299

Rhoslan Cromlech; Chamber tomb; SH483409

Lletty'r Filiast; Portal tomb; SH772829

Maen y Bardd; Chamber tomb; SH740718

Tan y Muriau; Portal dolmen; SH238288

Cerrig Pryfaid Circle; Stone circle; SH724713

Graig Lwyd Axe Factory; Axe quarry; SH717750

Denbigh

Allor Moloch; Portal tomb; SH793747

Tyddun Bleiddyn ; Long cairn; SJ007724

Capel Garmon; Chambered long tomb SH818543

Flintshire
Gop Cairn; Neo-BA Cairn; SJ086801

Merioneth
Cosygedol Cromlech; Long cairn;
SH602228
Hengwm Circles; Two stone circles;
SH616213
Bron-y-foel Isaf; Portal dolmen;
SH608246;
Llanbedr Church; Stone; Decorated
stone; SH585269
Gwern Einion Burial Chamber; Portal
dolmen; SH587286
Carneddau Hengwm; Severn C/Portal D;
SH613205
Dyffryn Ardudwy; Portal dolmen;
SH588229

Montgomery
Carrig Caerau and Lled Croen-yr-ych;
Two stone circles; SH903005

Radnorshire
Clap-yr-arian; Stone Cairn; SN936799
The four stones; Tomb/erratics; S)245608

Brecknock
Cwm Fforest Long Cairn; Long cairn;
SO183294
Ffostil Cairns; Two chambered cairns;
SO179349
Gwernvale Burial Chamber; Chambered
cairn; SO211192
Little Lodge; Severn Cotswold tomb;
SO182380
Pen y Wyrlod Llanigon; Severn Cotswold
tomb; SO225398
Pipton Tomb; Chambered cairn;
SO160373
Ty Illtud long barrow; Chambered cairn;
SO097263
Ty-isaf Chambered Tomb; Severn
Cotswold tomb; SO182290

Monmouthshire
Heston Brake Cairn; Chambered long
barrow; SO505886
Gaer/Garn Llwyd Burial chamber; Severn
Cotswold tomb; SO447968

Glamorgan
★Arthur's Stone (Maen Ceti); Gower;
Chamber tomb/erratic SS491905
Cae'r-arfau; Cairn; ST077821
Cerrig Duon Circle; Circle and rows;
SN852206
★Parc le Breos Cwm ; Gower; Severn
Cotswold tomb SS537898
★St Lythans Cairn; Chambered long
cairn; ST101723
★Tinkinswood Chambered Tomb; Severn
Cotswold tomb ST097733

Carmathen Pembrokeshire
Bedd-yr-Afanc; Chamber tomb;
SN108345
Careg Coetan Arthur; Portal dolmen;
SN159393
★Carreg Samson; Passsage tomb;
SM848335
Carn Turne; Chamber tomb; SM979272
Carn Llidi; Chamber tomb; SM735279
Carn Wnda; Chamber tomb; SM932392
Cerrig y Gof; Chamber tomb; SN037389
Cerrig Llwydion; Court Cairn/cist?;
SN374326
Clegr Boia; Settlement; SM737252
Dolwilym/Bwrdd Arthur/Gwalyfiliast;
Barrow Circle; SN170256
Gors Fawr; Stone circle; SN134294
Hanging Stone, Burton; Passage tomb;
SM972082
Meini Gwyr Stone Circle; Stone circle;
SN142266
★Pentre Ifan; Chambered cairn;
SN099370
Pendine Head Burial chambers; Four
chambered Tombs; SN222075
Waun Pwtlyn Long Cairn; Long cairn;
SN709260
Twlc y Filiast Cromlech; Chamber tomb;
SN343195
Mynydd Llanybyther ; Stone row;
SN549395

Scotland
Reading
Regional and site guides from *Historic
Scotland*, Audrey Henshall 1963, 1972
The Chambered Cairns of Scotland, vol 1
and 2. Edinburgh University Press.

Anna and Graham Ritchie 1998
Scotland: Oxford Archaeological Guides.
Euan MacKie 1975 *Scotland: an
Archaelogical Guide.*

Borders (Berwickshire-Roxburghshire)
Long Knowe; Long cairn; NY527862
Mutiny Stones, Longformacus; Long
  cairn; NY622590

Dumfries and Galloway, .Ayrshire, Lanarkshire
Balmalloch; Chambered cairn; NX263845
Ballochmyle, Catrine; Cup-ring rocks;
  NS511255
Cuff Hill; Chambered cairn; NS385550
Boreland; Long cairn; NX405690
*Cairnholy 1-2; Two cairns; NX517358
Carsphairn; Long cairn; ??
Dumtroddan; Cup-ring rock; NX362447;
  Standing stones; NX364443
Kirkdale; Horned cairn; ???
Mid Gleniron 1-2; Two chambered
  cairns; NX188610
Normangill, Crawford; Henge;
  NS972221
Slewcairn; Wood/stone tomb; NX924614
*Torhouskie; Stone circle; NX382564
White Cairn, Bargrennan; Rect. passage
  grave; NX351783
White Cairn, Corridow; Round cairn;
White Cairn, Glencairn; Long cairn;
  NX834873

Fife
*Balfarg (Glenrothes); Henge;
  NO281032
Balfarg (Glenrothes); Mortuary
  Enclosure; NO281031
Balbirnie (Glenrothes); Stone circle;
  NO281031
Lundun Linka; Standing stone ?BA;
  NO404127

Grampian (Banff-Kincardineshire, Aberdeenshire, Morayshire);
Broomend of Crichie, Inverurie; Henge-
  circle; NJ779196
Capo, Laurencekirk; Long cairn;
  NO633664
Cairn Catto; Long cairn; NK074421
*Cullerlie, Westhill; BA? Stone circle;
  NJ786042

Easter Aquhorthies, Inverurie; RSC;
  NJ832207
Garrol Wood, Mulloch; ?BA Stone circle;
  NO723912
Loanhead of Daviot, Oldmeldrum; RSC;
  NJ747288
Longman Hill; Long cairn; NJ737620
Old Keig, Alford; Stone circle; NJ596193
*Quarry Wood Henge; Henge; NJ185630
*Tomnaverie; RSC; NJ486034

Lothian
*Cairnpapple; Henge/Circle/Cairn;
  NS987717

Highland (Inverness, Ross and Cromarty, Skye Caithness, Sutherland)
Achadh a'Chuirn, Skye; Chambered
  cairn; NG664235
Achavanich, Latheron; Stone rows;
  ND187417
Mid Clyth; Stone rows; ND294384
*Balnuran of Clava; Two kerbed cairns;
  NH757444
*Cairn o'Get, Ulbster, Yarrows;
  Chambered cairn; ND313411
*Camster Long and Round; Cairns, Long,
  round; ND260440
*Clava Cairns; Passage grave; NH752439
Clava Cairns; Stone circles; NH760445
Cnoc Ullinish, Skye; Chambered cairn;
  NG324379
Cnoc Freicedain, Shebster; Long cairn;
  ND012653
Coil na Borgie, Bettyhill; Chambered
  cairns; NC715590
Skelpick; Chambered cairn; NC722567
*Corrimony, Glen Urquhart; Clava
  Cairn/Circle; NH383303
Embo, Dornoch; Chambered cairn;
  NH817926
*Hill o'Many Stanes, Lybster; Stone
  rows; ND295384
*Knoc Freceadain; Two horned long
  cairns; ND013654
Kensaleyre, Skye; Chambered cairn;
  NG420514
Liveras, Skye; Chambered cairn;
  NG642238
Muir of Ord; Henge II; NH527497
Ord, Lairg; Landscape/tombs; NC579062

Rudh'an Dunain, Loch Brittle;
  Chambered cairn; NG393163
Strath of Kildonan; Landscape/cairns/rows
  NC871291
Strathnaver, Bettyhill; Landscape/cairns;
  NC689416
Tulach an t'Sionnaich; Passage grave/long
  cairn ND070619

Perthshire
Carse, Dull; BA four-Poster circle;
  NN802487
Cleaven Dyke; Cursus/bank barrow;
  NO150410, NO177396
Croft Moraig; Stone circles; NN797472
Fairy Knowe, Bridge of Allen; Cairn —
  Neo-BA; NS796981
Pitnacree; Round barrow; NN928533

Strathclyde (Argyll Arran, Islay)
Achnabreck, Kilmartin; Cup/ring rocks;
  NR856906
Archnacree beag; Passage graves;
  NM922363; NM929363
Ballinaby, Islay; Standing stones;
  NR219672
Ballygowan; Cup/ring rocks; NR816978
Baluachraig; Cup/ring rocks; NR831969
Ballochroy; Stone rows; NR730524
Ballymeanoch; Henge/cairn; NR833963
Beacharra; Clyde cairn; NR692433
Blasthill, Kintyre; Chambered cairn;
  NR720092
Brackley; Clyde cairn; NR794418
Carnbaan, Kilmartin; Cup/ring rocks;
  NR838910
★Carn Ban Arran; Clyde cairn,façade;
  NR990262
Cultoon, Islay; Stone circle; NR195569
Craigabus, Islay; Clyde tomb; NR329451
Crarae House, Furness; Clyde cairn;
  NR985972
Dunchraigaig; Cairn; NR833968
Glebe; Cairn; NR832989
Kilmichael Glassery; Cup/ring rocks;
  NR857934
Kilmartin Glen; Circles, tombs;
  NR827977
Kintraw; Kerbed cairn; NM830050
Loch Nell South, Dalineun; Stone box
  chamber; NM889266
★Machrie Moor; Five stone circles;
  NR910324

Monamore; Chambered tomb; NS017288
★Nether Largie South, Kilmartin; Clyde
  cairn; NM838978; Cairn; NR830983;
  Cairn; NR831985
Port Charlotte, Islay; Cairn/chamber;
  NR248576
Ri Cruin; Cairn; NR825971
Strontoiller, Lorn; Cairn/stone;
  NM907289
Temple Wood, Temple Wood; Stone circle
  (?BA); NR826978
★Torrylin, Arran; Two Clyde cairns/por-
  tals; NR955210

Western Isles (Hebrides)
Barpa Langrass, N. Uist; Passage grave;
  NF838657
★Callanish/Calanais, Lewis; Stone circles,
  grave; NB213330; Four circles, stone
  visitor centre
Clettravel, N. Uist; Clyde Cairn;
  NF749713
Steinacleit, Lewis; ; Chambered cairn;
  NB396541
Unival, N. Uist; Passage grave;
  NF800668

Orkney Islands
The Orkney Islands have the greatest
concentration of Neolithic sites in northern Europe. Tombs, houses and settlements, as well as stone circles in evocative
and beautiful settings, make this the most
important location for appreciating tangible Neolithic monuments.

Reading
Anna and Graham Ritchie, *The Ancient
  Monuments of Orkney*, Historic Scotland.
Davisdon and Henshall 1989 *The
  Chambered cairns of Orkney*, Edinburgh.

Skara Brae, Mainland; Village; HY231187
Knap of Howar, Papa Westray; Houses;
  HY483518
Barnhouse, Mainland; Village; HY307127
Unstan, Mainland; Stalled cairn;
  HY282117
Midhowe, Rousay; Stalled cairn;
  HY372304
Knowe of Tarso, Rousay; Chambered
  cairn; HY404279

Blackhammer, Rousay; Chambered cairn; HY414276

Taversoe Tuick, Rousay; Chambered cairn; HY425276

Dwarfie Stone, Hoy; Rockcut tomb; HY243004

Isbister, South Ronaldsay; Stalled Cairn; ND470845

Curween Hill, Mainland; Chambered cairn; HY363127

Wideford Hill, Mainland; Chambered cairn; HY409121

Quoyness, Sanday; Chambered cairn; HY676378

Vinquoy, Eday; Chambered cairn; HY560381

Holm of Papa Westray South; Stalled/chambered Cairn HY509518

Maes Howe, Mainland; Chambered cairn; HY318127

Stones of Stenness, Mainland; Henge/circle; HY306125

Ring of Brodgar; Henge/Circle; HY294133

Shetland

Reading

Anna Ritchie 1997 *Shetland — Exploring Scotland's Heritage*. HMSO

Brough, Walsay; Carved rocks; HU555651

Gallow Hill, Mainland; Chambered cairn; HU258508

Gruting School, W. Mainland; Settlement; HU281498

Islesburgh, W.Mainland; Chambered heel cairn; HU334685

Jarslhof, Sumburgh; Settlement; HU398095

Loch of Strom; Settlement; HU403502;

March Cairn, W. Mainland; Chambered cairn; HU221789

Muckle Heog, Unst; Chambered heel cairn; HU631107

Pettigarths Field, Walsay; Settlement; HU586652

Pinhoulland, W. Mainland; Settlement; HU259497

Punds Water, W.Mainland; Chambered heel cairn; HU324712;

Roqnas Hill, N.Mainland; Chambered heel cairn; HU305834

Stanydale, W.Mainland; Settlement/land-scape; HU285502

Scord of Brouster, W. Mainland; Settlement; HU255526

Vementry, Mainland; Chambered heelcCairn; HU295609

Vementry; Chambered heel cairn; HU295609

Ireland

Reading

Duchas regional and site guides, *Irish Megalithic Tombs*.

Elizabeth Shee *Twohig*, Shire Publications.

Anthony Weir 1980 *Early Ireland — A field guide*, Blackstaff Press

Aubrey Burl 1993 *From Carnac to Callanish*, Yale; 2000 *The Stone circles of the British Isles*.

Peter Harbison 1992 *Guide National and Historic Monuments*, Gill and MacMillan.

Antrim

Ballintoy; Three passage tombs; D02 43 — 04 44

Ballylumford; Passage tomb?; D431016

Ballymacaldrack; Court tomb; D021182

Ballymarlargh; Court tomb; D140018

Ballyvennaght; Portal tombs; S20 36

Browndod; Court tomb; J205924

Carnanmore; Passage tomb; D218388

Cloghbrack; Court tomb; D213284

Craigs; Court tomb; C979175

Craigs; Passage tomb; C979173

Dunteige; Wedge tomb; D323079

Ticloy; Portal tomb; D232118

Armagh;

Annaghmore; Court tomb; H905178

Ballykeel; Portal tomb; H995213

Ballymacdermot; Court tomb; J066240

Clontygora; Court tomb; J098194

Slieve Gullion; Passage tomb; J025203

Carlow

Ardristan; Grooved stone; S84 71

Browne's Hill; Portal tomb; S75 77

Haroldstown; Portal tomb; S755768
Kernanstown; Portal tomb; S902778

Cavan
Cohaw; Double court tomb; H644125
Burren; Wedge tomb; H080351

Clare
Ballyganner North; Court tomb;
  R219956
Baur South; Wedge tomb; M217000
Caheraphuca; Wedge tomb; R392874
Derrynavahagh; Wedge tomb; M180054
NewGrove; Wedge tomb; R45 80
Parknabinnia; Wedge tomb; R264937
Parknabinnia; Wedge tomb; R265935
Poulaphuca; Wedge tomb; M264017
Poulnabrone; Portal tomb; M236003

Cork
Ahaglaslin; Portal tomb; W307363
Altar; Wedge tomb; W858303
Arderawinny; Portal tomb; V875307
Drombeg; Stone circle; W247352
Inchincurka; Wedge tomb; W233597
Island; Wedge tomb; W603908
Labbacallee; Wedge tomb; W772026
Keamcurravooly; Wedge tomb; W136677
Killickaforvane; Passage tomb; V221972
Kilmaclenine; Wedge tomb; R516058
Knockane; Wedge tomb; W328646

Derry
Ballybreist; Court tomb; H762886
Ballygroll; Burial complex; C533137
Boviel; Wedge tomb; C730078
Kilhoyle; Wedge tomb; C751162
Knockoneill; Court tomb; C819087
Tirnony; Portal tomb; C841017

Donegal
Bavan; Court tomb; G650755
Beltany Tops; Stone circle; C254003
Farranmacbride; Court tomb; G534854
Kilclooney More; Portal tomb; G732968
Malin More; Six portal tombs; G502825

Down
Audleystown; Court tomb; J562504
Ballynahatty; Passage tomb/henge and
  complex; J327677
Giant's Ring; Henge-cairn; J327677

Goward; Court tomb; J244310
Greengraves; Portal tomb; J445736
Kilfeaghan; Portal tomb; J232154
Legananny; Portal tomb; J288434

Dublin
Ballyedmonduff; Wedge tomb; O185212
Brenanstown; Portal tomb; O229242
Kilmashough; Portal tomb; O148237
Kilmashough; Wedge tomb; O198225
Kiltiernan; Portal tomb; O198225?

Fermanagh
Aghanaglack; Court tomb; H098436
Ballyreagh; Court tomb; H315504

Galway;
Crannagh; Portal tomb; M426059
Mweelin; Court tomb; H315504

Kerry
Caherard; Wedge tomb; Q390011
Cool East; Wedge tomb; V376758
Coomatloukane; Four wedge tombs;
  V507600
Drombohilly; Wedge tomb; V792605
Eightercua; Alignment/enclosure; V51 65
Gurteen; Stone circle/cist; W00 70
Lissyviggeen; Circle ?henge; V99 91

Kilkenny
Farnougue; Court tomb; S260122
Kilmogue; Portal tomb; S503281
Knockroe; Passage tomb; S408312

Leitrim
Corracloona; Court tomb; G996427
Kilnagarns Lower; Court and wedge
  tombs; G936256
Tullyskerny, Manorhamilton; Two court
  tombs; G90 37

Limerick
Duntryleague (Deerpark TD); Passage
  tomb; R78 28
Grange; Henge-circle; R640410
Lough Gur complex; Wedge tomb/settle-
  ment/circles, Grange Stone circle;
  R647403

Longford
Aghnacliff; Portal tomb; N263885

Louth
Arghnaskeagh; Portal tombs; J076137
Paddock; Wedge tomb; O048831
Proleek; Portal tomb; J082110
Proleek; Wedge tomb; J083110

Mayo
Alliemore; Court tomb; L761735
Ballyglass; Court tomb; G097381
Ballyglass; Court tomb; G098397
Behy; Court tomb, Ciede field systems;
   G050405
Cardadmore; Court tomb; G181326
Carrowkilleen; Two court tombs;
   G083168
Srahwee; Wedge tomb; L795745

Meath
Dowth; Passage tomb; O026737
Dowth Q; Henge; O34742
Fourknocks; Passage tomb; N019621
Knowth; Passage tombs; N994736
Loughcrew; Passage tombs; N587776
Newgrange; Passage tomb/circle;
   O007727
Tara; Passage tomb; N918597

Monaghan
Calliagh; Wedge tomb; H636267
Carn; Court tomb; H610260
Lisnadarragh; Wedge tomb; H724077

Roscommon
Drumanone; Portal tomb; G768024
Scregg; Passage tomb; M528552
Usna; Wedge tomb; G887016
Sligo
Achony; Boulder burial; G576140
Cabaragh ; Wedge tomb; G568248
Carrickglass; Portal tomb; G796157
Carrowkeel; Passage tombs; G755115
Carrowmore; Passage tombs; G663335
Clogcor; Portal tomb; G599438
Creevykeel; Court tomb; G721546
Deerpark/Magheraghanrush; Court tomb;
   G753367
Heapstown Cairn; Kerbed cairn ;
   G772162
Knocknarea; Passage tomb; G625344
Labby Rock, Carrickglass; Portal tomb;
   G795157
Lisnalurg; Henge-enclosure; G690387

Rathdoony Beg; Barrow cemetery;
   G661184

Tipperary
Baurnadomeeny; Wedge tomb; R846603
Loughbrack; Wedge tomb; R906592
Shandballyedmond; Court tomb;
   R844588
Shrough; Passage tomb; R841306

Tyrone
Balix Lower; Court tomb; H483963
Ballyrenan; Portal tomb; H373832
Ballywholan; Court tomb; H569470
Beaghmore; Stone circles; H685842
Clady Haliday; Court tomb; H342886
Creggandevsky; Court tomb; H643750
Knockmany; Passage tomb; H547559
Loughash; Wedge tomb; C517013
Sesskilgreen; Passage tomb; H612583

Waterford
Ballynamona Lower; Court tomb;
   X287835
Carriglong; Passage tomb; S590049
Gaulstown; Portal tomb; S539062
Harristown; Passage tomb; S675041
Knockeen; Portal tomb; S574163
Matthewstown; Passage tomb; S53 03
Munmahogue; Wedge tomb; S576060

Wexford
Ballybrittas; Portal tomb; S574163

Wicklow
Athgreany; Stone circle; N93 03
Baltinglass; Passage tomb; S885892
Castleruddery; Circle-henge; S925937
Glaskenny; Portal tomb; O196153
Moylisha; Wedge tomb; S930675
Seefin; Passage tomb; O073163

Museum collections

Too few museums make enough of their
Neolithic collections or have dynamic
exhibitions of their material, guided by
the mistaken belief that relatively recent
history is more interesting! However,
there is often much material stored

behind the scenes that can be studied, provided that arrangements are made with the archaeology/prehistory curator. Major Neolithic collections are starred.

England

Avebury: Alexander Keiller Museum
Barnard Castle: Bowes Museum
Bedford Museum and Art Gallery
Birmingham: City Museum and Art Gallery
★Brighton Museum and Art Gallery
★Bristol: City Museum and Art Gallery — SW collections
Buxton Museum
★Cambridge: Museum of Archaeology and Anthropology, Downing St
Cheltenham Museum
Chester: Chester Museum
Chichester: Chichester District Museum
Christchurch: Red House Museum
Colchester and Essex Museum, The Castle
★Devizes: Wiltshire Archaeological Society, Long Street
★Dorchester: Dorset County Museum
★Doncaster Museum Yorkshire collections
★Durham, Old Fulling Mill University Archaeological Museum
★Exeter: Royal Albert Memorial Museum
Gloucester: City Museum and Art Gallery
Guildford: Castle Arch, Quarry St
Hereford: Museum and Art Gallery
Hertford Museum
★Hull: Hull and East Riding Museum
Ispwich: Ipswich Museum
Kendal: Kendal Museum of Natural History and Archaeology
Letchworth: Museum
★Lewes: Museum of Sussex Archaeology
★London:British Museum
★London: Museum of London
Manchester Museum of Archaeology, University of Manchester
★Newcastle: Museum of Antiquities, University of Newcastle
Norwich:Castle Museum,
★Oxford: Ashmolean Museum

Oxford: Pitt Rivers Museum
★Peterborough: Peterborough Museum
Peterborough: Flag Fen Visitor Centre (information on Fengate)
Scilly Isles: Museum, St Mary's
Sunderland: Museum and Art Gallery
Truro: Royal Cornish Museum
Taunton, Somerset: Museum.
Norwich: Castle Museum
Worcester: City Museum and Art Gallery, Foregate Street
York: Yorkshire Museum
Sheffield: City Museum
Salisbury: Salisbury and South Wiltshire Museum, the Close
Weston-Super-Mare: The Time Machine Museum, Burkington Street
Worthing: Worthing Museum

Wales

★Cardiff: National Museum of Wales, Cathays Park
Bangor: Museum of Art and Archaeology
Aberystwyth: Ceredigion Museum

Scotland

Aberdeen: University Anthropological Museum, Marischal College
Dundee: Museums and Art Gallery
★Edinburgh: National Museum of Scotland,
★Glasgow: Hunterian Museum
★Glasgow: Kelvingrove Museum and Art Gallery
Inverness: City Museum
Kilmartin: Kilmartin House
Kirkaldy: Museum and Art Gallery
★Kirkwall: Orkney — Tankerhouse Museum
Lerwick: Shetland — Shetland Museum, Lower Hillhead
Montrose: Museum and Art Gallery
Port Charlotte: Islay — Museum of Islay Life
Stirling: The Smith Gallery and Museum
Stornoway: — Lewis Museum nan Eilean

Ireland
⋆Belfast: The Ulster Museum
⋆Dublin: National Museum of Ireland
Ceide Fields Visitor Centre, Mayo
Bru na Boinne, Donore, Co Meath
Carrowmore Visitor Centre, Sligo
Armagh
Cork
Enniskillen
Limerick
Monaghan

Journals with regular items on Neolithic Britain and Ireland

Archaeology Ireland
Current Archaeology
Proceedings of the Prehistoric Society
Proceedings of the Society of Antiquaries of Scotland
Proceedings of the Royal Irish Academy
County archaeological society journals

Societies and further study

Societies

The following societies are always pleased to include new members regardless of their professional or amateur status.

County Archaeological Societies (for example the Sussex Archaeological Society and the Wiltshire Archaeological Society) — enquire at local museums or libraries

The Prehistoric Society (current address — Institute of Archaeology, University College London, Gordon Square, London, WC1H 0PY) offers members a friendly and dynamic programme of lectures, tours, conferences, and the excellent *Proceedings*.

The Neolithic Studies Group – a friendly specialist group offering annual conferences, tours and publications. Enquiries to Professor Tim Darvill, School of Conservation Studies, University of Bournemouth, Fern Barrow Campus, Poole, Dorset BH12 5BB, and to Dr Gordon Barclay, Historic Scotland, Longmore House, Salisbury Place, Edinburgh EH9 1SH.

Council for British Archaeology, Council for Scottish Archaeology (CBA) — national organisations coordinating policy, activities and publicity for archaeology. Annual membership offers local groups, monthly magazine, newsletter, listings of courses, excavations and events. Contact through WEB, or Bowes Morell House, Walmgate, York, YO1 9WA/ Council for Scottish Archaeology, Royal Museum of Scotland, Chambers St, Edinburgh, EH1 1JF.

Members are elected to The Society of Antiquaries of Scotland (enquires to the Society) at the Royal Museum of Scotland, Chambers St, Edinburgh, EH1 1JF.

The Society of Antiquaries of London elects its members, but does offer, by arrangement, access to its library, some events and meetings, and fieldwork grants. Enquiries to the Secretary, The Society of Antiquaries of London, Burlington House, Piccadilly, London W1.

Membership can be taken out annually with Cadw (Wales) English Heritage, Historic Scotland, Ulster (DOENI) and Duchas in Ireland, permitting access to guardianship of sites such as Stonehenge, Newgrange and Maes Howe as well as all other sites in state care. The National Trust has similar schemes, although most sites are freely accessible on National Trust land.

Courses and further study

There are two main types of academic courses available on Neolithic Britain and Ireland. Extramural courses are programmed annually in Departments of Continuing Education attached to Universities, Colleges and Institutes. Many courses offer general introductions to Archaeology, Prehistory, and sometimes to Neolithic topics, and normally are part of the Credit Accumulation and Transfer (CATS) scheme, which enables students to study gradually towards certificates, diplomas and sometimes part-time degrees. CATS points may sometimes be added to degree courses as part of the required credit.

Other courses are more formal University degree courses leading to BA, MA, M.Sc., M.Phil and Ph.D. degrees. Neolithic studies are covered in almost all general archaeology degrees at the many universities now offering them. However, strong traditions for Mesolithic-Neolithic-Bronze Age research are offered at: Bangor, Birmingham, Bournemouth, Cambridge, Cardiff, Durham, Edinburgh, Exeter, Glasgow, Lampeter, Leicester, Liverpool, London, Newport, Manchester, Newcastle, Nottingham, Oxford, Reading, Sheffield, Southampton, and Winchester. Most courses are full-time, although part-time degrees and distance learning are being introduced and prospective students should inquire at the relevant institution and through UCAS for current information on courses and entrance requirements.

Practical experience and participation can often be arranged through local museums, archaeological societies, county and regional archaeological units and trusts. These may offer training excavations, handling sessions and courses, and some may welcome assistance with survey, finds processing and other archaeological work.

Archaeological sites, legislation and preservation

Virtually all the sites in the site lists are Ancient Monuments, protected through legislation (in England and Wales — The Ancient Monuments and Archaeological Areas Act 1979, and in Scotland and Northern Ireland by similar legislation. The Republic of Ireland has its own strict legislation). Sites are regularly inspected by the relevant bodies, some are under state care as Guardianship monuments allowing public access, others are on private land and their use is regulated by the relevant bodies (eg CADW, DOENI, English Heritage, DUCHAS and Historic Scotland). Over the centuries, megalithic stones have been torn down and removed, earthworks have been ploughed and damaged, and many Neolithic sites are now very partial reflections of their former size or state. Excessive landuse, tractors, motorbikes, feet, rabbits, horses, poaching by farm animals, tree-roots, erosion and outright vandalism are all threats to these important and relatively delicate sites. If your visit to a site identifies recent damage or threat, please inform the relevant local authority (usually through the Sites and Monuments Archaeological Officer).

Bibliography

Abbreviations:
Antiqs.J.-Antiquaries Journal
CBA — Council for British Archaeology
PPS — Proceedings of the Prehistoric Society
PSAS — Proceedings of the Society of Antiquaries of Scotland.
PRIA — Proceedings of the Royal Irish Academy
Arch. J. — Archaeological Journal

Abercrombie, J. 1912 *A study of the Bronze Age pottery of Great Britain and Ireland*, 2 vols. Oxford, Oxford University Press.

Allen, M.J. 1997 'Environment and landuse: The economic development of the communities who built Stonehenge (an economy to support the stones)', in Cunliffe, B. and Renfrew. C. (eds) *Science and Stonehenge*. Proceedings of the British Academy, 92. Oxford. 115-44.

2000 'High resolution mapping of chalkland landscapes and landuse', in Fairbairn A. (ed) *Plants in Neolithic Britain and beyond*. Oxbow. 9-26.

Ammerman, A.J. and Cavalli-Sforza, L.L. 1973 A population model for the diffusion of early farming in Europe. In Renfrew, A.C. (ed) *The Explanation of Culture Change*. London, Duckworth. 343-57.

1984 *The Neolithic transition and the genetics of populations in Europe*. Princeton, Princeton University Press.

Andrevsky, W. 1998 Lithics: macroscopic approaches to analysis. Cambridge Manuals of Archaeology. Cambridge. Cambridge University Press.

Ashbee, P. 1966 'The Fussells's Lodge Long Barrow excavation 1957' *Archaeologia*. C, 1-80.

1974 *Ancient Scilly*. London, David and Charles.

1984 *The Earthen Long barrow in Britain* (second edition), Norwich, Geo Books.

2000a Coldrum revisited and reviewed. *Archaeologia Cantiana* CXXI, 1-41.

2000b The Medways' Megalithic long barrows. *Archaeologia Cantiana* CXXI 319-345.

Ashbee, P. Smith. I.F. and Evans, J.G. 1979 Excavation of three barrows near Avebury, Wilsthire. *PPS* 45, 207-300.

Ashmore, P. 1995 *Calanias: The Standing Stones*. Edinburgh. Historic Scotland.

1996 Neolithic and Bronze Age Scotland. London, Batsford.

Atkinson, R.J.C. Wayland's Smithy. *Antiquity* 32, 126-33.

Bamford, H.M. 1985 *Briar Hill excavation 1974-87*. Northampton, Northampton Development Corporation.

Barber, M. Field, D. and Topping, P. 1999 *The Neolithic Flint Mines of England*. London, RCHM(E), English Heritage.

Barclay, A. Gray, M. and Lambrick, G. 1995 *The excavations at the Devil's Quiots, Stanton Harcourt, Oxfordshire 1972-3 and 1988*. Thames Valley Landscapes: The Windrush Valley, Vol 3. Oxford, Oxford Archaeological Unit.

Barclay, A. and Harding, J. (eds) 1999 'Pathways and ceremonies: the cursus monuments of Britain and Ireland' in *Neolithic Studies Group seminar papers 4*. Oxford, Oxbow.

Barclay, G. 1983 Sites of the third millennium bc to the first millennium AD at North Mains, Strathallen, Perthshire. *PSAS* 113, 122-281.

1996 Neolithic Houses in Scotland, in Darvill, T. and Thomas, J. (eds) *Neolithic Houses in Northwest Europe*.

1999 'Cairnpapple revisited' in 1948-98 *PPS* 65, 17-46.

2001 Neolithic enclosures in Scotland. In Darvill and Thomas (eds) *Neolithic enclosures in Atlantic north-west Europe*. 155-70.

Barclay, G. and Maxwell, G.S. 1998 *Cleaven Dyke and Littleour: monuments in the Neolithic of Tayside* Society of Antiquaries of Scotland, Monograph Series no. 13.

Barker, G. and Webley, D. 1978 'Causewayed camps and Early Neolithic Economies in Central Southern England' in *PPS* 44, 161-86.

Barnatt, J. 1990 *The Henges, Stone circles and ringcairns of the Peak District* Sheffield Archaeological Monographs 1.

Barnatt, J. and Collis, J. 1996 *Barrows in the Peak District: recent research*. Sheffield. J.R.Collis Publications.

Barrett, J. Bradley, R. and Green, M. 1991 *Landscape, Monuments and Society: the prehistory of Cranborne Chase*. Cambridge, Cambridge University Press.

Bar-Yosef, O. and Valla, F.R. 1991 *The Natufian culture in the Levant*. International Monographs in Prehistory. Archaeological Series 1. Ann Arbor, Michigan.

Beckensall, S. 1986 *Rock carvings of northern Britain*. Princes Risborough, Shire.

1999 *British Prehistoric Rock Art*. Stroud, Tempus.

Bell, M. Fowler, P.J. and Hillson, S.W. 1996 *The Experimental Earthwork Project 1960-1992*. York, CBA research report no. 100.

Berg, S. 1995 *Landscape of the monuments*. Stockholm, Riksantikvariameber Arkeologiska Undersöknigar.

Bowden, M. 1991 *Pitt River: the life and archaeological work of Lieutenant General Henry Lane Fox Pitt Rivers*. Cambridge, Cambridge University Press.

Bowman, S. 1995 *Radiocarbon Dating*. London, British Museum.

Bradley. R. 1993 'Altering the earth: the origin of monuments in Britain and continental Edinburgh.

1997 *Rock Art and the prehistory Atlantic* Europe. London, Routledge.

1998 *The Significance of Monuments* Routledge. London.

Bradley, R. and Edmonds. M. 1993 *Interpreting the Axe Trade*. Cambridge, Cambridge University Press.

Brodie, N. 1994 *The Neolithic-Bronze Age transition in Britain*. Oxford, British Archaeological Reports 238.

Britnell, W.J. 1979 The Gwernvale long cairn, Powys. *Antiquity* 53 132-4.

1980 'Radiocarbon dates from the Gwernvale chambered tomb, Crickhowell, Powys' *Antiquity* 54 147.

Britnell, W. J. & Savory, H. N. et al. 1984 *Gwernvale and Penywyrlod: two Neolithic long cairns in the Black Mountains of Brecknock* Cambrian Archaeological Monographs. Cambrian Archaeological Association Bangor 2.

Burl, A. 1993 *From Carnac to Callanish: the prehistoric stone rows and avenues of Britain, Ireland and Brittany*. New Haven, Yale University Press.

1991 *Prehistoric Henges*. Princes Risborough, Shire.

1997 *Prehistoric Astronomy and Ritual*. Princes Risborough, Shire.

2000 *The Stone Circles of Britain, Ireland and Brittany*. New Haven, Yale University Press (new edition).

Campbell Smith, W. 1963 'Jade axes from sites in the British Isles.' *PPS*. XXIX 133-72.

Case, H. 1982 'Introduction' in Case, H. and Whittle, A. (eds) *Settlement patterns in the Oxford Region: excavations at Abingdon causewayed enclosure and other sites*. 1-9.

Case, H.J. and Whittle, A.W.R. 1982 *Settlement patterns in the Oxford region: excavations at the Abingdon causewayed enclosure and other sites*. CBA Research Report 44. Oxford.

Childe, V.G. 1925 (1957 sixth ed). *The Dawn of European Civilisation*. London, Routledge.

1934 *New Light on the most Ancient East*. London, Kegan Paul.

1931 *Skara Brae: A Pictish village in Orkney*. London, Kegan Paul.

Childe, V.G. and Grant, W.G. 1939 'A stone-age settlement at Braes of Rinyo, Rousay, Orkney' (First report) *PSAS* 73. 6-31.

1947 'A stone-age settlement at Braes of Rinyo, Rousay, Orkney.' (Second report) *PSAS* 81. 16-42.

Childe, V.G. and Smith, I.F. 1954 'The excavation of a Neolithic Long Barrow on Whiteleaf Hill, Bucks.' *PPS*, XX part 2, 212-30.

Clare, T. 1986 'Towards a reappraisal of henge monuments'. *PPS* 52, 281-316.

1987 'Towards a reappraisal of henge monuments: origins, evolution and hierarchies.' *PPS* 53, 457-78.

Clark, A. 1996 *Seeing beneath the soil*. London, Batsford.

Clark, J.G.D. 1935 *The Mesolithic settlement of northern Europe*. Cambridge.

1936 'The timber monument of Arminghall and its affinities.' *PPS* II, 1-51.

1963 'Neolithic bows from Somerset, England, and the prehistory of Archery in north-western Europe.' *PPS* 29, 50-98.

1965 'Radiocarbon dating and the expansion of farming culture from the Near East over Europe.' *PPS* XXXI, 58-73.

Clark, J.G.D. and Longworth, I. 1960. 'Excavations at the Neolithic site at Hurst Fen, Mildenhall, Suffolk.' *PPS* 1960, XXVI. 202-45.

Clarke, D.V., Cowie, T.G. and Foxton, A. 1985 *Symbols of Power at the time of Stonehenge*. Edinburgh. HMSO.

Clarke, D.V. 1976a 'The Neolithic village at Skara Brea, Orkney.' *Excavations 1972-3: An interim report*. HMSO. Edinburgh.

1976b 'Excavations at Skara Brea: A summary account.' In Burgess, C. and Miket, R. (eds) *Settlement and economy in the third millennium BC*. BAR British Series 33. Oxford.

Clarke, D.V. and Sharples, N. 1990 'Settlement and subsistence in the third millenium bc.' In C. Renfrew (ed) *The prehistory of Orkney* (second ed). Edinburgh University Press, 54-82.

Cleal, R. Walker, K and Montague, R. 1995 *Stonehenge in its landscape: twentieth century excavations*. London, English Heritage.

Cleal, R. and MacSween, A. 1999 *Grooved ware pottery in Britain and Ireland*. Neolithic Studies Group Seminar papers. 3. Oxford, Oxbow.

Clifford, E.M. 1936 Notgrove Long Barrow, Gloucestershire. *Archaeologia* LXXXVI, 119-61.

Clough, T.H.McK. and Cummins, W.A. (eds) 1979 *Stone Axe Studies*. Vol 2. London, CBA Research Report 23.

1988 *Stone Axe Studies*. Vol 3. London, CBA Research Report 28.

Coles, J. 1973 *Archaeology by Experiment*. London. Hutchinson.

Coles, B. and Coles, J. 1986 *Sweet Track to Glastonbury*. London, Thames and Hudson.

Coles and Simpson, D. 1965 'The excavation of a Neolithic Round Barrow at Pitnacree, Perthshire, Scotland.' *PPS* XXXI 34-57.

Colt Hoare, R. and Cunnington, W. 1812 *The history of Ancient Wiltshire (north and south)*. London.

Connah, G. 1965 'Excavations at Knap Hill, Alton Priors.' *WAM* 60,1-23 [Reports by Annabal, K.F. Denston, C.B. Fowler, P.J. Smith, I F. and Sparks, B.W.S.

1969 'Radiocarbon dating for Knap Hill'. *Antiquity* 43 304-5.

Coombs, D. 1976 Callis Wold round barrow, Humberside. *Antiquity* L 198, 130-31.

Cooney, G. 1999 A boom in Neolithic Houses. In *Archaeology Ireland*. Vol 13, 47, 13-16.

2000 *Landscapes of Neolithic Ireland*. London, Routledge.

Cooney, G. and Mandal, S. 1998 *The Irish Stone Axe Project*. Monograph 1. Dublin, Wordwell.

Corcoran, J. 1969 'The Severn Cotswold Group.' In Powell, T.G.E. et al. *Megalithic Inquiries in the west of Britain*. Liverpool.

Cummins, W.A. 1980 Stone Axes as a guide to Neolithic communications and boundaries in England and Wales. *PPS* 46, 45-60.

Cunnington, M.E. 1911 'Knap Hill Camp'. *Wiltshire Archaeol Natur Hist Mag* 37(1), 1911 42-65.

1931 The Sanctuary on Overton Hill, Avebury: being an account of the excavations carried out by Mr and Mrs B.H. Cunnington in 1930. *Wiltshire Archaeological Magazine 45*, 300-35.

Cunliffe, B.W. 1993 *Wessex to 100 AD*. London. Longman.

Curwen, C. 1929 *Prehistoric Sussex*. London, the Homeland Association.

1930 'Neolithic Camps.' *Antiquity*. 4; 22-54.

1934 'Excavations at Whitehawk Neolithic camp, Brighton.' *Antiqs. J.* 14, 99-133.

1936 'Excavations at Whitehawk camp, Brighton. Third season 1935.' *Sussex Arch. Colls*. 77; 60-92.

Daniel, G. 1950 *The prehistoric chambered tombs of England and Wales*. Cambridge University Press.

Darvill, T. 1987 *Prehistoric Britain*. London, Batsford.

1989 The circulation of stone and flint axes: a case study from Wales and mid-west England. *PPS* 55, 27-43.

1996 Neolithic Buildings in England and Wales and the Isle of Man. In Darvill and Thomas (eds) *Neolithic Houses in North-west Europe*. 77-112.

1997 'Ever increasing Circles: the sacred geographies of Stonehenge and its landscape.' In Cunliffe and Renfrew (eds) *Science and Stonehenge*. 167-202.

Darvill, T. and Thomas, J. (eds) 1996 *Neolithic Houses in northwest Europe and beyond*. Neolithic Studies Group Seminar Papers 1, Oxford, Oxbow.

2001 *Neolithic Enclosures in Atlantic North-west Europe*. Neolithic Studies Group Seminar Papers 6, Oxford, Oxbow.

Davison, J.L. and Henshall, A.S. 1989 *The chambered Cairns of Orkney*. Edinburgh, Edinburgh University Press.

1991 The chambered cairns of Caithness. An inventory of their structure and contents. Edinburgh, Edinburgh University Press.

De Valera, R. and O'Nuallain, S. 1961 *Survey of the Megalithic tombs of Ireland*, Vol 1.Co, Clare. Dublin.

1964 *Survey of the Megalithic tombs of Ireland*, Vol 2.County Mayo. Dublin.

1980 *Survey of the Megalithic tombs of Ireland*, Counties Galway, Roscommon, Leitrim, Longford, Westmeath, Laosghis, Offaly, Kildare, Cavan. Vol 3. Dublin.

1982 *Survey of the Megalithic tombs of Ireland*, Vol 4. Counties Cork, Kerry, Limerick, Tipperary. Dublin.

Dawson, M. (ed) 2000 *Prehistory, Roman and Post-Roman landscapes of the Great Ouse valley*. CBA Research Report.

Dixon, Philip 1981 'Crickley Hill [Gloucestershire]' *Curr Archaeol* 7, 1981 145-7.

Dixon, Philip 1988a 'Crickley Hill 1969-87' *Curr Archaeol* 10, 1988 73-8.

1988b 'The Neolithic settlement on Crickley Hill.' In Burgess, C., Mordant, C. and Maddison, M. (eds) *Enclosures and defences in the Neolithic of western Europe*. Oxford, BAR. 75-87.

Drewett, P. 1975 *The excavation of an oval burial mound of the third millennium bc at Alfriston, East Sussex, 1974.*
 1977 'The excavation of a Neolithic causewayed enclosure on Offham Hill, East Sussex. 1976.' *PPS* 43 201-41.

Edmonds, M. 1993 'Interpreting causewayed enclosures in the past and present.' In Tilley, C. (ed) *Interpretative Archaeology.* Oxford, Berg. 99-142.
 1995 *Stone tools and society: working stone in the Neolithic and Bronze Age Britain.* London, Batsford.
 1999 *Ancestral Geographies of the Neolithic.* London, Routledge.
Edmonds, M. and Seaborne, T. 2001 *Prehistory in the Peak.* Stroud, Tempus.
Edwards, K. and Whittington, G. 1998 'The Palaeoevironmental Background: pollen studies at Rae Loch.' In Barclay, G. and Maxwell, G. (eds) *The Cleaven Dyke and Littleour.*
Eogan, G. 1984 *Excavations at Knowth, 1.* Dublin, Royal Irish Academy.
 1986 *Knowth and the Passage-tombs of Ireland.* London, Thames and Hudson.
Eogan, G. and Roche, H 1997 *Excavations at Knowth 2.* Dublin, Royal Irish Academy.
Evans, C. 1988a 'Acts of Enclosure: a consideration of concentrically-organised causewayed enclosures.' In Barrett, J.C.and Kinnes, I. (eds) *The archaeology of context in the Neolithic and Bronze Age.* Sheffield. Department of Archaeology, University of Sheffield, 85-96.
 1988b 'Monuments and Analogy: the interpretation of causewayed enclosures.' In Burgess, C.; Topping, P. Mordant, P. and Maddison, M. (eds) *Enclosures and defences in the Neolithic of western Europe.* Oxford. BAR, 47-73.
Evans, J.D. 1971 'Habitat change on the calcareous soils of Britain: the impact of Neolithic Man' and 'Notes on the environment of early farming communities in Britain' in Simpson, D.D.A. (ed) *Economy and settlement in Neolithic and early Bronze Age Britain.* Leicester. Leicester University Press, p.27-73 & p.11-26.
Evans, J.G. and O'Connor, T. 1999 *Environmental Archaeology: Principles and Methods.* Sutton Publishing. Stroud.

Fairbairn, (ed) 2000 *Plants in Neolithic Britain and beyond.* Neolithic studies Group Seminar Papers 5. Oxford, Oxbow.
Fairweather, A. and Ralston, I. 1993 'The Neolithic timber hall at Balbridie, Grampian Region, Scotland: the building, the date, the plant macrofossils.' *Antiquity* 67, 313-23.
Fox, C. 1938 *The personality of Britain.* Cardiff. National Museum of Wales.

Glass, H. 2000 'White Horse Stone: A Neolithic Longhouse.' *Current Archaeology* 168, May 2000, 450-3.
Gibson, A. 1986 *Neolithic and Early Bronze Age pottery.* Aylebury, Shire.
Gibson, A. 1998 *Stonehenge and timber circles.* Stroud, Tempus.
 1999 *The Walton Basin Project: Excavation and Survey in a prehistoric landscape 1993-7.* York, CBA Research Report 118.
Gibson, A. and Simpson, D. (eds) 1998 *Prehistoric Ritual and Religion.* Stroud, Sutton.
Gibson, A. and Woods, A. 1997 *Prehistoric Pottery for the Archaeologist.* Second ed. Leicester University Press. Leicester.
Green, F.S. 1996 Mesolithic and later houses at Bowman's Farm, Romsey, Hampshire, England. In: Darvill, T. and Thomas, J. (eds*) Neolithic Houses in North-west Europe and Beyond.* 113-22.
Green, M. 2000 *A Landscape Revealed: 10,000 years on a Chalkland Farm.* Stroud, Tempus.
Green, S. 1980 *Flint Arrowheads of the British Isles* Oxford. British Archaeological Reports 75.
Grogan, E. 1996 'Neolithic Houses in Ireland.' In Darvill, T. and Thomas. J. (eds). *Neolithic Houses in Northwest Europe.* 41-60.

Harding. A.F. 1981 Excavations in the prehistoric complex near Milfield, Northumberland. *PPS* 47, 87-136.
Harding, A.F. (ed) 1982 *Climatic Change in Later Prehistory.* Edinburgh University Press.
Harding, A. and Lee, G. 1987 *Henge Monuments and related sites of Great Britain: Air Photographic evidence and catalogue.* Oxford. British Archaeological Reports 175.
Hartnett, P.S. 1957 Excavation of a passage grave at Fourknocks, Co. Meath. *Proceedings of the Royal Irish Academy,* 58C, 197-277.
Hartwell, B. 1998 The Ballynahatty Complex. In Gibson, A. and Simpson, D.D.A (eds) *Prehistoric Ritual and Religion.*
Hedges, J. 1984 *Tomb of the Eagles.* London, John Murray.
Henken, H. O'N. 1939 'A long cairn at Creevykeel, Co Sligo.' *Journal of the Royal Society of Antiquaries of Ireland* 69, 53-98.
Henry, D.O. 1998 *From Foraging to farming: the Levant at the end of the Ice Age .* University of Pennsylvania Press.
Henshall, A. 1963 *The chambered tombs of Scotland.* Edinburgh, Edinburgh University Press. Vol 1 (North and East).

1972 *The chambered tombs of Scotland*. Edinburgh, Edinburgh University Press. Vol 2 (South and West).

Herity, M. 1974 *Irish Passage Tombs*. Dublin, Irish University Press.

Hey, G. 1997 Neolithic settlement at Yarnton, Oxfordshire. In Topping, P. (ed) *Neolithic Landscapes*. 99-112.

Hodder, I. 1990 *The domestication of Europe*. Oxford, Blackwell.

Hodder, I. And Shand, P. 1988 The Haddenham Long Barrow: an Interim Statement. *Antiquity, 62*, 349-53.

Holgate , R. 1991 *Flintmines*. Princes Risborough, Shire Publications.

Houlder, C. 1968 The henge monuments of Llandegai. *Antiquity* 42, 216-21.

Jones, C. and Gilmer, A 1999 Rougham Hill: a final Neolithic/early Bronze Age landscape revealed. *Archaeology Ireland* 13, No. 47, 30-2.

Kinnes, I. 1976 'Monumental function in British Neolithic burial practices.' *World Archaeology* 7, 16-19.
1979 *Round Barrows and Ring-ditches in the British Neolithic*. British Museum Occasional Papers 7.
1992 *Non-Megalithic Long Barrows and Allied Structures in the British Neolithic*. London, British Museum Occasional Papers 52.

Kinnes, I. Schadla Hall, T. Chadwick, P and Dean, P. 1983 'Duggleby Howe reconsidered.' *Arch. J.* 140, 83-108.

Kinnes, I. and Varndell, G. (eds) 1995 'Unbaked urns of rudely shape.' *Essays on British and Irish Pottery for Ian Longworth*. Oxford, Oxbow Monograph 55.

Lambrick, G. 1988 *The Rollright Stones: Megaliths, Monuments and settlement in the prehistoric landscape*. London, English Heritage.

Lee, R.B. and Devore, I. 1968 *Man the Hunter* Chicago, Aldine.

Legge, A 1981 'Aspects of cattle husbandry.' In Mercer, R. (ed) *Farming practice in British Prehistory*. Edinburgh, Edinburgh University Press. 169-81.

Liddell, D. 1930 'Report on the excavations at Hembury Fort, Devon 1930.' *Proc. Devon Archaeological Exploration Society* I(2) 39-63.
1931 'Report on the Excavations at Hembury Fort, Devon. Second Season. 1931.' *Proc. Devon Archaeological Exploration Society* 1(3) 90-120.
1932 'Report on the Excavations at Hembury Fort. Third season 1932.' *Proc. Devon Archaeological Exploration Society* I(4) 162-90.
1935 'Report on the excavations at Hembury Fort, Devon fourth and fifth seasons 1934-1935.' *Proc. Devon Archaeological Exploration Society* II(3) 135-75.

Lord, J. 1993 *The Basics of Lithic technology*. Norfolk, John Lord.

Loveday, R. 1985 Cursuses and related monuments of the British Neolithic. Unpublished PhD thesis, University of Leicester.

Lubbock, J. 1865 *Prehistoric Times*. London.

Lynch, F. 1991 *Prehistoric Anglesey*. Llangefri, Anglesey Antiquarian Society, 2nd Edition.
1997 *Megalithic Tombs and Long Barrows in Britain*. Princes Risborough, Shire.

Lynch, F. Aldhouse-Green, S. and Davies, J. 2000 *Prehistoric Wales*. Stroud, Sutton Publishing.

Mackie, E. 1977 *Science and Society in Prehistoric Britain*. London, Paul Elek.

MacSween, A. 1995 'Grooved ware from Scotland.' In Kinnes and Varndell (eds) *Unbaked urns of rudely shape* 41-9.

Malone, C. 1989 *Avebury*. London, English Heritage, Batsford.
1999 'Processes of Colonisation in the central Mediterranean.' *Accordia Research Papers* London vol 7, for 1997-9, 37-57.

Manby, T.G. 1963 'The excavation of Willerby Wold Long Barrow.' *PPS* XXIX 173-205.
1976 'The Excavation of Kilham Long Barrow, East Riding of Yorkshire.' *PPS* 42, 111-60.
1988 'The Neolithic in Eastern Yorkshire.' In Manby, (ed) *Archaeology in Eastern Yorkshire. Essays in Honour of T.C.M. Brewster*. Sheffield, Sheffield University Press.

Mauss, M. 1954 *The Gift*. London, Cohen and West.

Megaw, V. and Simpson, D.D.A. 1979 *Introduction to British Prehistory*. Leicester. Leicester University Press.

Masters, L. 1973 'The Lochill long cairn.' *Antiquity* XLVII, 96-100.

Mercer, R. 1980 *Hambledon Hill: A neolithic landscape*. Edinburgh, Edinburgh University Press.
1981a Excavations at Carn Brea, Illogan, Cornwall 1970-3 'A Neolithic fortified complex of the third millennium bc.' *Cornish Archaeology* 20, 1-204.
1981b 'The excavation of a late Neolithic henge-type enclosure at Balfarg, Markinch, Fife. Scotland.' *Proc. Soc. Antiq. Scotland*. 111, 63-171.
1988 'Hambledon Hill, Dorset, England.' In Burgess. C.; Topping, P. Mordant, P. and Maddison, M. (eds) *Enclosures and defences in the Neolithic of western Europe*. Oxford. BAR, 89-106.

1998 *Causewayed Enclosures*. Princes Risborough, Shire

2001 Neolithic enclosed settlements in Cornwall: the past, the present and the future. In Darvill. T. and Thomas, J. (eds) *Neolithic Enclosures in Atlantic North-west Europe*. 43-49.

Mercer, R. and Healy, F. forthcoming *The excavations of the Neolithic enclosure complex at Hambledon Hill, Dorset*. London, English Heritage Reports.

Miket, R. 1976 'The evidence for Neolithic activity in the Milfield Basin, Northumberland.' In Burgess, C., and Miket, R. (eds) *Settlement and Economy in the third and second millennia B.C.* British Archaeological Reports 22, 113-47.

Morgan, F.De V. 1959 'The excavation of a long barrow at Nutbane, Hants.' *PPS* 35, 15-51.

Moore, A. Hillman, G. and Legge, A. 2000. *Village on the Euphrates: from foraging to farming at Abu Hureyra*. Oxford, Oxford University Press.

O'Kelly, M.K. 1982 *Newgrange: Archaeology, art and legend*. London, Thames and Hudson.

O'Riordain, S. 1954 'Lough Gur excavations: Mesolithic and Bronze Age houses on Knockadoon.' *PRIA* lvi (c) 297-459.

O'Sullivan, A. 1996 'Neolithic, Bronze Age and Iron Age woodworking techniques.' In Raftery, B. *Trackway Excavation in the Mountdillon Bogs, Co Longford. 1985-1991*. Dublin, Irish Wetland Unit Transactions 3, 291-342.

Oswald, A., Dyer, C. and Barber, M. 2001 *The creation of monuments. Neolithic causewayed enclosures in the British Isles*. Swindon. English Heritage.

Palmer, R. 1976 'Interrupted ditch enclosures in Britain: the use of aerial photography for comparative studies.' *PPS* 52, 161-86.

Parker-Pearson, M. and Ramilisonina. 1998. 'Stonehenge for the ancestors: the stones pass on the message.' *Antiquity*, 72, 308-26.

Piggott, S 1937 'Excavation of a Long Barrow in Holdenhurst Parish, near Christchurch, Hants.' *PPS*. III, 1-14.

1940 'Timber Circles: a re-examination.' *Arch. J.* 96, 193-222.

1954 *Neolithic cultures of the British Isles*.

1952 'The Neolithic Camp on Whitesheet Hill, Kilmington Parish' *Wiltshire Archaeological and Natural History Magazine* 54 (197) 404-10 [Appendix by Jackson, J.W.S.].

1962 *The West Kennet Long Barrow* London. HMSO.

1971-2 'Excavation of the Dalladies Long Barrow, Fettercairn, Kincardinshire.' *Proc. Soc. Antiqs. Scotland* 104, 23-47.

1973 'Dalladies Long Barrow; NE Scotland.' *Antiquity* XLVII, 32-6.

Pitt-Rivers, A. 1898 *Excavations on Cranborne Chase*. Vol IV.

Pitts, M. 1996 'The Stone Axe in Britain.' *PPS*. 62, 311-71.

2000 'Return to the Sanctuary.' *British Archaeology* 51, 15-19.

1998 *Hengeworld: life in Britain as revealed by the latest discoveries at Stonehenge, Avebury and Stanton Drew*. London, Century.

Pollard, J. 1992 'The Sanctuary, Overton Hill, Wiltshire: a re-examination.' *PPS*, 58, 213-26.

1995 'Inscribing space: formal deposition at the later Neolithic of Woodhenge, Wiltshire.' *PPS* 61, 137-56.

Powell, T.G.E. 1938 'The passage graves of Ireland.' *PPS*. iv. 239-48.

Powell, T.G.E. and Daniel, G.E. 1956 *Barclodiad y Gawres*. Liverpool.

Pryor, F. 1974 *Excavations at Fengate, Peterborough, England. The first report*. Toronto. Royal Ontario Museum Monograph 3.

1984 *Excavations at Fengate, Peterborough, England. The fourth report*. Northampton. Northampton Archaeological Society Monograph 2.

1988 'Etton, near Maxey, Cambridgeshire: a causewayed enclosure on the fen-edge.' In Burgess, C.; Topping, P. Mordant, P. and Maddison, M. (eds) *Enclosures and defences in the Neolithic of western Europe*. Oxford. BAR, 107-126.

1999 *Etton; Excavation at a Neolithic Causewayed enclosure near Maxey, Cambridgeshire, 1982-7*. London, English Heritage.

Redman, C. 1976 *The Rise of Civilisation*. San Francisco, Freeman.

Renfrew, A.C. 1973 'Monuments, mobilisation and social organisation in Neolithic Wessex.' In Renfrew, C. (ed) *The explanation of culture change: models in prehistory*. London, Duckworth. 539-58.

1985 (2000 ed) *The Prehistory of Orkney*. (third impression)Edinburgh, Edinburgh University Press.

1979 *Investigations in Orkney*. London, Society of Antiquaries of London Research Report/Thames and Hudson.

Renfrew, C. and Bahn, P. 2000 Archaeology: theory and practice. Cambridge, Cambridge University Press.

Richards, C. 1988 Altered Images: a re-examination of Neolithic mortuary practices n Orkney. In Barrett, J.C. and Kinnes. I.A. (eds) *The Archaeology of Context in the Neolithic and Bronze Age: recent trends*. Sheffield, Department of Archaeology, Sheffield University. 42-56.

1990 'Postscript: the late Neolithic settlement complex at Barnhouse Farm, Stenness.' In Renfrew (ed) *The Prehistory of Orkney*. Edinburgh University Press. Edinburgh. (reprint of 1985 edition with postscript.) 305-16.

1996 'Henges and Water: towards an elemental understanding of monumentality and landscape in late neolithic Britain.' *Journal of Material Culture* 1, 313-35.

Richards, J. 1990 *The Stonehenge Environs Project*. English Heritage.

1991 *The English Heritage Book of Stonehenge*. London, Batsford.

Ritchie, A. 1983 'Excavation of a Neolithic farmstead at Knap of Howar, Papa Westray, Orkney.' *Proc. Of Soc of Antiquities of Scotland* 113, 189-218.

(ed) 2001 Neolithic Orkney in its European Context. Cambridge, McDonald Institute Monographs.

Robertson Mackay, R. 1987 'The neolithic causewayed enclosure at Staines, Surrey: excavations 1961-63.' *PPS* 53, 23-128.

Robinson, M. 2000 'Colopteran evidence for the Elm Decline, Neolithic activity in woodland, clearance and the use of the landscape.' In Fairbairne. A. (ed) *Plants in Neolithic Britain and Beyond*. Neolithic Studies Group Papers 5. Oxbow, Oxford.

Roe, F. 1979 Typology of Stone Implements with shaftholes. In Clough and Cummins (eds) Stone Axe Studies, 23-48.

Ruggles, C.1999 *Astronomy in Prehistoric Britain and Ireland*. New Haven, Yale University Press.

Ruggles, C. and Barclay, G. 2000 'Cosmology, calendars and Society in Neolithic Orkney: a rejoinder to Euan Mackie.' *Antiquity* 74, 62-74.

Ruggles, C. and Whittle, A. 1981 *Astronomy and Society in Britain during the period 4000-1500 BC*. Oxford, British Archaeological Reports 88.

Sahlins, M.D. 1968 *Tribesmen*. New Jersey, Prentice Hall.

1972 *Stone Age Economics*.

Saville. A. 1990 *Hazelton North: the excavation of a Neolithic long cairn of the Cotswold-Severn Group*. London, English Heritage Archaeology report no. 13.

Savory, H.N. 1952 'The excavation of a Neolithic dwelling and a Bronze Age cairn at Mount Pleasant Farm, Nottage (Glam).' *Trans. Cardiff Naturalist's Society* 89, 9-25.

Scourse, J.D. 1997 Transport of the Stonehenge bluestones: testing the glacial hypothesis. In Cunliffe, B. and Renfrew, C.(eds) *Science and Stonehenge*. 271-314.

Shanks, M. and Tilley, C. 1982 'Ideology, symbolic power and ritual communication: a reinterpretation of Neolithic mortuary practices.' In Hodder, I. (ed) *Symbolic and structural archaeology*. Cambridge. Cambridge University Press.

Sharples, N. 1991 *Maiden Castle: excavation and field survey 1985-6*. London, English Heritage.

Shee Twohig, E. 1981 *The megalithic art of western Europe*. Oxford, Clarendon.

1990 *Irish Megalithic Tombs*. Princes Risborough, Shire.

Sheridan, A. 1985-6 Megaliths and Megalithomania: an account and interpretation of the development of passage tombs in Ireland. *Journal of Irish Archaeology*, 3, 17-30.

1992 'Scottish Stone Axeheads: some new work and recent discoveries.' In Sharples, N. and Sheridan, A. (eds) *Vessels for the Ancestors*. Edinburgh, Edinburgh University Press. 194-212.

1995 'Irish Neolithic Pottery: the story in 1995.' In Kinnes and Varndell (eds) *Unbaked urns of rudely shape* 3-22.

Sherratt, A. 1997 Economy and Society in Prehistoric Europe. Edinburgh, Edinburgh University Press. (Section III – Discovering the Secondary Products Complex).

Smith, B. 1995 *The emergence of Agriculture*. New York. Freeman, Scientific American Library.

Smith, I.F. 1965 *Windmill Hill and Avebury: excavations by Alexander Keiller*. 1925-1939. Clarendon, Oxford.

1971 'Causewayed Enclosures.' In Simpson, D.D.A. (ed) *Economy and settlement in Neolithic and early Bronze Age Britain*. Leicester. Leicester University Press. 89-112.

Smith, R. 1984 The ecology of neolithic farming systems as exemplified by the Avebury region, Wiltshire. *PPS*, 50. 99-120.

Speak, S. and Burgess, C. 1999 'Meldon Bridge: a centre of the third millennium BC in Peebleshire.' *Proc. Soc. Antiq. Scotland* 129, 1-118.

Startin, W. 1978 'Linear pottery culture houses: reconstruction and manpower.' *PPS* 44, 143-57.

Startin, W. and Bradley, R.J. 1981 'Some notes on work organisation and society in Prehistoric Weseex.' in Ruggles,C. and Whittle. A (eds) *Astronomy and Society in Britain during the period 4000-1500 BC*. Oxford. BAR Brit. Ser 88. 289-96.

Stukeley, W. 1740 *Stonehenge*. London.

1743 *Abury*. London.

Thomas, J. 1988 The Social significance of Cotswold-Severn burial practices. *Man*, 23. 540-59

1999 *Understanding the Neolithic*. London, Routledge.

Thomas, J. and Whittle, A. 1986 'Anatomy of a tomb: West Kennet revisited.' *Oxford Journal of Archaeology*. 5, 129-56.

Thom, A. 1967 *Megalithic Science in Britain*. Oxford, Oxford University Press.

1971 *Megalithic lunar observatories*. Oxford, Oxford University Press.

Thorpe, I. 1984 'Ritual, power and Ideology: a reconstruction of earlier Neolithic rituals in Wessex.' In Bradley, R. and Gardiner, J. (eds) *Neolithic Studies*. Oxford, BAR 133. 41-60.

1986 'Ethnoastronomy: its patterns and archaeological implications.' In Ruggles and Whittle (eds) *Astronomy and Society in Britain during the period 4000-1500 BC*. Oxford. British Archaeological Reports, Brit. Ser 88. 275-88.

Tilley, C. 1994 *A phenomenology of Landscape*. Oxford, Berg.

Topping, P. 1992 'The Penrith henges: a survey of the Royal Commission on the Historical Monuments of England.' *PPS*, 58, 249-264.

(ed) 1997 *Neolithic Landscapes*. Neolithic Studies Group Seminar papers 2. Oxford, Oxbow.

Thorpe, R.S., Williams-Thorpe, B., Jenkins, D.G. and Watson, J.S. 1991 'The Geological sources and transport of the bluestones of Stonehehenge, Wilshire, UK.' *PPS* 57(2) 103-58.

Ucko, P. Hunter, M. Clark, A., and David, A. 1991. *Avebury Reconsidered: from the 1660s to the 1990s*. London, Unwin Hyman.

Vatcher, F.de. M. and Vatcher, L. 1965 'East Heslerton Long Barrow, Yorkshire: the eastern half.' *Antiquity* XXXXIX, 49-52.

Vyner, B. 1984 'The excavation of a neolithic cairn at Street House, Loftus, Cleveland.' *PPS* 50, 151-96.

1988 'The Street House Wossit: excavation of a Later Neolithic and Early Bronze Age palisaded ritual monument at Street House, Loftus, Cleveland.' *PPS* 54, 173-202.

Wainwright. G.J. 1979 *Mount Pleasant, Dorset, Excavations 1970-81*. Society of Antiquaries of London, Research Report 37.

1989 *The Henge Monuments: ceremony and society in prehistoric Britain*. Thames and Hudson London

Wainwright, G.J and Longworth, I.H. 1971 *Durrington Walls 1966-8*. Society of Antiquaries of London, Research Report 2.

Whittle, A.W.R. 1991 Wayland's Smithy, Oxfordshire: excavations at the Neolithic tomb in 1962-3 by R.J.C. Atkinson and S.Piggott. *PPS* 57, part 2. 61-102.

1996 *Neolithic Europe: the creation of New Worlds*. Cambridge, Cambridge University Press.

1997 *Sacred Mound Holy Rings: Silbury Hill and the West Kennet palisade enclosures: a later Neolithic complex in north Wiltshire*. Oxford. Oxbow Monograph 74.

Whittle, A, W. R. Pollard, J. and Grigson, C. 1999 *The Harmony of Symbols. Windmill Hill*. Cardiff Studies in Archaeology, Oxford, Oxbow.

Whittle, A.,W.R. Keith-Lucas, M., Milles, A., Noddle, B., Rees, S. and Romans, J. 1986 *Scord of Brouster: an early agricultural settlement on Shetland*. Oxford Committee for Archaeology, Oxford.

Whittle, A.W.R. and Wysocki, M. 1998 Parc le Bros Cwm transepted long cairn, Gower, W Glamorgan: date, contents and context. *PPS* 64, 139-82.

Wilkinson, T.J. and Muphy, P. 1995 *The archaeology of the Essex Coast*. Volume 1. The Hullbridge Survey Project. East Anglian Archeaology 71.

Wilkinson, T.J. and Murphy, P. forthcoming. *The Archaeology of the Essex Coast*. Volume 2. Excavations at the Stumble. East Anglian Archaeology.

Williams, A. 1953 'Clegyr Boia, St David's (Pembrokeshire) Excavations in 1943.' *Archaeologia Cambrensis* 102, 20-47.

Willock, E.H. 1936 'A Neolithic site on Haldon.' *Proc. Devon Archaeologcal Exploration Society* 2; 244-63.

1937 'A further Note on the Neolithic site of Haldon.' *Proc. Devon Archaeological Exploration Society*. 3, 33-43

Wysocki, M. and Whittle, A.W.R. 2000 Directionality, lifestyle and tirues: new biological and archaeological evidence from British earlier Neolithic mortuary assemblages. *Antiquity* 74, 591-601.

Index

Page numbers in **bold** denote the location of illustrations